TORRES STRAIT

THURSDAY IS.

GULF OF
CARPENTARIA

GROOTE
EYLANDT

○Weipa

CAPE
YORK
PENINSULA

Mitchell R.

○ Cooktown

RN
LY
BLELAND

385

Karumba○

Atherton
Tableland ○Cairns
GREEN ISLAND
DUNK ISLAND

592

Flinders R.

○Townsville

RY

Mt. Isa○ ○
Mary
Kethleen

596

Georgina R.

Bowen○
Proserpine○
HAYMAN ISLAND
SOUTH MOLLE ISLAND
LINDEMAN ISLAND
BRAMPTON IS.
○Mackay

400

Fitzroy R.

BARRIER REEF

iver

Longreach○

QUEENSLAND

Emerald○
433
○Rockhampton
HERON ISLAND
○Gladstone

IMPSON
DESERT

THE CHANNEL
COUNTRY

○Birdsville
STURTS
STONY
DESERT

Cooper's Cr.

Charleville○

358

370

○Roma

477

Bundaberg○
FRASER IS.
○Maryborough

Kingaroy○

SOUTH

STRALIA

LAKE
EYRE

Cunnamulla○

Moonie○
○Toowoomba
Warwick○

○BRISBANE
Southport
○Surfers Paradise
○Coolangatta

Gold Coast

ndamooka

Woomera○
○Wilpena
Pound

LAKE
TORRENS

NEW

Bourke○

Darling R.

Narrabri○ Armidale○

○Grafton

PACIFIC

ugusta○

Broken
Hill○

Wilcannia○

SOUTH

Macquarie R.

Tamworth○

○Kempsey
○Port Macquarie

ort Pirie

BAROSSA
VALLEY

Renmark○

○Mildura

WALES

Lachlan R.

Parkes○

○Dubbo

○Bathurst

○Newcastle

○
Murray
Bridge

Swan Hill○

Hay○

Griffith○

Murrumbidgee R.

○SYDNEY
○Wollongong

OCEAN

DELAIDE○

SPENCER
GULF

KANGAROO
IS.

346

466

578

Bendigo○

VICTORIA

Ballarat○

MT.
GAMBIER

Geelong○

Shepparton○

Wagga
Wagga○

○Albury

○CANBERRA
○Cooma

Healesville○

○MELBOURNE

Phillip
Island

683

BASS STRAIT

KING IS.

TASMAN SEA

FLINDERS
IS.

Burnie○
Devonport○
Queenstown○

BELL
BAY
○Launceston

TASMANIA

HOBART○ ○Port Arthur

VS

ed mainly by modern jet and turbo-jet aircraft.

Land of Fortune

LAND OF FORTUNE
A Study of the New Australia

JONATHAN AITKEN

Atheneum
New York 1971

Printed in Great Britain by Morrison and Gibb Ltd
London and Edinburgh
First American Edition

CONTENTS

PREFACE

This book is a contemporary study of Australia written by a British journalist normally resident 12,000 miles away from his subject. As such it has many of the weaknesses, but hopefully some of the strengths, of an outsider's portrait.

I first visited Australia in December 1965. At the time I was private secretary to the Right Honourable Selwyn Lloyd, who was touring the country in his then capacity as Opposition spokesman for Commonwealth Affairs.

As a junior observer on this VIP tour I was fascinated to see some of the changes that were then beginning to sweep through the Australian continent. The economic explosion, the dramatic developments, the migrant melting-pot, the altering attitudes to everything from Art to Asia, and the overall spirit of national optimism and self-confidence, added up to a story that was largely unknown and certainly unappreciated in the northern hemisphere.

I persuaded my publishers in London and New York to let me try and tell this story. On receiving their commissions I made four subsequent visits to Australia in four years, each trip consisting of six or seven weeks of round-the-country travelling and reporting. The text of this book thus represents the labour of over 500 interviews, some 250,000 miles of air travel and innumerable days of on-the-spot and in-the-library research.

Profiling a country of 13 million people with a land area the same size as that of the continental USA is in one sense an impossible task, for the author's sins of omission will inevitably be extensive. All that I can hope to do is to present the flavour of today's Australia. Certainly this is very different from the Australia of a decade ago, and it also contrasts sharply with the contemporary scene in Europe and the United States. Australia is often said to be a derivative and imitative society, and this is undoubtedly true of many of its aspects, yet my fundamental reason for wishing to write a book about the country was a desire to communicate something of the originality and unconventionality of this rising star of Western civilization. Australia is too often overrated by those who live in it, and underrated by those who live outside it. Its somewhat mediocre past is an unworthy harbinger of its undoubtedly glittering future. Its present is full of contrasts and paradoxes.

Australia lacks individual excellence yet aspires to collective greatness. Though economically rich, it is only beginning to rise above the cultural poverty-line. Though half its population is under the age of thirty, many of its key jobs are held by men over sixty. Though its domestic policies are stable its international role as an Asian neighbour is fraught with unknown possibilities. One could go on cataloguing dichotomies like these for several pages, but paradoxes miss the point. Australia is changing itself so fast that interpretative pontification about its virtues and vices is apt to have a built-in obsolescence. All one can say for certain is that Australia is now enjoying an economic, social, cultural and political era of rising standards that appears to be unrivalled by any other comparable nation. How and why this is happening, I have tried to explain in the ensuing 270 pages.

ACKNOWLEDGEMENTS

This book could never have been written without the co-operation, interest, kindness, and in some cases generous hospitality of hundreds of Australians. It seems almost invidious to single a few of them out for mention in this preface, but special thanks are undoubtedly due to Frank and Elayne Mills (to whom this book is dedicated) for taking me into their home within hours of my arrival on Australian soil, lending me an apartment in Sydney for all of my visits, and generally providing me with all imaginable help, encouragement and friendship during my prolonged researches.

Similar thanks are owed to Peter Janson who was many times a most munificent host to me in Melbourne.

I am also particularly grateful to Sir Peter Heydon, Mr Holt Boardman, and other officers of the Federal Department of Immigration who assisted me with my chapter on migrants and arranged key interviews for me in all parts of the continent.

In addition I would like to thank the following people who went out of their way to help me when I was preparing this book: Lord Casey; the Hon. Charles Court and the Department of Industrial Development of Western Australia; Mr Peter Grose; Sir William Gunn; Mr John Haddad; Mr Jack Joel; Sir Charles Johnston; Sir Frank Packer and the librarians of the *Sydney Daily Telegraph*; Mr Angus McLachlan and the librarians of the *Sydney Morning Herald*; Mr John Ulm and Qantas Airways; Mr Glenister Shiel, and Mr Dennis Wren.

Beyond those mentioned there were literally hundreds of individuals in all parts of the continent who gave up their time to welcome me, answer my questions, and show me around. Collectively they proved to me the truth of the old axiom that Australians are just about the friendliest and most hospitable people in the world.

Although almost all my book was researched first-hand on the spot in Australia, I inevitably consulted the works of authors who have written earlier books on this subject. In particular I must gratefully acknowledge my debt to Mr Craig MacGregor's *Portrait of Australia*, Mr John Pringle's *Australian Accent*, and Mr Donald Horne's *The Lucky Country*. I am grateful to all these authors for permission to quote from their works.

Likewise I am grateful to the Editors of the *Bulletin*, the *Australian*, and the *Listener* for permission to quote from certain articles which they originally published and which are acknowledged in my text. I would also like to thank Mr Charles J. V. Murphy of Washington, DC, for giving me access to his unpublished researches on King Ranch Australia. Finally I owe a great debt of gratitude to my dedicated secretary, Mrs Evelyn Hicks, who efficiently transcribed all my original tape-recorded notes and interviews, and typed out the entire manuscript in its draft, corrected, and final forms.

Although my obligation to all these friends and helpers is considerable, the final responsibility for all facts and opinions is of course my own.

1

GLIMPSES OF THE THIRD CENTURY

Australia enters her third century as a nation undergoing a quiet revolution. Quiet, because its changes have gone largely unnoticed in the outside world. A revolution because many hitherto unquestioned facts and opinions about Australia are being turned upside down.

The force behind the revolution has been a wave of physical discoveries and developments which date from the middle of the 1960s. Taken at face value they represent a degree of dramatic innovation unequalled in Australia since those heady years just after the arrival of the early settlers. Yet the real importance of the innovation has been its social and political impact in awakening a new national mood.

Some of the early symptoms of this mood have been mildly destructive, for since the mid-1960s tumbrils bearing some of Australia's most established images and values have been rolling towards the guillotines of history. Already overthrown is the economic infrastructure of a country dominated by agricultural industry and the concept of Australia as a deferential trade satellite of Britain. On trial are such touchstones of Australian life as political conservatism and cultural philistinism, while serious and not unsuccessful attempts are being made to storm the antipodean Bastilles of literary censorship, restrictive immigration and moral illiberalism.

The forces behind these changes are many and varied. A mineral explosion, a rising influx of immigrants, a flood of foreign capital, an economic involvement with Asia, a fresh awareness of the outside world through improved communications and a burying of old inferiority complexes are only some of the factors involved. But whatever the process, the effect has been to transform both the physical face and the psychological atmosphere of contemporary Australia.

L.O.F.—1*

It is temptingly easy to generalize about this transformation. Every week half a dozen eulogistic editorials in Australia's newspapers sound ringing trumpet fanfares on such themes as: 'a new air of national self-confidence', 'undreamed of levels of personal affluence', 'major breakthroughs in our relationship with Asia', 'stronger links with the United States', 'impressive improvements in cultural and social sophistication', 'dazzling opportunities to make a fortune', 'new dimensions in cosmopolitan life-styles' or 'growing international excitement about our country'. These panegyrical labels sound far too good to be true, yet on close examination the hard facts about the New Australia go a fair way towards justifying the national self-enthusiasm.

Up to the middle of the 1960s, there did not seem to be any particular cause for great enthusiasm about Australia. The twelve million inhabitants were thought to be hopelessly isolated both in geography and outlook; their economy was almost exclusively dependent on primary produce from agriculture; their politics and trading activities were tightly tied to Britain's apron-strings, and there was little reason to suppose that any of these trends would alter.

The first blow for change was struck by a succession of sensational mineral discoveries which have triggered off a boom the like of which has not been seen since the days of the Klondike gold rush. In the last seven years the island continent whose economy was once thought to depend exclusively on its 140 million sheep has been transformed into the world's new mining Eldorado, for during the late sixties Australia discovered the world's largest deposits of iron ore, uranium, nickel and bauxite. Enough oil has been struck to cater for 70 per cent of the nation's domestic needs. There have been massive finds of world-class phosphate, lead, zinc, natural gas, coal, copper and manganese. Prospectors have also discovered significant commercial deposits of tin, cobalt, tungsten, silver, wolfram, rutile, titanium, bentonite, ilmenite and zircon. Hardly any of these discoveries had been dreamed of, let alone commercially developed, before 1963.

Hearing today's incredible statistics for the present and future value of these minerals, seeing the new mines, ports, roads, railways and townships that are now springing up in the most desolate parts of the outback, and talking to the men whose vision inspired and led the superboom are experiences which leave visiting outsiders reeling with astonishment and a few lucky Australians insiders laughing all the way to the bank.

Stock exchange dramas apart, the effects of these mineral discoveries are still only just beginning to be felt, yet already, as a direct result, Australia's economy has, in the last five years, completely shifted its emphasis towards mineral production and exports; Japan has replaced Britain and the USA as Australia's leading trading partner; the Australian stock market has become the world's most go-go casino for international investors; large desert wildernesses are becoming populated; a flood of overseas capital has poured into all Australia's development industries, particularly mining; handsome personal capital gains from the boom have become widespread at all social levels and have created a new plutocracy in Australia; the prospecting and exploration scene has become hysterically energetic; and above all the atmospheric excitement of the mining boom has changed the whole mood of Australia, away from caution and complacency towards innovation and boisterous self-confidence.

But if the mining boom was the only facet of the revolution that makes up the New Australia, the effect on the national character would be about as insignificant as Canada's nickel strikes were to the Canadian character during the 1950s. Fortunately, there are many additional ingredients in the Australian melting-pot today that make for fascination. For instance, 180,000 immigrants were arriving each year in Australia by the end of the 1960s, accounting for 48 per cent of the annual population growth; 85,000 of these came from continental Europe, 79,000 from Britain, 3,000 from the USA and 3,000 from Asia. The impact of these new settlers has been extraordinary. The comparatively small number of Americans, who tend to arrive bursting with risk capital and pioneering zeal, have completely transformed certain types of Australian agriculture, notably cattle and cotton. The continentals, or 'New Australians', have created a sophisticated gastronomic world of *haute cuisine* and chic restaurants in a land whose staple diet used to be steak or mutton. The British have helped to revitalize broadcasting and journalism (at least six major quality newspapers have started up in Australia in the last five years), and are also thought to be partly responsible for the amazing phenomenon of Australia's book sales—which are higher per capita than in any other country in the world. And all migrant groups have contributed heavily to Australia's rapidly improving cultural life and to the leftward political swing which could well bring the 22-year-long reign of the conservative Liberal Party to an end at the next election.

But it is important not to leave the impression that Australia is being changed exclusively by outsiders, for the real force behind the antipodean revolution is the willingness to pounce eagerly on new ideas. One finds this in businessmen, government officials, sharebrokers and real estate men, just as much as in migrant restaurateurs and artists. Because Australia was already 'The Lucky Country' in terms of standards of living, home ownership statistics and leisure facilities long before the post-1965 wave of mineral-induced prosperity came along, the main effect of the present superboom is to make enlightened Australians highly receptive to new ideas for improving the quality of life in their own country. The most exhilarating aspect of contemporary Australia is the attitude that no bright idea should ever go unheard or uninvestigated, that no new project is ever too farfetched to be unworthy of 'giving it a go'. Want to cure your drought by pumping rivers backwards across a mountain range? Want to make a harbour by blowing out the rock obstacles with an atomic bomb? Want to have a top-class arts festival even if it means flying half your performers 12,000 miles across the world? Want to irrigate the desert by constructing $100 million worth of dams in an uninhabited wasteland? Want to build the world's most expensive and ostentatious opera house? Australia is your country. All the above 'mad' ideas have been or are being implemented in Australia, and although some of them are expensive mistakes, the effect of having tried them at all creates an atmosphere whose keynote is daring innovation. This atmosphere is unique to Australia. The developing countries of Africa and Asia might like to emulate it, but they do not have the wherewithal to do so. Oil-rich states like Kuwait or the Gulf sheikhdoms are more comparable, but their wealth is so colossal and their populations so small that their developmental extravaganzas have become meaningless. As for the English-speaking world, in Britain change tends to bring decay; in North America change tends to bring problems; only in Australia does change mean pure unadulterated excitement.

To conjure up Australia's current atmosphere of action, development, excitement and national pride is difficult for a reporter schooled in the disciplines of factual journalism. Matthew Arnold, when asked on one occasion to define 'the grand style', replied that it could not be described, but only felt. The same is true of the New Australia.

At first glance, enthusiastic feelings about Australia are tempered by the continent's general tone of couldn't-care-less superficiality, for although there is a great deal of glamour, drama and profundity about the present era of change in Australia, the people tend to be woefully inarticulate in expressing it. If a visitor is taken round some impressive new development, his guide will dutifully recite all the record-breaking statistics, the highest-ever prices, the soaring production figures, and maybe even some quotations from other visitors about the beauty of the local scenery. But following this slightly arid catalogue, a pregnant silence is apt to fall. If the Australian fills it at all, he will say something on the lines of 'She'll be right then—until the roof falls in, I suppose.' A remark like this after a tour of a city's new arts centre or a visit to a $50 million nickel mine just clawed out of the most rugged outback desert gives an impression of over-casual nonchalance. In fact, the cynicism cloaks a passionate Australian pride which would be embarrassing for emotion-hating Anglo-Saxons to put into words. Basically, this national pride stems from a sense of achievement at building a new civilization from the ground upwards on a landmass that is still partly un-known and untamed. Despite numerous attempts to label Australia as 'getting very Americanized', or 'still very British', or even 'in hock to the Japanese', the intriguing truth is that Australia is developing a distinctive life-style of her own which differs substantially from any other civilization. The influences of Britain, America and now South-East Asia are certainly strong, but one could convincingly argue that Australia has simply borrowed the best ideas from her 'great and powerful friends' and is moulding them together in her own Australian image. Certainly many Australians themselves believe this, and are appreciative when visitors accept this interpretation, for the quickest way to an Aussie's heart is through his patriotism.

But patriotism has not prevented Australia from suffering the burden of a poor international image. Despite the massive growth in trans-Pacific jet travel, ignorance about the Eldorado that Northern Hemisphere travel agents insist on calling 'Down Under' is still caused by isolation. Because of its geographical situation, nobody 'stops over' in Australia en route for other destinations. International reporters and TV crews are rare visitors, as Australia's news is usually quiet and good. Although the financial communities of the world have now got the message that Australia is a jumping country, those who do not play the stock market and have no special interest in the Antipodes still think of

'Down Under' in terms of koala bears, kangaroos, sheep and wide open spaces.

The Australian image is further dented by the under-informed comments of overseas intellectuals, who tend to be vaguely critical of antipodean illiberalisms, such as the 'White Australia' immigration policy, licensing restrictions, and literary censorship. There is enough half-truth in some of these criticisms for the mud to stick. As a waspish New York magazine editor once put it, 'Who wants to know about a sleepy, puritanical, farming country which doesn't dare let in Negroes or *Tropic of Capricorn*?'

Certainly there are unattractive aspects of Australia. The mindless conformity of suburbia; the exploitation of some of the Aboriginal tribes; the high infant mortality rate in country districts; the environmental squalor of areas within some cities; the absence of compassion for genuine hardship cases not covered by the government's inadequate social security programme; the excessive puritanism and philistinism; the old-fashioned snobberies and political shibboleths—all are easy and justifiable targets for criticism. Yet there would have been many more targets five years ago, for Australia's pace of change has been so rapid and its effects so profound, that the country is today almost unrecognizable as the country I first landed in in 1965.

These changes have certainly brought about many important material and physical improvements in modern Australia, but the really remarkable difference between the Australia of the sixties and Australia of the seventies is the transformation of attitudes, life-styles and atmosphere. Because these are somewhat intangible changes for a reporter to capture with the written word, perhaps it will be permissible to borrow a device from the world of films and spend the rest of this opening chapter pretending to be a TV camera zooming in on several documentary sequences which give the flavour of life in the New Australia.

OPENING SEQUENCE—RINGSIDE SEATS AT THE MARKET

The scene opens on what appears to be a good old Australian punch-up. A miscellaneous collection of brawny workers, mothers with squawking babies, ink-spotted schoolboys with slide rules, country farmers in shorts and bushie hats and sharp-looking city gents carrying smoked-salmon packed lunches are jostling uncomfortably together on two or three tightly crammed benches. All are craning their necks to see something ahead of them, some have binoculars, and two of the sharp gents have got their own little step-ladder, which they keep mounting in order to peer into the distance. Suddenly there is pandemonium. Shouts of 'Is that 2 dollars or 3 dollars, Chalkie? Can't yer bloody well write straight!' When Chalkie's hieroglyphics become clear, two of the brawny workers stampede towards a nearby telephone, knocking over the step-ladder and trampling on a schoolboy who is using his slide rule to send furious tic-tac signals. Meanwhile, a weeping woman has made it to the telephone. She is elbowed out of the way by a city gent, who in turn is pulled away by a pugnacious taxi-driver. Fists fly and oaths fill the air. Can this be a race meeting? A rowdy election rally? A demonstration? No, it's just the public gallery of the Sydney Stock Exchange on a day when one mining company announces encouraging nickel drilling results from its Western Australian leases. The brokers have chalked up gains of $3 on its share price, and potential buyers and sellers are getting gripped with the nickel fever. One of the doorkeepers says genially, 'They're a bit rough today, but my word you should have seen the gallery on the day when Tasminex went from $3 to $90 to $18 and back to $40 all in one morning. It was worse than the bloody gladiators in Ben Hur.'

SEQUENCE 2—A 1970-MADE AUSTRALIAN MILLIONAIRE

Cut to a palatial suite of air-conditioned offices six storeys high on Pitt Street—the Wall Street of Sydney. A tall, bouncy, 37-year-old stockbroker, David Constable, is telling me the story of his own gilt-edged rise to multi-millionairedom. Around us is a scene of feverish action and variegated accents. A hurricane of telephone orders to buy and sell are keeping the order clerks' telephone consoles flashing with the winking lights of piled-up waiting calls. Telex machines chatter away with instructions from international customers. Teenage apprentices are tuning up their stretching muscles to Olympic standards as they clamber around a huge wall-chart marking in the latest movements in share prices. Around the office one hears the fruity aristocratic tones of Olde England from 30-year-old David Wheeler, who made a fortune in the City of London and is now repeating his achievement in Sydney as Constable's partner; the sharp Atlanta twang of US-born Roger Planalp, who now lives permanently in Australia working as Chief Geologist to the Constable-financed Target Group of exploration companies; while over the telephone wires from small migrant

customers come exclamations like 'Mamma mia!', 'Mein Gott!'
or more familiarly the dinky-di strine squawks of 'No risk, mate!',
'She'll be right' or 'Go for yer life, boy.' In the centre of this
maelstrom sprawls the rangy figure of David Constable. He is
cradling two telephones under his chin and talking simultaneously
to London and Perth, pausing briefly to order himself a new
$20,000 Jensen motor-car and a dozen Sydney rock oysters for
each of his lunch guests. David Wheeler leafs through the day's
list of small share orders from housewives and working men,
repeats the old Wall Street adage, 'When the lift boys are in, it's
time to be out,' and then gloomily observes to no one in particular
that the market looks quite out of control. Another partner slaps
him cheerfully on the back and says, 'Don't say that until my
Tasminex have come good and made me a few hundred thousand
please, David.' At this point a posse of pretty waitresses usher in a
delicious lunch starting with oysters and champagne. Here perhaps
is the *dolce vita* of Australia's high finance.

Times were not always so good for David Constable. Son of a
department-store manager, he was a drop-out from Sydney
University, and worked his way round the world doing drudgery
labour as an office-boy for stock-exchange firms in various international cities. When he took the typically dashing plunge of
starting up on his own in 1961, he had considerable difficulty in
scraping together the $28,000 fee for a seat on the Sydney Stock
Exchange. But today, Constable & Co. is a legendary success
story, employing an executive staff of 60 and controlling its own
merchant bank and a stable of mineral companies. By taking skilful
positions on the stock market as a share trader, Constable has
multiplied his capital 40 times during the last four years, while his
revenue earned in sharebroking commissions has increased 20
times over during the same period. Even the 1970 shakeout has
barely dented his prosperity.

A lot of Constable's success is due to a company called Target
Petroleum. His merchant banking company underwrote 20 million
shares at 10 cents each when this mineral exploration company was
first floated early in 1969. After the market sagged a few months
later, Target's shares slumped to 2 cents. Constable went on
buying, picking up a personal holding of 1.5 million shares.
Following the big nickel strike by Poseidon, Target's chief
geologist, Roger Planalp, advised the purchase of several leases in
the same area, a move which sent Target's shares rocketing ahead
to 80 cents, thereby making a fortune for the prescient founder

(who has paid practically no tax at all on his gigantic profits, since all oil investments are tax-deductible in Australia— a concession which was withdrawn in the last budget). Since he also had some 12,000 shares in Poseidon, bought at prices between $1 and $18 and sold at prices between $150 and $250, David Constable must now be one of the richest young self-made men in Australia. He has no idea how he will spend his millions. 'Not on art—I'm a pretty good Philistine, really. After I've finished building my new waterfront house, I reckon I'll travel a lot setting up a network of international Constable & Co. branches, trying to make a few bob for my clients, and building up the companies of which I'm a director. You can't go wrong in this country now in the long term.'

SEQUENCE 3—THE WONDER MINE

Cut to Windarra, where my chartered Piper Comanche is swooping low over the site of Poseidon, the nickel mine named after the sea god of Ancient Greece. Poseidon has now passed into the mythology of modern mining, for its massive nickel strike in September 1969 broke stock-market records all over the world, making it the greatest mining share gusher of all time with prices fluctuating widly from $1 to $250 and back to $30, all in a few months of hectic trading.

From the air, Poseidon looks like a technological Stonehenge, for suddenly rising up out of the arid wastes of the Simpson Desert one sees weird aluminium formations of a circle of drilling rigs, flanked by caravans, cranes, bulldozers, power units and other bulbous metallic lumps of exploration equipment. In the shimmering 110° noonday heat which forces even the most muscular workmen to take a siesta, a ghostly stillness falls on the drilling area, giving the rigs the appearance of silver sepulchres which could well be imagined as the shrines of desert druids rather than the excavation tools of avaricious financiers. Certainly there are few hints at Windarra of the hysterical reactions that have caused fights on the floors of stock exchanges and created a new army of both Australian millionaires and Australian bankrupts.

But 24 miles across the rugged spinifex scrub from the drilling rigs, one comes upon the tiny hamlet of Laverton, otherwise known as 'Poseidon City', and here is a spot which really does exude the nickel rush fever. Laverton (pronounced Lay-ver-ton) looks as though it is straight out of the film set of a 1930s Western featuring a 'one-horse town'. It is literally a one-street town, for apart from

a ramshackle old pub, a quaint fly-blown post office, a general
store, a police station and one or two dilapidated houses, there
was precious little else in Laverton until the nickel boys started
up their activities. But today, thanks to Poseidon, Laverton has
struck it rich. The town's 80 inhabitants got wind of the potential
nickel discovery during the spring of 1969 due to the comings and
goings of geologists, some of whom made optimistic comments over
their evening beers in the neighbourhood's one and only pub. As a
result of these alcoholic indiscretions, just about everyone in the
Laverton district from Constable Griffith, the local policeman, to
'Fanny Annie', the local lady of easy virtue, picked up a few
Poseidon shares, which were then selling for around 60 cents.
Several weeks later, Poseidon confirmed that it had made a major
nickel strike.

The first result was pandemonium on the stock markets. At the
Sydney Stock Exchange the mining boards collapsed under
pressure from the stamping feet of brokers, clerks fainted and
strong men wept in the public galleries as the shares rocketed from
60 cents to a peak of $32. Constable Griffith made an overnight
profit on his 800 shares of more than $25,000. The biggest
individual shareholder, Poseidon's 48-year-old chief executive,
Norman Shierlaw of Adelaide, made $6 million in four days, and
shared his fortune-making inside knowledge with several lucky
friends. Even the waitress in his local steakhouse took his advice.
'Gee, Mr Shierlaw, thanks for the tip on your shares,' she said,
'I've made enough money in three days to go around the world.'
Similar killings were made by investors from Los Angeles to
London. A Harrods store assistant, Miss Irene Apolonoff, who on
an earlier visit to Western Australia had bought herself 2,000 shares
at 4 cents each, suddenly found herself with a paper profit of
$250,000. Even a syndicate of 16-year-old Melbourne schoolboys
pooled their pocket money and savings and made $5,000. But
unlike some previous Australian glamour mining stocks, Poseidon
really did have the proof of its big strike. Geologists confirmed an
orebody at Mt Windarra of several million tons of disseminated
nickel sulphides and around one million tons of massive sulphides.
On reading the geological reports, several experts insisted that the
real value of Poseidon was much higher than even the already
astronomical share prices suggested. In late October 1969, a
respected firm of Melbourne investment analysts, Argus Investment Service, made the following bold prediction which was
reprinted in Britain's *Investors' Chronicle*: 'Poseidon not only will

be the "star" of 1969 but looks like being the stock of the century. We have previously said that the shares would range from $25 to $100. We would now like to amend our minimum target to $80 and, of course, the maximum price is lifted to $100 plus. For the nervous clients who sold at $25 we offer this advice . . . buy back Poseidon . . . and don't be frightened of selling stocks like BHP and Peko to do so. Already the back-room boys of the various broking houses are working out their facts and figures and we can tell you the price forecasts for Poseidon shares are fantastic. We are content to say that the shares have a $100 PLUS potential.'

Poseidon at first lived up to its advance legend, for the shares rose as high as $250 and spent almost a year at prices of over $100. At the time of writing they have fallen in the general world depression of stock markets to around $30 (still making a healthy profit for anyone who bought them at 60 cents) but despite the disappointments in such a fall, there is enough nickel at Windarra for the shares to be seen by respected financial institutions as a long-term solid investment. Poseidon's dramatic share price fluctuation partly reflects the great Australian love of gambling, for the company's success not only sent its own shares soaring, it also temporarily doubled and trebled the prices of many other small and speculative mining companies. It is these small exploration outfits that gave Laverton its frontier spirit, for the town has been inundated with pegging teams, geologists, financiers and general fast-buck-chasers from all over the world. Light air-craft, charabancs, horse-drawn wagons, Land-Rovers, cars and tractors have poured into the district, carrying a motley horde of exotic characters who might have stepped straight from the lines of Robert W. Service's gold-rush poetry. Prospectors and prostitutes, adventurers and alcoholics, speculators and share analysts, builders, brokers, jailbirds, jokers, rich men, poor men, beggarmen and thieves—all are to be found sitting round the social melting-pot of the evening camp fires in Laverton, dreaming of making a Poseidon-sized fortune.

The chances of these gold-diggers hitting some sort of a jackpot are better than one might at first imagine, for under Australia's remarkably casual rules of mineral prospecting (described more fully in the following chapter) just about anyone who has paid 50 cents for a 'Miner's Right' licence can go out into the desert and peg any number of 300-acre claims. The individual pegger's profits depend on whether or not he is able to convince a mining company that his claims are worth buying. Under normal con-

ditions, nickel claims will only find a purchaser if there is some
hard evidence of nickel-bearing rock formations on the ground.
However, in the immediate post-Poseidon era, almost any claim
within 100 miles of Windarra would fetch a high price unseen from
one of the more incautious mineral exploration companies, while
the mineral rights for land that did contain a few hopeful-looking
'gossans' (rocks giving a vague clue to the possibility of nickel)
would fetch colossal sums, upwards of $20,000 per claim. These
conditions were a prospector's dream, but some of the more
unscrupulous entrepreneurs were not above helping the dream
along still further with sharp practices. Drinking in the Laverton
pub, I met a young prospector called Bert, reputed to have made
over $300,000 in three months by staking claims. How had he
done it? My question was greeted by hoots of ribald laughter from
the successful prospector's drinking companions, who urged him
to tell me the true story. After much coyness, the story emerged
that Bert had hit on the bright idea of improving the value of his
claims in the Simpson Desert by driving some 300 miles southwards to Kambalda (where the Western Mining Corporation has
a rich nickel mine in full production) and picking up some genuine
nickel rocks there. He transported these rocks back to Laverton
and showed them to visiting representatives of mining companies
as if they had been found on his claims near Windarra. Although
some mining companies were smart enough to know that Bert
was pulling a fast one, several were not, and as a result Bert made
himself a fast fortune. How typical this sort of activity is, no one
knows, but the fact that it goes on at all means that for the small
investor, backing shares in the Australian mining boom is even
more of a gamble than is already apparent.

SEQUENCE 4—ANOTHER GAME OF CHANCE

Cut to West Point, Tasmania, where work is starting on the
foundations of Australia's first casino. In a country that is mad
about all forms of gambling, it would seem a simple matter to
extend the regulations to cover roulette. Not in Tasmania, where
the granting of the casino licence has been the biggest and most
hotly disputed event since the discovery of the island. After
thirteen years of preliminary negotiations, eight continuous weeks
of passionate debates in the State Parliament, angry sermons from
pulpits, pro and anti campaigns throughout the mass media, and
a public referendum, the Federal Hotel Group has just been given

the go-ahead to build a $4 million hotel with a casino room seating 150. Even now the argument still reverberates on. John Haddad, the 32-year-old business whizz kid who is General Manager of the $200 million Federal Hotel Group, proudly proclaims, 'This venture will put Tasmania on the map. The island's stagnant economy is at present being harmed by the large number of Tasmanians who escape to the mainland or go overseas for their holidays. Fiji's second name is "Greater Tasmania" because so many of the people go there. We think this development will encourage residents to stay in Tasmania and will attract thousands of tourists.' Retorts one old-timer, 'A tourist is a person who arrives in Tasmania with a pound note and a dirty shirt and changes neither. We don't want 'em.'

The scene around Tasmania is one of immense natural beauty, wide open spaces, unexplored forest country and marvellous facilities for swimming and sailing. Yet one has the impression that the inhabitants of the Apple Isle are slightly out of tune with the twentieth century. Watching the middle-aged generation perform their dainty waltzes and foxtrots at an hotel dance, the image is distinctly Victorian. But according to the manager of the West Point Hotel, the sex life of Tasmania's youth makes Peyton Place look tame. 'The main reason we need a casino here is to keep the boys and girls out of real trouble,' he said. 'In some of these quiet, sleepy little villages they're shockers! Not only do we have the highest illegitimacy rate in Australia, we have incest, sodomy, rape by 12-year-old boys—the lot. These larrikins get up to some stuff, my word they do. The sooner a bit of modern progress cools them off a bit the better.'

SEQUENCE 5—THERE'S GOLD IN THEM THERE BOOKS

Cut to a book-lined basement office in one of the seedier parts of the unfashionable Sydney suburb of Darlinghurst. It is the southern hemisphere headquarters of the famous international literary agency, Curtis Brown Ltd, and I am talking to its manager and founder, 31-year-old ex-journalist Peter Grose. When he set up shop on February 8th, 1968, neither he nor anyone else knew what to expect, as there had never been a literary agent in Australia before. Yet within a few weeks of opening, Grose could see that he was on to a winner, for a flood of profitable business started pouring into his office immediately, much of it unsolicited. Although the publicity given to Curtis Brown's arrival caused a wearying flow of unrequested and largely unpublishable manuscripts (arriving at a rate of over 20 a week), Grose managed to separate the wheat from the chaff successfully enough to turn over $60,000 during his first year of operation and $120,000 during his second. He confidently expects to double this figure again in the present year, and thereafter to maintain an impressive annual growth in profits. Already this branch of Curtis Brown is comfortably in the black and employing a staff of four. It is still the only literary agency in Australia, but its success in this role has been so startling that it has revolutionized the opportunities and rewards open to Australian writers. As Peter Grose puts it, 'We arrived here at exactly the right time, because it was the perfect moment to start riding the crest of the nationalistic wave. We now push through ten or twelve book contracts each month and the bulk of these are non-fiction Australiana. Today, we're getting really solid advances for this sort of work, in the $3,000 to $5,000 range and upwards. In other fields, fiction is still a weak market unless, of course, it's a contract for a client like Patrick White, Thomas Keneally or Frank Hardy. But thanks to our activities, newspaper serialization prices in Australia have just about doubled, and television rights have become astronomical. We've had some advances as high as $250,000 for TV work, and we've also put through good contracts for 10 or 12 films. The whole market here is going through a big period of expansion.'

Peter Grose seems to be a young man whose dreams are coming true. He went to Curtis Brown Australia from the job of being London correspondent on Rupert Murdoch's *The Australian*, returned to his native Sydney, and built up a unique business with a speedy degree of success that amazed the literary world. The future ahead of him in Australia looks golden, for he could clearly go on building up his empire for decades ahead, living an agreeable and profitable life as a powerful figure in the literary world he loves. Yet the baffling thing about Peter Grose is that he is determined, within the next two or three years, to hand over Curtis Brown Australia to someone else, and to return to London. Ask him why he wants to abandon the climatic and commercial joys of Sydney to become a member of the large British colony of expatriate Australian intellectuals and Peter Grose mumbles vague answers like 'London is so much more stimulating.' Is there something wrong with him, or with Australia?

SEQUENCE 6—ART FOR CASH'S SAKE

Cut to the Rose Skinner Art Gallery in Perth. It is the opening week of the City's 1970 festival, and thanks to the munificence of Sydney dealer Rudy Komon, art lovers of the West are about to be treated to their first ever Fred Williams exhibition. Williams is one of the leading landscape painters in Australia, and some of his aficionados argue passionately that he is the finest artist of his type in the world. Yet despite Williams' undoubted talent and eminence, it is striking that few of the 150 Perth plutocrats present at the opening seem anxious to talk to the young artistic genius who stands shyly at the perimeter of the champagne scrum, conspicuously mundane in his baggy off-the-peg brown suit. But while Williams is left in unsplendid social isolation, the opening ceremony is being performed by a lean and fanatical-looking young man in sideboards and a clerical collar. He is the Reverend John Hazlewood, the Anglican Dean of Perth. At first, one cannot hear a word of his speech, but gradually murmurs like 'Cor, this bloke's got a bee in his bonnet' quieten the Bacchanalian buzz. It becomes clear that the Dean is not so much opening an exhibition as preaching a sermon, and that he is condemning to the cultural equivalent of hell-fire and damnation just about every person in the room.

'I am concerned by the morality of those who grow fat and prosperous by exploiting the skills of an artist. There are grave dangers in allowing paintings to be prostituted by commercial interests. I am utterly opposed to the practice of buying art as an investment, and regard the acquisitive nature of those members of our society who follow this despicable fashion as utterly revolting and disgusting,' cries the Dean. After much more in this vein, the choleric cleric ends in a flurry of theatrical gestures with the peroration, 'That the majestic panoply of our country can be exploited as an investment is a vicious debauchery of our artistic heritage and must be stopped.'

At the end of this withering attack, the audience (many of whom ought to have been turning pale or at least shifting uneasily in their well-heeled shoes) breaks into thunderous applause. From behind the Onassis-like dark glasses of arch-investor Rudy Komon comes the surprising cry 'I quite agree with everything the Dean said.' Someone retorts, 'You can afford to, Rudy, seeing that every picture got sold at $10,000 a time before you even opened.'

After more badinage, the champagne drinkers swiftly turn their backs on the majestic panoply of Fred Williams'pictures, and talk to each other. Their conversation is largely about comparative capital gains in the stock market and the art market.

SEQUENCE 7—THE WINE KING

Cut to the lush green pastures of the Hunter Valley near Newcastle in New South Wales, where an eleven-man syndicate of wine investors from Sydney has assembled to taste the 1970 vintage from their newly inaugurated Rothbury vineyard. These investors, headed by Australia's leading wine expert, Len Evans, recently bought 1,000 virgin acres of land in the Pokolbin district, thought to be one of the best wine-growing areas on the continent on account of its rich volcanic soil and its summer cloud formations which produce a very gradual ripening of the grapes. The syndicate (whose members include two surgeons, two dentists, two drapers, an art-gallery owner and a TV compère) is an enthusiastic collection of amateur wine-lovers who claim to put quality before profits. Even so, they are not doing badly, for although their land cost them $200 an acre to buy, and $2,000 an acre to install and cultivate the vines, after four years of cultivation each acre will be producing more than 2,000 bottles of wine annually, selling at a wholesale price of around $1.25 per bottle.

The moving spirit behind the Rothbury syndicate—and for that matter behind a great deal of Australia's booming wine industry—is a wild Welsh dynamo with a connoisseur's palate, Len Evans. He started out life in Britain as a golf professional, but got fed up 'with teaching weak-wristed Jewesses at Potters Bar Golf Club how to swing a mashie', and came to Australia in search of adventure. He arrived in Sydney in 1957 as a glass-washer in a pub, got interested in wine, found he had a first-class palate and graduated via spells as beverage manager in leading hotels to becoming Australia's Number One wine pundit. Today, he writes a regular weekly wine column for *The Bulletin* magazine, compères two regular TV shows, has produced four wine books in four years, owns a fashionable restaurant at which he delivers a speech on the wine of the day his patrons are drinking, is wine consultant to the Qantas airline and four hotel companies and is chairman of four wine companies. As effervescent in character as the finest French champagne, Len Evans sees the wine boom as a major ingredient in the development of the Australian national character despite the recent imposition of a heavy new wine tax.

'In the last ten years, Australia's annual wine consumption has gone from 12 million bottles to 72 million bottles, and the rate of increase is over 15 per cent a year. This remarkable growth is due to five main factors: increasing affluence at all levels; energetic promotion by the wine industry; the profound influence of the continental migrants on drinking habits; the growth of sophisticated and cosmopolitan tastes, mainly among those Australians who have spent some time overseas; and the general acceptance of the fact that Australia today is a rich country able to enjoy its Mediterranean-style leisure. Although some Australian wine has been cheap plonk that's only one degree better than beer, there is also a tremendous and growing emphasis on quality. The good Australian wines are second only to the very finest French vintages, and our general average standard of wine-making here is often better than Europe's. Producing high-quality wines has become a great emotional thing here, and this Rothbury syndicate shows it. This is the wrong district to make big money in. The capital costs are exorbitant, we've spent far more money than we need have done in getting the very best wood for our equipment, and we're spending a long time in careful cultivation of the vines before we move into commercial production. But the point is that we're going all out for the highest standards. You find this happening a lot in Australia now—enlightened people looking beyond the maximum profits they've made many times before anyway, and using their money to seek out a little bit of Australian excellence.'

SEQUENCE 8—THE NEW PRESS LORDS

Cut to three conversations with newspaper proprietors who have founded major Australian publications in the last 18 months. In the left corner Mr Gordon Barton, proprietor of Melbourne's only Sunday newspaper—*The Observer*. His is a particularly intriguing appearance on the Australian publishing scene, because *The Observer*'s political viewpoint is far and away the most left-wing among mass-selling antipodean journals. In an age when the editorial policy of all Australia's newspapers is politically right of centre (*The Australian* is the only arguable exception), *The Observer* swims steadily against the stream by regularly reprinting four pages of London's socialist weekly *The New Statesman*, by crusading against the Vietnam war, and by generally espousing all liberal causes, such as anti-censorship, or the right of the Australian communist journalist, Wilfrid Burchett, to be granted an Australian passport. Such campaigns are dear to the heart of Gordon Barton, a lean ascetic-looking intellectual in his early forties who describes his present political views as 'mildly left-wing and pro-pacifist'. Barton achieved the unusual academic distinction of successfully reading for three degrees simultaneously during his three years as an undergraduate at Sydney University, but even this gruelling scholastic task was an insufficient challenge to his prodigious energies, so he devoted additional parts of his college days to working as a divorce-court judge's clerk and also to starting a small trucking business.

This trucking business, which he built up into the road transport giant known today as IPEC, made Gordon Barton a multi-millionaire. He has since branched out into other fields, such as finance, tourism and book publishing (he is chairman of Tjuringa Securities, the Federal Hotel Group and the publishing house of Angus & Robertson) and has unsuccessfully tried to beat the Australian government's ban on starting up a third domestic Australian airline. Yet amidst all this capitalism, Barton has remained faithful to his socialist and pacifist convictions. In recent years he has helped to finance an abortive attempt to set up a major new national political group, 'The Australia Party', and his other altruistic gestures include paying for full page anti-Vietnam advertisements in the press at the time of L.B.J.'s Australian visit. Barton decided to start *The Observer* in mid-1969 'to fill an obvious gap'. So far, the most obvious gap has been the gulf between the paper's high costs and low revenue, for due to a restrictive practice agreement between Melbourne's newsagents and established newspaper proprietors, *The Observer* is not allowed to be sold from news-stands. Despite this overwhelming handicap, the paper manages to sell a creditable 150,000 copies each Sunday and is currently fighting the restrictive practice agreement in the courts. If this battle succeeds, as it is expected to do, newsagent sales should push *The Observer* circulation upwards of 500,000, but even with this triumph in his sights, Gordon Barton remains pessimistic about the chances of spreading his own political gospel. 'I don't think many people will buy the paper for its politics. It's the strip cartoons and the sports pages which will bring in the readers. This is still a highly conservative country, but

I think I've done a bit to promote a few alternative ideas to those of the present establishment.'

The philosophy of *The Observer* and of Barton's left-of-centre *Sunday Review* would be anathema to Peter Wright and Lang Hancock, the Perth-based tycoons who in 1969 founded *The Independent*—Western Australia's first new paper for 70 years—in order to promote their own ideals of free enterprise, *laissez-faire* capitalism and anti-bureaucracy. Hancock and Wright are the leading discoverers and developers of the gigantic iron-ore resources in the Pilbara district of the North West. Their royalties from these discoveries run comfortably in excess of $10 million annually, and they decided to spend some of this wealth in starting a Sunday newspaper 'because we disliked the existing monopoly newspaper set-up and reckoned that a competitor would quite simply be helping the development of Australia'. On the day the paper was born, Peter Wright said that he hoped 'to raise the interest of the people around us by fighting socialism and the woolly thinking that goes with it; monopolies whether government or private, and government in secret or by regulation, clique or bureaucrat'. Lang Hancock declared: 'A policy of "free bread and free theatres" has led to the ruination of nations in the past, so therefore, in order that it doesn't happen here I would like to help spread the gospel of freedom and initiative to such an extent that enthusiastic people will voluntarily bring their brains, energy and honest goodwill to aid in the production of this newspaper.'

The people of Western Australia have given *The Independent* their blessing (not yet to such an extent as to make it profitable but what's a few thousand dollars loss to two iron-ore barons?) for the circulation now tops 100,000 and is steadily rising. As with *The Observer*, *The Independent*'s cartoons are probably more responsible than editorial policy for the paper's readership growth, but whatever the causes, the success of both these politically opposed ventures deserves salutation on account of their high journalistic standards (both papers are superbly laid-out web-offset tabloids), the new opportunities for news and feature coverage both have opened up, and for the commendable vision of the proprietors' readiness to lose big money in the early stages in order to found good newspapers.

The Independent's first managing-editor was the maverick genius of Australian journalism, Mr Maxwell Newton. He has, in his astonishing career, inspired the creation of more top-class publications than any other working journalist in his half of the world, having been the editor or managing-editor at the birth of the Fairfax Group's *Australian Financial Review*, Rupert Murdoch's *Australian* and Hanwright's *Independent*, and since 1969 the proud founder and proprietor of a group of over 15 country newspapers, newsletters and financial weeklies which he owns himself. 'I got sick of other bastards telling me what to say, so I reckoned on giving owning papers a go myself. I haven't regretted it. My little show is only a year old, but already I'm making marvellous profits, turning over $100,000 a month and paying out a wages bill of $7,500 a week to a staff of over 100.'

Newton's little show began with a shoestring-run series of newsletters which purported to give inside information to their subscribers on subjects such as patterns of economic trade, mining shares and political trends. At one point this information nearly put Newton inside, when one of his newsletters reprinted a government document, thereby causing the Australian Security Police to raid the publisher's Canberra home and to put him on an Official Secrets charge. However, Australia has more sense in these matters than some other countries for the local magistrate threw the charge out at first instance saying there was no case to answer. Newton sent a cheeky telegram to Prime Minister Gorton saying merely 'Ho-Hum!', but his message might well have read 'Thanks for helping my business', as the attendant publicity caused many more people to want to buy the newsletters. Thanks to his rising revenues, Max Newton bought himself a web-offset printing press in the Canberra suburb of Fyshwick, acquired a chain of local country newspapers and started up a go-go financial weekly specializing in the tipping of mineral shares. This paper *The Australian Miner* rocketed away to a 50,000 plus circulation, as did *Jobsons*, another Newton acquisition in the financial field. The proprietor of this diverse empire looks and talks like a real dinkie-di Aussie, complete with an armoury of adjectival expletives, the muscular build of a prize-fighter, and wearing the typical bushie shorts even in office hours. But the rugged rural exterior conceals the brain of a Cambridge First in economics and the energy and prejudices of a latter-day Beaverbrook. For all his cussedness and erratic eccentricity, Newton could yet become the most influential Australian press baron of his day. As he himself puts it, 'Journalism here is just starting to open up after being a long-established closed shop. From here on it looks like being excitement all the way.'

SEQUENCE 9—A TAKEOVER BID BY TOKYO

Cut to a department store in Melbourne early in 1970 where 77 Japanese supermarket executives are being given the grand tour. They are not salesmen—they have come to buy. 'We're used to seeing the little yellow men signing contracts with our big mineral companies for raw materials,' confides an Australian sales director of the store, 'but this is the first time the Japs have shown an interest in buying finished products from us over the counter. It's bloody well amazing.'

Amazing is an understatement when one discovers what this deputation from Tokyo is really up to. Sponsored by the Japan Retailing Centre, the executives have come to examine the prospects for buying $1,000 million worth of supermarket goods a year from Australia from 1975 onwards. Explains Mr Takahashi, the deputy leader of the mission: 'By 1975 Japan's supermarkets and stores will have annual sales of about $20,000 million. About half of that must come from other countries, and of that $10,000 million we would like to buy 10 per cent or $1,000 million worth from Australia. We are particularly interested in some of your manufactured goods and also in your food products. Australia is the only country in Asia equipped with mass-production techniques and familiar with bulk supplying, so you could be very helpful to us. Australian food products will soon become very popular in Japan, because even in our traditional eating habits, Japanese tastes are now getting very Westernized. Australia may easily become our biggest import market.'

As Mr Takahashi's wobbly metallic voice drones out these predictions, the Australian sales director has gone into a mock fainting fit. 'Strewth,' he gasps, 'a thousand million bucks worth of supermarket orders a year! At the moment, we sell less than $500 million worth of minerals and half the country starts crying that we're an economic colony of the Japs. If this lot have their way, we'll soon be Tokyo's offshore island. Where's my order book now?'

SEQUENCE 10—LONG LIVE OUR FUTURE KING

Cut to Buckingham Palace, where the future King of Australia is giving me an off-the-record interview. The Royal Family's Assistant Press Secretary, Mr David Gallagher, politely tells me beforehand that he is 'astonished' at the Prince of Wales' affirmative response to my written request to see him, adding, 'I think it must be because he's so very interested in Australia himself.'

Gallagher and I reach the Prince's first floor sanctum via an antiquated lift and enter a large room furnished in the time-honoured tastes of university and school studies—sporting prints, a desk piled with work books, sprawling armchairs and a cavernous white sofa. Prince Charles is dressed in the mufti of an impeccably tailored Guardee, with a herringbone tweed jacket, dark blue tie and dark grey terylene trousers broadening down to flapping turnups. He is relaxed, friendly and has a good line in under-graduate humour. It is clear from the start that he likes talking about Australia. He feels that his spell at Timbertop School in Victoria was a turning point in his life, because before that time he had been unhappy at Gordonstoun and had virtually no self-confidence. Ironically, Timbertop turned out to be a much tougher establishment than Gordonstoun, as it was run on Out-ward Bound lines with routines such as two cross-country runs a week, trekking, hiking, wood-chopping and pig-feeding. Prince Charles arrived feeling very worried about this tough regime and nervous at the prospect of being thrown to the kangaroos, but in addition to enjoying the school's spartan life, he soon found that the most wonderful aspect of an education in the Victorian bush was the way in which people came up to him and talked openly and unaffectedly. Having spent most of his schooldays wrapped in the inevitably unnatural social cocoon of being heir to the throne, this free-and-easy atmosphere of Australia came as a major personal breakthrough. Prince Charles still remembers rather wistfully small incidents such as the time when he was able to walk over to a Melbourne airport drink vendor and have a long informal chat with him on equal terms. Such moments are hard for him to come by in Britain, but friendliness, informality and a complete absence of artificiality were the keynotes of all his relationships in Australia, and as a result he enjoyed his time there so much that he personally extended his stay at Timbertop to a second term.

The other big development in the Prince of Wales' life in Australia was that for the first time in his Royal career he was performing his duties completely on his own. With the Queen and the Duke of Edinburgh 12,000 miles away, there was no parental guidance to teach him how to handle lunches with Governors and

Governors-General, meetings with Prime Ministers, confrontations with applauding crowds and speech-making visits to remote settlements. Although it is assumed that Royal personages learn all about these things at the cradle, Prince Charles was as nervous as any débutante in carrying them out for the first time. On an occasion when he began an address to a form at Timbertop, 'Unaccustomed as I am to public speaking', the boys roared with laughter, but the joke was true. However, the discovery that his unaided performance of official duties was going down rather well gave another massive boost to his self-confidence.

The Prince of Wales certainly looks back on the Australian part of his education with gratitude, and consequently expects to have a special interest in Australia in the years ahead. As yet, he has no positive ideas as to what form this special interest will take. With characteristic modesty he prefers to say that he still knows very little about Australia and is far too inexperienced to decide what he wants to do there. He is attracted by the possibility of extending his countryside-preservation activities in Britain to similar environmental causes in the Antipodes, and certainly hopes to visit Australia much more frequently than the present quin-quennial schedule of royal tours permits. Already his 1970 visit is his third sortie to Australia in three years—the other two being to Timbertop and to the funeral service for Prime Minister Harold Holt. This last sad visit was the first time the Prince of Wales had officially represented the Queen overseas, and he asked to be allowed to make the trip within minutes of hearing about Holt's disappearance on the 8 a.m. news at Windsor.

As for the thorny issue of Australian Republicanism, the Prince of Wales feels this is something of a phantom movement. He jokes about the poet chap who leads the campaign for the overthrow of the monarchy (Geoffrey Dutton of Adelaide), and believes that a majority of the young Australians still have the feeling that Britain is 'home'. I thought that my royal interviewee, for under-standable reasons, might be showing a trifle too much optimism on this point, yet three weeks later the Sydney *Daily Mirror* published a remarkable Gallup poll which said that 65 per cent of all Australians look forward to seeing King Charles reign over their country, and that even among Australia's under-25s (thought to be the most fractious age group of anti-monarchists) 53 per cent are loyal royalists. It seems that the admiration between Australians and their future monarch is entirely mutual.

SEQUENCE 11—EXIT OF A PRIME MINISTER

Cut to the gardens of The Lodge, Canberra, official residence of
Australia's Prime Ministers, on the morning of March 11th, 1971.
John Gorton is strolling around his herbaceous borders for the
last time, talking candidly to reporters about his resignation the
day before from the political leadership of Australia. He is saying:
'I feel like a galley slave who has been set free. But I've heard of a
lot of galley slaves who got so used to the job that they don't want
freedom, so I've mixed emotions.'

Under some sharp questioning from Mr John Sorrell of the
Melbourne Herald as to what brought about his downfall, the
ex-Prime Minister snaps: 'I hope this campaign to vilify me by
some fly-by-night magazines will now cease. There has been a
definite attempt to destroy me. Those people would make up and
invent any charge against me. It's been sickening—like looking
into a cesspool. I'm astonished that people could do it.'

From this outburst, an observer might conclude that the departing leader had been turned out of office as a result of some major
private scandal. But although John Gorton's mildly Rabelaisian
style had indeed resulted in a few rumours about Prime-
ministerial peccadilloes with birds and bottles, his exit from The
Lodge was the climax of a long-simmering row about policies and
methods of government.

John Gorton was a rugged individualist who liked to behave as
though he was Australia's first President. He centralized his control
of government, built up a powerful White-House style executive
department, and was apt to make important pronouncements on
policy without consulting his cabinet. This highly personalized
form of administration infuriated those of Gorton's supporters
who expected Australia's 18th Prime Minister to follow the constitutional pattern of his predecessors. So when a quarrel erupted
between the Prime Minister and the Defence Minister, Malcolm
Fraser, some Liberal Parliamentarians turned it into an outright
assault on the leadership. There had been attempts at similar *coups*
before, but this one succeeded because of the growing popularity
of the Labor opposition and the consequent restlessness among
Liberals about Presidential-style Gortonism.

Cut to the Parliament buildings in Canberra where the new
Prime Minister, 63-year-old William McMahon, is basking in the
sunlight of his ascent to the top job. He is Australia's fifth Prime

Minister in five years, a surprisingly turbulent record for a nation which prides itself on its political stability. By the new leader's side is his elegant wife Sonia, an ex-model aged 38, who would outpace even the glamorous 22-year-old Madame Trudeau in any beauty contest for international politicians' wives.

Billy McMahon has enjoyed more of the best jobs and the worst disappointments in a long career than any other Australian politician, and the general view is that it's good to see this able professional technocrat fulfil his highest ambition at last.

'I can only express my joy that I am where I am,' Australia's 19th Prime Minister tells reporters. The next move he makes is to announce that the Prime Minister's Department will shed many of its functions and that the Department of the Cabinet Offices (hitherto attached to the Prime Minister's Office) will have a new head and less responsibilities. Australian Presidential Government, it seems, is a thing of the past.

SEQUENCE 12—A MIGRANT'S VISION

Cut to a Sydney pub just off Bondi Beach where in one corner four young professional men are singing a beery version of *God Save the Queen*. One of them was born in Turin, one in Athens, one in New Orleans and one in London. All are migrants. I ask them why they like Australia. The Englishman replies, 'I'm much better off here. I read in the paper today that the average wage in Britain is only 24 quid. Here it's 35 quid (70 dollars) and I'm making much more than that.' The Greek says, 'Beaches and sunshine as good as in Greece and no fascist colonels to imprison people for political reasons'. The Italian claims, 'Here I have my own house looking onto the sea. I can afford to drink more wine and eat better food than I could when I worked for Fiat.' The American says, in a slow Confederate drawl, 'Ah figure Australia's now like what the United States were like fifty years ago. Lots of wide open spaces. Not too much overcrowding. No Negroes to go muggin', and burnin', and lootin', and rapin' the women. And more chances of making a fortune than in any other country on this earth.'

Feeling as though I was listening to a series of recorded comments for a Department of Immigration TV commercial, I asked what they disliked about their new homeland. There were a few predictable grumbles about Australia's uncouth bad manners, high taxation and shortage of cultural quality. But the Greek migrant stopped us all in our tracks. 'In my country there is a famous temple, the Parthenon. When you're right up close to it, you find a lot of imperfections. Crumbling stones, broken carvings and so on. But walk round it and survey it with imagination and with vision and you will see why the Parthenon becomes, for many people, the most beautiful building in the world. You can do the same with Australia. This is a changing country. Close to it, you will find many minor imperfections and even a few big faults. But travel all over it, look at it with vision and you will see why the Australians themselves believe that they have the luckiest, happiest and potentially greatest country in the world.'

Sceptical, but curious, I took his advice.

2

MINERALS AND
MINING TOWNS

THE NICKEL BELT

'In this part of Australia, dearie, nickel is a girl's best friend,' said Cleopatra of Kalgoorlie as she gave a suggestive hitch to her gold lamé negligée. Cleo was sitting in a tent pavilion lined with purple silk, illuminated by an ormolu candelabra, and perfumed by an aerosol can fuelled with Chanel No. 5. Her affluence, which she claimed to be an income of $30,000 and a share capital of $100,000, is the product of the world's oldest and newest professions—prostitution and punting on nickel shares.

There's nothing unique about Cleopatra in Kalgoorlie. Even her exotic accommodation is duplicated in at least a dozen similar field-of-the-cloth-of-lust pavilions fronting on to Hay Street, the town's legendary red light district which is discreetly tolerated by the local authorities.

Yet although there are obvious differences in Kalgoorlie between the courtesans and the artisans in the ways they *earn* money, the only distinction between the two groups when they *make* money is that the more respectable citizens listen to their share tips standing up.

Whatever the recipient's posture, Kalgoorlie is undoubtedly the best place in Australia for picking up nickel exploration 'info'. Standing 371 miles due east of Perth on the edge of the barren baking dust-bowl that is the Great Victoria Desert, 'Kal' is a marvellous monument to human greed. In 1893 an itinerant Irishman, Paddy Hannan, discovered gold on the site of the present town, thereby triggering off a boom that led to the creation of a Kalgoorlie City which in 1900 had 70,000 inhabitants, six newspapers, two racecourses and a plethora of hotels, schools, breweries, clubs and civic buildings. This superstructure long outlived the

gold rush, although the mines on 'Golden Mile' discovered by
Hannan are still producing $20 million worth of the precious
yellow metal each year. This output was enough to guarantee Kal's
survival as a semi-ghost town for three-quarters of a century, but
by 1966 the run-down in population had fallen as low as 18,000,
and there was much pessimism about the dwindling gold reserves.
Old-timers in Kal were apt to pooh-pooh these doldrums, saying
that it was only a matter of time before the Eastern gold-fields
would 'come good' again, and how right they were! For ever since
the Perth-based Western Mining Corporation made a major nickel
strike at Kambalda just 40 miles south of Kalgoorlie in 1966, the
region has been jumping with exploration excitement. Today,
Kalgoorlie is the undisputed capital of the 1970s nickel boom. Its
population has shot up to 30,000, and its rate of building permits
now runs at $150,000 worth a month (compared to $10,000 worth
a month three years ago). Its hotels are booked solid for weeks in
advance. Its streets are lined with grotesquely overloaded Land-
Rovers, jeeps, station wagons, caravans and drilling-rig trucks
which set off each morning in pursuit of the desert's elusive
minerals, looking like a twentieth-century equivalent of Hannibal's
armigerous elephants going into battle. Its airfield is so busy with
stockbrokers' private jets, extra scheduled flights from Perth, and
Cessnas chartered by prospectors that one might almost be at
Gatwick or La Guardia. Yet impressive though the physical
indications of the nickel rush may be, they're nothing compared
to Kal's feverish atmosphere of speculation, which is best sampled
by visiting the Palace Hotel's Steak House Bar. Through this air-
conditioned oasis pours a steady stream of geologists, prospectors,
surveyors, metallurgists, promoters, company directors and share
buyers. All have dry throats, most have long ears and some have
loose tongues, a combination which gives the Steak House Bar
Australia's coldest beer and hottest rumours. It has been said that
the right word to three or four of the bar's key 'regs' (regulars)
can within half an hour start a run on the London and New York
Stock Exchanges. What is certainly true is that almost any sort of
word can get several drinkers hot-footing it down the street to buy
or sell shares at Kalgoorlie's only stockbroking office where the
overworked proprietor, Mr Rex Reed, considerately posts a list of
share price movements on the outside of his building, a gesture
which has resulted in the wearing down of the adjacent strip of
pavement and caused the corner to be re-named 'The Wailing
Wall'.

But although some speculators get their fingers burnt by this sort of hysterical activity, the overall atmosphere in the Steak House Bar is one of boundless optimism. Hearty strangers in shorts slap you on the back and tell you of the 'cert' nickel rock samples they've just brought back from a claim they pegged 80 miles away in the spinifex scrub. Bushily moustached financiers boast loudly of the leases their new exploration company will be floating on the market next week. Perhaps the best people to buy a beer for are the professionally qualified geologists working for established companies. One of these I talked to was a British migrant, 26-year-old Malcolm Humphreys. Holding a B.Sc. Honours degree in geology from Swansea University and a Ph.D. gained in South Africa when on a scholarship from The Anglo-American Corporation, Humphreys came to Australia a year ago and began working for a medium-size exploration company, Hawkstone Minerals, at a salary of $8,000 a year. He spends most of his time working in the field, advising on the pegging of claims, doing geological assay work and checking out interesting information brought in by amateur prospectors. He manages to save about two-thirds of his salary, and with this capital, like most geologists working in Australia, he punts heavily on the stock market, showing to date 'a gain of about 30 per cent every two or three months'. On the overall mining boom picture in the nickel belt, Humphreys commented: 'Geologically, this whole region is very exciting and very promising. In terms of real exploration very little has yet been done. Although more and more professionally qualified people are coming in, this State alone is now short of 2,000 geologists, and at the rate that promising mineral areas are now being prospected, in three or four years time we will be 10,000 geologists short. In this area, the geological evidence does suggest that there may be a major nickel shield running for hundreds of miles, so the chances of finding more Poseidons or Western Minings look very hopeful. But why don't you get out in the field and see for yourself?' That sounded good advice, so equipped with digger hat, snake-bite kit, bushie shorts and water bottle, I chartered a light aircraft and flew round the nickel belt.

First landing was at Kambalda, the Western Mining Company town perched on top of the 20 million-plus tons of high-grade nickel ore that was discovered in 1966. Before that discovery, Kambalda was virgin desert. Now it is an immaculate piece of transported suburbia with a population of 3,500 (rising to 6,000 by 1973). Swimming pools, shopping areas, hotels, drive-in cinemas and a town planner's dream layout make Kambalda an attractive place to visit, but as the turnover in single male mine workers is well over 100 per cent a year, the attractions can't be so obvious to those who live there. Nevertheless, Kambalda is the proof that the nickel boom can mean real developments and real profits. The present production of 65,000 tons of ore per month refines down to an annual nickel metal output of 30,000 tons (worth around $2,500 a ton at current prices), and as these figures and the estimate of ore reserves are mere fractions of the ultimate potential, it is no wonder that Western Mining shares have shown a fifty-fold increase since 1966.

After the reality, the dreams. A 180-mile flight took me to Leonora (population 130), an oven of a village (2 inches of rainfall in the last 18 months) with the temperature nudging 110° in the shade. After lowering several pints of ice-cold lemon-squash at the pub, I called on Mr Sid Winchcombe, Leonora's red-bearded Clerk of the Petty Sessions, Registrar for Births, Deaths and Marriages and Registrar of Mines. It is the last job that's keeping him really busy these days, for Sid Winchcombe's district takes in some 400 square miles of the Eastern Goldfields, including Windarra, the site of wonder mine Poseidon. Sid was the second man in the world to know about Poseidon and he never made a cent out of his knowledge. The veteran prospector, Ken Shirley, called in to the Leonora Mines Office early in 1969 to register the claims he ultimately sold to Poseidon, and said to Winchcombe, 'I've spent forty years looking for something as good as this, and now I think I've found my mine'. Shirley made similar remarks to other local friends, some of whom took action. Leonora's butcher, Keith Biggs, snapped up 10,000 Poseidon shares at 60 cents and an additional 15,000 at $1.20; today his 25,000 shares are worth around $130 each. Although Biggs bought bigger than anyone else, there are at least 10 Poseidon-made millionaires in Leonora today, including two garage mechanics and a hotel bartender.

Some Leonora residents who missed out on the actual Poseidon bonanza have done almost as well since it happened by pegging claims. One of these is Mrs Amy Freeman, a middle-aged widow who until late 1969 worked as a cook in Leonora's pub. When the Poseidon story broke, Mrs Freeman took two Aboriginal boys out into the desert and pegged 71 claims. Pegging a claim can be done by anyone holding a Miner's Right (available on application by paying 50 cents) and the act of pegging consists simply of sticking four poles into the ground at the corners of a rectangle which must not exceed 300 acres. Mrs Freeman ('I'm no expert, but my natives knew some good areas') performed this operation 71 times, registered her claims, and then sold the whole lot off to two mining companies (one of which, Nickelfields of Australia, gave her a seat on the board) for shares and cash reputed to be worth well over 500,000 dollars. It is not quite such easy money as it sounds, for Mrs Freeman spent almost four months in the blazing heat of the desert, sleeping rough and living off the land. She put her entire savings into the purchase of a 'ute' (utility truck) and borrowed several thousand dollars to register her claims (the fee is $187 per claim), although at the time there was never the slightest guarantee that any mining company would want to buy them. But early in 1970, almost anyone who had pegged a claim in the Kalgoorlie-Kambalda-Leonora-Laverton nickel belt found buyers pounding on their door. Newspapers like the *Kalgoorlie Miner* were full of advertisements such as 'Representative of well-known Melbourne Mining Company seeks claims. Apply Room Number—Palace Hotel'. Once enough claims have been purchased by a promoter, his company, if it is as unscrupulous as many have been, can float a share issue on the stock exchange without any geological investigation of the claim areas. In such a case, the prospectus describing the share issue is often inevitably vague, merely describing the company's interests in obscure but optimistic South Sea Bubble phrases such as 'several promising mineral leases near Windarra'. Yet these magic words have been quite enough to send the issue price soaring away at an immediate premium of three or four hundred per cent, thanks to the gullibility of Australia's myriad small investors hoping to be in on 'the next Poseidon'.

The share which, for one brief moment, looked most likely to earn this accolade was Tasminex, a nickel exploration company drilling less than 90 miles from the site of Poseidon in the Great Victoria Desert. When I visited it in February 1970, I was angrily turned away by the site foreman, a most un-Australian gesture which became explicable only in the light of Tasminex's subsequent catastrophe. The story of this ill-fated concern is a cautionary tale to all would-be investors in Australia's nickel rush, beginning with the three Aborigines from the Wongi tribe who sold their mineral claims at Mt Venn to a disbarred solicitor turned mining entrepreneur for the pittance of $100. After some hard bargaining, the new owner of the claims resold them to Mr 'Plugger Bill' Singline, a Tasmanian earth-moving contractor turned company promoter. The price paid was 250,000 shares in Plugger Bill's exploration company, Tasminex NL (no liability), whose quote on the Melbourne Stock Exchange was then 50 cents per share. Tasminex began drilling at Mt Venn in January 1970, the share price by this time having risen to $4. On January 27th, rumours of a strike sent the shares soaring to $15. At this juncture, a Melbourne newspaper sent a reporter round to interview Tasminex's chairman. Plugger Bill was celebrating with champagne and he told the reporter, 'We have struck massive sulphides . . . this could be bigger than Poseidon.' That was a phrase to start a stock-exchange riot, and in London as Singline's words came over the tape, the share price went through the roof to $90. In twenty-four hours of lunatic trading at both ends of the world, the quote zoomed and plummeted alternately, ending up at $20 when Plugger Bill (who had not been out to the drilling rigs himself) amended his forecast to, 'I think it's there, but I don't know.' Other experts, however, were considerably less sanguine. Tasminex's consultant geologists publicly disassociated themselves from the Chairman's comments, and three weeks later the directors of the company had to issue a statement indicating that drilling results showed only minute and virtually worthless traces of nickel. The shares crashed to $3.

At the time of writing, various authorities are still probing Tasminex's strange affairs, but the immediate effect of the crash was to cause a fairly widespread shake-out in all nickel exploration companies, particularly those which had been more active in mining the stock market rather than their claim. Early in 1971, as the world economic recession hit Australia, several small mining companies collapsed completely, and there was one disaster on the scale of Britain's Rolls Royce bankruptcy when the prominent Sydney mining finance house, Mineral Securities, went into liquidation. Disasters like these have rightly strengthened demands for an Australian Securities and Exchange Commission with powers to stamp out the most flagrant forms of negligence or dishonesty but no one will ever stamp out the tendency of some Australians to treat the stock market as a casino. Yet despite the short-term consequences, no one in Australia doubts that more nickel deposits will be found in the coming years, and it is expected that nickel fever will soon be on the rampage again for many more seasons and in many more areas. Paradoxically, nickel is not particularly important to the national economy, for Australia as yet produces less than 200,000 tons of nickel concentrates each year and exports only $50 million worth of nickel metal. The continent's iron-ore exports, and the import savings of the new oil fields, are worth twenty times as much. However, nickel retains its glamour partly because of its high price of around $5,000 a ton, and partly because of the ease with which it is theoretically possible for one prospector to make a Poseidon-sized fortune just be picking up one nickel-bearing 'gossan' rock. It is this element of luck which hypnotizes the gambling-loving Australians into punting their savings on almost any old exploration company which sounds as though it might conceivably be on to a good thing, and the fact that many small investors ultimately lose their savings in this way is regarded as all part of the fun. As a former Federal Treasurer (Finance Minister) Sir Arthur Fadden put it, 'Possums and parrots are protected in Australia, but mugs are not.'

LEWIS WEEKS—AUSTRALIA'S AMERICAN OIL DIVINER

Although many of Australia's other mineral exploration projects have not proved to be a mug's game—anyway, by nickel search standards—nevertheless, an element of muggishness played a helpful role even in so solid an achievement as the discovery of Australia's oil by the nation's largest public company, Broken Hill Proprietary Ltd.

This development occurred, according to the country's foremost mineral financier, Sir Ian Potter, because BHP originally hired an expert 'to prove that there wasn't any oil in Australia'. The man assigned for this task was a retired American geologist, Lewis G. Weeks. It is no exaggeration to say that he is probably the major individual contributor to the new prosperity and national self-confidence that is now characteristic of contemporary Australia, for against great odds and considerable expert advice, Weeks personally inspired, planned and executed the discovery of the mammoth offshore oil and gas field in the Bass Strait.

The political and commercial significance of this achievement is enormous. Up to 1966, Australia's domestic oil production was minuscule. Some 98 per cent of the national petroleum requirements had to be imported across potentially vulnerable Pacific shipping routes at an annual cost of $350 million in foreign exchange. But when the Bass Strait oil wells get into full production (scheduled for 1972) it is predicted that they will supply over 70 per cent of Australia's petroleum needs, and will provide at least two-thirds of the population with natural gas. Moreover, the Bass Strait find set off an avalanche of immensely rewarding mineral prospecting activity throughout Australia, and in particular there are now definite signs that the companies using Weeks' methods in other Australian offshore areas will soon be finding more oil in commercial quantities.

Lewis Weeks, the proud instigator of this mining boom, is the living rebuttal of the biblical suggestion that the age of man should be three-score years and ten, for the climax of his work in the Bass Strait came when he was 73. Now in his 78th year, he lives in hectically busy retirement at Westport, Connecticut, where I visited him on a sweltering afternoon in the late summer of 1969. As we sipped iced tea in his spacious sun lounge with a splendid view over Long Island Sound, he told the full story of his historic Australian discovery.

Like so many of Australia's recent mineral developments, the Bass Strait oil strike began entirely by chance. Lewis Weeks had retired from his post as Chief Geologist of Standard Oil, New Jersey, in 1958, and was operating from his home as a freelance geological consultant, when he was approached in 1960 by the giant Australian steel company, Broken Hill Proprietary Ltd. BHP were worried about a problem concerning some lucrative coal mines they owned in the Sydney area. Put simply, BHP had received vague reports that there could be an oil field in the Sydney Basin and they feared that any drilling or discovery of oil in this area might threaten their coal mines, which were vital to the future of their steel refineries at Newcastle and Port Kembla. Would Lewis Weeks come out and make a report on oil prospects in the Sydney Basin? Weeks assured the BHP executive who called on him, that from studying geological maps he could categorically state that there was no oil in the Sydney Basin, and added 'It's not worth your while to pay my air fare for me to come and look.' However, BHP persisted, offered Mrs Weeks an air ticket as an additional inducement, and eventually the man who has been described as 'the most distinguished geologist in the United States' arrived in March 1960 on Australian soil. Within a few days of on-the-spot research, Lewis Weeks was able to repeat his previous diagnosis that there was definitely no oil in the Sydney Basin. As Australia's leading mineral financier, Sir Ian Potter, puts it: 'BHP originally hired Weeks to prove that there wasn't any oil in this part of Australia. When he confirmed this, they were delighted with him.'

Two nights before Weeks and his wife were due to return to
New York, they were given a friendly farewell dinner by some
BHP executives in the Australia Hotel, Sydney. During the course
of this meal Weeks casually remarked, 'Would you people be
interested in really looking for oil in Australia? If you were, I have
some ideas about where you might find it.' Weeks says that it had
only at that moment occurred to him to ask this question, since
he had always regarded BHP as a steel-orientated company which
had never shown any serious interest in the field of oil exploration.
Pressed for details by the electrified BHP men, Weeks explained
his theory: 'I told them that I had felt sure, ever since 1931, that
there must be oil in the Bass Strait. Australia is a continent of old
rocks, and 91 per cent of the world's oil reserves are in young
sediments, so the prospects for onshore oil strikes do not look too
good. But young sediments of the type that are prolific in petroleum
are clustered in the Bass Strait. There had already been over one
hundred unsuccessful oil wells drilled along the South Australian
and Victorian coast, and for that reason no one was still seriously
interested in the Bass Strait, as the oil industry's rule is, generally
speaking, "No offshore search begins until onshore oil has been
found." But I thought this was a mistake, because it seemed to
me when I studied the surveys and talked to one of the drilling
companies in 1931 that the edge of the oil-bearing basin along the
coast had probably been flushed out by water coming down from
Victoria's rivers and mountains. I reckoned that a few miles off
the coast there would be an untouched petroliferous basin in the
Bass Strait. For three decades this idea had been a small gleam
in my geologist's eye.' The BHP executives reported this conversation to the company's chief executive, Sir Ian McLennan.
Weeks flew down to the BHP head office in Melbourne the next
day, again expounded his theory and outlined on a map an area
of 63,000 square miles in the Bass Strait in which he thought oil
fields would lie. 'My logic,' says Weeks, 'was like that of a half-wit
who managed to find a horse by saying to himself, "If I was a
horse where would I go?"'

This equine reasoning impressed Sir Ian McLennan enough
for him to end the discussion by saying, 'Right then, let's give
this one a go.' The BHP regular Friday board meeting was taking
place later on the same day, and the project was given an immediate blessing by the directors. To the astonishment of Lewis
Weeks, who was accustomed to international oil companies
spending months and sometimes years of research before taking

up leases, the applications for oil leases and drilling permits were
laid before the governments of Victoria, Tasmania and South
Australia only forty-eight hours after the original conversation in
the Australia Hotel dining-room. The first step in an oil search
which was to revolutionize Australia's economy had been taken.

In the initial stages of planning the operation BHP wanted to
hire some large international oil company to do all the work for
them in return for a massive share of the profits. Weeks strongly
advised against it. 'I say spend the money yourselves, and it will
be worth many times what it costs you. Right now, all you've got
is a lot of water and my enthusiasm. The big companies are certain
to be unimpressed because no onshore oil has been found. The
best you'll get from them is some rather half-hearted seismic work.
Once we've got some results, the oil companies will get very
curious, and that's the moment to start offering terms.'

BHP took this advice, and once the leases had been granted,
Weeks and a specially gathered team of Australian and American
experts began a schedule of detailed basic geologic research work
which lasted for four years. The results of the unsuccessful coastal
drill holes were carefully analysed, 18,000 air miles were logged by
aircraft doing surveys with an aerial magnetometer, and on the
basis of the magnetometer's results some 6,000 miles of seismic
shooting were carried out. Weeks was virtually in complete control
of all these activities, although he returned to America for periods,
leaving a deputy in command of the project. BHP did everything
he advised and asked for and never questioned his judgment. When
Weeks showed Sir Ian McLennan the seismic records indicating
the fields that are now major oil-producing areas, the BHP Chief
Executive's only comment was, 'It all looks like witchcraft
to me.'

But the witchcraft soon turned to magic. Sixteen of the world's
leading oil companies made serious studies of Weeks' results, and
many sent their own geologists to the Bass Strait. Some of them
remained sceptical, but in the end there was little difficulty in
arranging the 'farm-out' (oil industry jargon for partnership).
Thanks to an experienced American lawyer brought in by Weeks,
BHP negotiated an immensely favourable deal with Esso Petroleum
Ltd, which gave the Australian company almost every conceivable
option in profit-taking (eventually they took a straight 50-50
partnership). Drilling began in 1965, after a drill ship, the
Glomar III, had arrived in the Bass Strait following a hazardous
voyage from the Louisiana coast through two hurricanes. Just 15

miles from the coastline which had produced 140 dry wells, an offshore drilling rig christened Barracuda was set up and the *Glomar III* set to work.

Three months later in April 1965, Lewis Weeks was back in Connecticut attending an evening meeting of the Westport Men's Garden Club, to which he had only just been elected. The topic under discussion was 'Woodland Flowers', and as the evening wore on some of Weeks' fellow horticulturalists must have begun to wonder whether the new member was a trifle too important for such a localized subject. For during the course of the meeting, Weeks was repeatedly dragged away to the telephone in order to answer a flood of long-distance telephone calls from the other side of the world. The callers all brought the same good tidings. At the Barracuda rig the *Glomar III* had struck a large oil field at a depth of 3,460 feet.

Good news has been flowing from the Bass Strait ever since. Major oil and gas strikes have been made in at least six places (one of them as far out as 55 miles from the coast), all of them in structures located by Weeks' seismic shootings. Bass Strait reserves are now conservatively estimated at 5 billion barrels of oil (a barrel is 42 gallons) and 12 trillion cubic feet of natural gas. These reserves will probably turn out to be at least three times the present estimates, as there are some fifteen promisingly petroliferous structures pinpointed by Weeks' surveys which have yet to be drilled. Moreover, the Bass Strait oil exploration costs were the lowest in the history of the oil industry. At the moment of the Barracuda strike, BHP had invested only $1½ million, over 40 per cent of which they recovered through the Australian Government's subsidy for oil search operations. On Weeks' original operational area of 63,000 square miles, the costs work out at 3 cents an acre, or $20 per square mile—figures which leave oil experts gasping with incredulity at their cheapness. It is hardly surprising that Broken Hill Proprietary's shares soared by 600 per cent within two years of the first strike, thereby creating several new millionaires among stockholders.

Lewis Weeks himself will be able to live out his octogenarian years in immense affluence as a result of his achievements in the Bass Strait, since the agreed reward for his work is a payment of a 2½ per cent royalty on the value of the oil and gas produced. This should put him in the million dollar a year income bracket by the early 1970s, and as a result he is already being inundated with begging letters, but no one in Australia begrudges him a cent

of this impending fortune. As one senior BHP executive put it,
'Weeks is a genius. His imagination, enthusiasm and expertise
created a project which most authorities believed was impossible.
If he had asked for a royalty of 10 per cent at the beginning, we
would happily have agreed to it, for this man has revolutionized
our company and the whole Australian economy.'

LANG HANCOCK

After Lewis Weeks, the most important individual discoverer of
Australia's minerals is a 60-year-old square-jawed Western
Australian farmer, Langley George Hancock. He personally
located the massive Hamersley iron-ore deposits on Mt Tom
Price, standing 1,400 miles north-east of Perth in an area which,
until 1965, was a barren wilderness populated only by dingoes,
kangaroos and rock pythons.

The Hamersley deposits are the most valuable of their kind in
the world both in terms of quantity and quality, for Mt Tom Price
alone (named after the American geologist who confirmed Hancock's find) is a 2,000-million-ton colossus of high-grade hematite
iron ore from which 22 million tons are now being exported
annually at a price of around $10 a ton f.o.b. Lang Hancock's
share of this wealth under his 2½ per cent royalty agreement with
the mining companies is an annual income in excess of $8 million,
a sum which makes him Australia's biggest individual taxpayer
by a comfortable margin. But as Hancock himself is the first to
admit, his initial moves towards the acquisition of his fortune
happened entirely by luck.

Lang Hancock was originally a wealthy pastoralist, the owner
of an inherited 750,000 acre sheep station (by no means an exceptional size for Western Australia) at Mulga Downs in the
northern foothills of the Hamersley Mountains.

He was also a part-time prospector, and to facilitate both his
prospecting and pastoral activities he took up flying, obtaining his
first pilot's licence some 39 years ago when there were only three
other private aeroplanes in Australia.

In 1952, Hancock, accompanied by his wife, was crossing the
Hamersley mountain range in an Auster when a sudden build-up
of low cumulus cloud caused him to come down to an alarmingly
low height in order to get under the bad weather.

Forced beneath the cloud he found himself skimming the
mountain tops, and as the conditions worsened he was compelled

to dive down and fly between the mountain gorges. Fortunately, he knew the Hamersleys well from boyhood days and was able to pick out a path to safety by following the course of a river.

Previously, he had always flown several thousand feet above this particular terrain and as he navigated his aircraft through the narrow gorges at this hazardous altitude he saw for the first time that the mountain walls were a deep ochre red. Although on this expedition Hancock's mind had to remain on his flying he formally registered the thought he might just have chanced to see iron ore in them there hills.

A year later, in the winter of 1953, he returned to the Hamersleys, flew along the walls of the same red gorges for some 70 miles and eventually landed on an unprepared patch of scrub where he collected samples which proved that he had indeed discovered a sensational iron ore deposit.

Armed with this information Hancock proceeded to keep silent about it for seven years. The reason for this remarkable discretion lay in the harsh State regulations which gave the government of Western Australia automatic ownership of iron-ore rights regardless of who had actually discovered the iron.

But in due course this regulation was changed, partly thanks to pressure from Hancock who then attempted to get national and international mining companies interested in his find, although he refused to disclose his hand until protection of some kind for his own rights had been guaranteed.

The best response and guarantee of protection came from the British-owned Rio Tinto Zinc mining giant, whose Australian subsidiary, Conzinc Rio Tinto, finally moved into action in 1960 after their initial scepticism had been overcome by Hancock making a personal appeal to the RTZ London chairman, Mr (now Sir) Val Duncan.

'They all seemed to think I was Billy Muggins from the bush,' recalls Hancock, 'and I had to fight like hell to get anyone interested even when I went over to Melbourne to bash their door down. But Duncan was a good bloke and he got the message. He sent out his top geologist and then the Kaiser Steel Corporation part of the Rio Tinto consortium sent out their top geologist, Tom Price. I flew him round Hamersley and he nearly fell out of the aeroplane with excitement. That was the turning point, and we had a deal within days after that.'

The deal was that Hancock should receive 2½ per cent of the value of each ton of minerals found anywhere in the Pilbara district by Rio Tinto. It is said that when Rio Tinto executives signed this agreement they thought the Pilbara district was a strip of land around the actual visible ore, whereas it is, in fact, an 8,000-square-mile tract of territory in which the chances of further mineral finds (and thus further royalties for Hancock) are extremely good. If that happens, Lang Hancock will be in the Rockefeller-Getty class, but as it is he is not exactly short of loose change and he does not intend to rest upon his financial laurels.

When I interviewed him in his modest Thomas Street offices in Perth, I asked him how he was going to spend his new fortune. In personal luxuries? 'No, I'm just a knockabout Joe Blow—your clothes probably cost more than mine do. I'm not an extravagant type.'

In endowing charitable or educational institutions, like universities? 'Give money to universities—that would be asking for trouble. All those places do is turn out more Communists.'

Would he then sit back and let the government take it all in taxation? 'Not on your life. The Government is getting too rich from minerals without doing any work for it. All they do is spend money on civil servants. We've got one civil servant for every 3·8 per cent of the working population,' he claimed indignantly.

What then would he do with his wealth? 'I'm going to finance several new iron projects which will make even Tom Price look small. What's more, I'm going to keep the equity of them mostly in Australian hands. Although we owe a lot to the foreign companies for all the know-how they've contributed, and although Australia has got all kinds of benefits from those companies such as high wages, good training and new development, we need to get greater Australian participation in the equity that controls these mineral developments. If this can happen, the standard of living in this country could double in 15 years.'

In the months since he voiced this optimistic prediction, Lang Hancock has been striving mightily to make it come true. He has developed his initial lucky break of finding iron ore by aerial reconnaissance into a proper scientific technique which he calls 'geo-botany'—the systematic search from the air for certain botanical, geological and physical signs indicating the probability of an iron-ore deposit. This technique has produced remarkable results, for up to mid-1970 Hancock had located 510 significant deposits in the north-west of Western Australia (300 of them in the Pilbara), and several of these are known to be as big, or bigger, than the existing iron-ore mines.

With his ascetic partner, Peter Wright, Hancock is now working on putting these new discoveries into production. Both men champion the cause of Australian participation in the mining boom, and are insisting on a large slice of the equity being made available to Australian shareholders. Since two 1970-discovered Hanwright deposits, Rhodes Ridge and McCamey's Monster, are known to be larger than all the existing iron-ore mines in Australia put together, the owners are in a strong position to extract the best possible deal from their overseas partners who put up the lion's share of the capital for the railways, harbours and mining equipment. As Peter Wright puts it: 'Our new deposits are so huge and have such a high grade of ore that the world has become a seller's market from our point of view.'

Outside his mammoth mineral enterprises, 'No-neck' Hancock (his schoolboy nickname is still appropriate to his prize-fighter's profile) has become increasingly militant in the promotion of his political views. These can be described as being only slightly to the left of George Wallace's, for Hancock is at times noisily contemptuous of liberals, Canberra politicians, civil servants and anyone who supports the slightest relaxation in the White Australian policy. Hancock is also an entrenched opponent of the influential Minister for Industrial Development in Western Australia, Mr Charles Court. Court's development plans for opening up the Pilbara iron-ore fields have been savagely attacked in Hancock's Sunday paper *The Independent* and described as 'Creeping Socialism'.

Because of such opinions, and his own recently founded newspaper to promote them, Lang Hancock is not popular with large sections of Western Australia's establishment, and his pugnacious criticisms of those he disagrees with win him many enemies. But this controversial 'Billy Muggins from the bush' is worshipped in the booming north-west mining areas which he discovered and is now striving to expand. In the bar of the Mt Tom Price Motel, many a toast is drunk in the evenings to Langley George Hancock. The compliment is deserved, for without his chance flight through the Hamersley gorges, Australia's iron-ore riches might well to this day lie undiscovered.

THE SMALL-TIME PROSPECTORS

Anybody can look for minerals in Australia, and there are times when it seems as though just about everybody does. Isolated bars and hotels in the north and west are often packed out with adventurous optimists who have paid 50 cents to the local Council Office for a Miner's Right—a document which enables a prospective prospector to wander over anyone else's land in search of minerals. If the holder of a Miner's Right thinks he is on to something, he can peg a claim and then apply for a lease, but most small-timers do not reach these advanced stages, and instead live off a diet of extravagant hope. Sometimes they manage to supplement this un-nourishing menu by doing prospecting work on commission for mining companies with leases in the area.

Now that mineral exploration in Australia has become a big and highly professional business, it is fashionable to write off the slightly eccentric fossickers, gougers and panners who still roam the outback with sieves and shovels strapped onto their backs, frequently living in excruciatingly primitive 'humpies'—sackcloth and corrugated-iron hovels. Their mission in life is to scratch the earth for mineral ores, particularly gold, and often they find enough small quantities of these substances to keep themselves in beer and board. Every fossicker dreams of the day when he will make a big strike and some occasionally still do, although nowadays the first move a lucky finder makes is to sell his rights in a deposit to one of the big companies. Fossickers like to tell the story of how two farmers, John Morgan and George Cowcill, one day picked up nickel-bearing rock samples near Kambalda in Western Australia which earned them an immediate $50,000 reward from the Western Mining Corporation (whose Kambalda nickel fields discovered as a result of those samples are now conservatively estimated to be worth more than $700 million). Bar talk in the bush is often centred on how Old Harry got paid $10,000 the other day for info he gave to Swiss Alumina or how Mt Morgan are sending a geologist tomorrow to look at Pedro's claim. A lot of this is pure frontiersman fantasy, but all gold-rush rumours get rapt attention over the evening beer, and even when they are nonsense they often make good listening.

The country wastelands are also roamed by large numbers of week-end prospectors who enjoy a modicum of success, usually by the practice known as 'gouging'. Gouging consists of finding a small deposit of some sort of mineral ore, shovelling it into a truck, and selling it off to one of the mining companies. One popular centre for week-end gougers is Mt Isa, the isolated mining town in northern Queensland. Energetic inhabitants of the town are apt to make a regular practice of digging out the small surface copper deposits which are scattered in plenitude all around the area. One Mt Isa miner explained to me the economics of his own gouging activities: 'Me and my mate go out every Friday night into the bush and most times we find ore very quick. The best ore has about 15 to 20 per cent of pure copper in it, and when we reckon we've found a bonza (first-class) pile we dig like hell and shovel it into the back of the ute (utility truck). If we're lucky, and if we've gone easy on the beer, we may come back on a Sunday night with five or six tons. We can sell it off to the mine for two or three hundred bucks if the quality's right. That's big money, and it all helps towards the house I'm going to buy down south one day.'

Gougers, fossickers and panners still have a role to play in Australia's mineral development, for although their private scratchings are normally of little importance there is always the chance that they may stumble over something big. This certainly happened when a former Adelaide hospital matron, Mrs Gwen Stevens, discovered the world's richest uranium deposit early in 1970. 'I was looking for something else,' she explained, after her major prospecting activities around the Nabarlek district 170 miles east of Darwin in the Northern Territory caused her to unearth a deposit of some 60,000 tons of high-grade uranium oxide, conservatively valued at around $800 million. Fairy-tale finds like that of Matron Stevens (who is expected to earn around $8 million as a result of her good luck) are likely to continue, for Australia's surface is still ludicrously under-prospected. In the Northern Territory, which is known to be one of the world's most promising mineral-bearing regions, only twelve resident geologists work in 520,000 square miles. Even the arrival of some fifty company prospecting teams is doing little to cover this potentially lucrative Texan-sized land mass, so the opportunities for amateur small-timers still look good, although one's view of the future success of individual prospectors is apt to change after meeting them.

On my own visits to the north, the fossickers struck me as a weird collection of what in local jargon are called 'ratbags, alkies, larrikins, galahs and dills' (approximate translation: nut-cases, alcoholics, scoundrels, bird-brains and half-wits). The doyen of them all was an octogenarian called Sam Summerfield (recently deceased), whose main claim to fame, apart from his 40 years of unsuccessful search for gold, was that he held British Air Licence Number 12 and had been the RAF instructor who taught King George VI how to fly. How Summerfield ended up at

Tennant Creek in the Northern Territory remained a mystery, as indeed did the origins of many of the Runyonesque characters I met with names like Chinky Charlie, Bert the Bludger, Scratcher O'Reilly, Moaner Jones and Tiger Wotto. 'They're all bonza fellers in their own ways,' said one barman darkly, 'but you don't want to ask them too many questions.' I neglected this advice, but attempts at coherent conversation with fossickers proved singularly unfruitful. I was not in the least surprised to be told later in Darwin by the surgeon in charge of the Flying Doctor Service that the most serious medical problem in the Northern Territory was the high incidence of mental illness.

Yet the amateur prospecting scene is changing. Frustrated city workers from the south with a yen for adventure are quitting their office desks to come north as three- or four-man exploration syndicates. At Port Hedland in the north-west, I met an English migrant and his son who had sunk their savings into the purchase of a Land-Rover laden with geiger counters, spectrographs and other sophisticated pieces of technical mining equipment. University students reading geology are spending their vacations on the prospecting trail. Light-aircraft owners are now apt to head for the mining areas to see if they can spot an attractive deposit from the air as Hancock did. Many of these new prospectors have caught the sweet smell of success, for during the frenzied months of the nickel boom, some of them made fortunes by pegging claims and selling off information to exploration companies. Since 90 per cent of Australia's minerals were discovered either through 'outcrops' (a professional's term meaning that part of the deposit was lying visible on the surface of the ground) or through clues in rock formations picked up on the ground, it is clear that smart or lucky prospectors have as good a chance as anyone of making themselves millionaires. Their activities certainly help to create an exciting Klondike-type atmosphere, which can best be captured by visiting some of the mining towns.

MT ISA

You know you've arrived at Mt Isa when, after flying 1,000 miles north-west of Brisbane over some of the bleakest and hottest scrubland in the world, you see from the aircraft window a gigantic phallic symbol looming high over the spinifex. This is the 503-foot smelter chimney of Mt Isa Mines, and the landmark for one of Australia's oldest established and most celebrated mining centres. The 18,000 local inhabitants, 4,500 of whom are directly employed by Mt Isa Mines, burst with pride about their town, known since its discovery in 1927 as 'The Isa'.

The mine, they tell you, is the richest by value in Australia (not too wild a claim with reserves conservatively estimated at 120 million tons of copper ore and 100 million tons of silver lead zinc), and now has an output of 120,000 tons of ore a year. The wages are the highest in Australia (including prosperity bonuses, it is quite possible for an underground shift worker to take home over $200 a week). The city's surface area of 15,000 square miles makes it the largest in Australia (only if you assume, as the locals do, that neighbouring townships like Cloncurry, 80 miles away, and Camooweal, 117 miles away, are suburbs). The rate of car ownership—$1\frac{1}{2}$ people per car—is the highest in Australia and the third highest (after Los Angeles and Chicago) in the world, and the local motorists' tastes are so expensive that part of the car park has to be labelled 'Pontiacs Only'. The regular food and drink delivery journeys are the longest in the world, with milk and groceries coming from the Atherton Tableland, 800 miles away, and the town has Australia's highest per capita consumption of beer (delivered from Melbourne, 2,000 miles away).

Listening to such outpourings of local patriotism, the punch-drunk observer tries to discover if there are any unfavourable aspects of life at The Isa. Is anyone worried by the isolation? 'Hell no, it only takes a day to get to Townsville (400 miles away) or two days to get to Brisbane.' Do you miss the kind of social life that is found in the big cities? 'This town has the best social life in Australia,' said the wife of the company personnel manager indignantly. 'There are at least twenty social clubs and fifteen sports clubs. And what with all these Sirs about the place, getting presented to the Governor-General, and interesting people passing through all the time, this is becoming a very sophisticated city.' Why are there so many wrecked cars lying about the streets? 'There have only been four or five smashes this week-end,' said one surprised miner, adding enthusiastically, 'You see, we have the highest accident rate in Australia, because a lot of the migrants save up their wages and buy their first-ever cars here. As they haven't any idea how to drive, it's London to a brick they'll have a knock or two in the first week.'

The high wages are undoubtedly Mt Isa's biggest attraction. Immigrants of over 30 nationalities account for some 55 per cent of the Mines' work force, at least half of which turns over once a year. It's a great coming and going town, and for all the local pride the fact remains that most inhabitants do not want to stay permanently at The Isa. Men come for the money (many supplement their wages with profitable weekend activities such as gouging and kangaroo-shooting), are put off by the flies, the heat, the isolation and the rather staid atmosphere of the long-established company town. When they've saved up enough money for a deposit on a house or whatever their economic objective may be, then they return to the cities of the south. Yet Mt Isa nevertheless retains a stable permanent population of around 8,000, whose community spirit is a driving passion. On the subject of passion, it is interesting to note that of The Isa's 18,000 inhabitants, 5,000 are children under 10, a statistic indicating that there is at least one corner of Australia (still unreached by television) which is doing its best to live up to the slogan 'Populate or Perish'. It's also a good town for single girls. Recently, twelve female teachers were drafted into Mt Isa's schools by the Queensland government. Within ten months all of them were married.

Mt Isa is particularly important because it is the prototype for many of the new mining centres further north. If Australia's outback is to be opened up by real communities, as opposed to temporary shanty towns, then the planners of the new mining areas must emulate and even excel The Isa's comforts such as air-conditioning in every home, high wages and cheap accommodation for single men, an Olympic swimming pool, a million-dollar hospital, good bars and hotels, spacious streets and high-quality schools. And if these facilities can be matched with the friendliness, sociability and community pride that characterizes The Isa, then Australia will look like succeeding in its attempts to create a network of permanent and prosperous population centres in regions which until now have been barren and hostile wildernesses.

THE IRON-ORE TOWNS

In the 1,000-square-mile corner of Western Australia which stands north of the 26th parallel and inland from Port Hedland, there is enough iron ore to supply world needs for the next 150 years without touching the reserves in other countries. It is in this strip of rugged territory known as the Pilbara that the excitement of the nation's mineral boom becomes really apparent, for this is where Australia's new frontier begins.

Port Hedland, which stands on the north-west coast 1,400 miles from Perth, is a good starting place for a tour of the frontier. Seven years ago it was a dilapidated shipping village of around 800 people. Today it is the bustling capital of the Pilbara's mineral developments, with a population of 6,000 (scheduled to rise to 30,000 over the next decade) and a rate of industrial expansion unequalled in Australia. A visitor is shown the town's specially dredged new deep-water harbour, already exporting some 20 million tons of minerals to Japan each year; the railhead terminals where the ore arrives (at economy class transportation costs of less than 1 cent per ton mile) from mines like Mt Goldsworthy and Mt Newman, respectively 80 and 260 miles away in the desert. One visits the operations of a California-owned salt company, exporting over 1 million tons of solar salt from Port Hedland's tidal flats; the innumerable construction projects; the stacked rows of prospectors' and construction workers' caravans and the pubs with notorious reputations for brawling and boozing. If after this tour an observer needs any reminder that Port Hedland is Australia's chief port for iron exports, he soon gets it from the clouds of dust which swirl across the town from the loading wharves, and turn a white shirt chocolate-coloured within half an hour. 'No one's going to complain about it until the ore starts to clog our cash registers,' says the President of the Port Hedland Shire Council cheerfully, and after seeing how shops, hotels, real-estate sales and all small businesses are booming, one realizes why the local merchants are happy to put up with the appalling air pollution and overcrowded housing conditions.

Happiest of all are the pub-keepers. 'Pay-day night at the Port is an experience you'll remember all your life,' said a friendly bartender. 'Along the waterfront the blokes smash an average of 2,000 glasses on Fridays and you'll see more fighting here than you would in Vietnam. I often carry the cash to the bank the next morning with my knuckles split open and maybe a few bashes on the old face, but what the hell, I'm making a bloody fortune.' After much predictable rhetoric about how Port Hedland was the best town in Australia, the barman added helpfully, 'Incidentally, if you come and take a decko tonight, don't let on you're a Pom (an Englishman). We had two Poms in a couple of weeks ago who started giving themselves airs and saying the Port wasn't as nice as Surrey or some place. By the time they'd got out of the row that started, they'd got so many bloody bruises that you could have mistaken them for a pair of bloody Abos.'

Unnerved by this description of the fate that befalls patriotic Englishmen, I took a discreet back seat in the beer garden of Port Hedland's toughest pub. The scene lived up to the frontier legend. Some 3,000 construction workers, miners, wharfies and labourers universally clad in shorts and singlets poured into the bars around 6 p.m., their pockets stuffed with the week's wages—anything up to $200—which they appeared to be determined to pour down their throats in liquid form before the next morning. In the 90° heat, tempers grew shorter as the drinks got longer. Many arguments seemed to get settled with fists, even when on such unemotive topics as the reserves of iron ore at Mt Newman (officially estimated at somewhere between 345 million and 1 billion tons), or whether or not the Port needed a newspaper. There was much shouting about plans for a wild-turkey hunt in the morning, and still more about the woman hunt that was planned when the boys went on an excursion next month to Perth. A babel of foreign languages rose from various immigrant workers' tables, which annoyed one fair dinkum Aussie so much that he finally seized a jug of beer and poured it over the heads of four noisy Chianti-drinking Italian miners. As they scuttled away to dry themselves out, their belligerent assailant turned his xenophobic eye to other parts of the room and demanded angrily, 'Now where are the bloody Yugoslavs?'

Next to drinking, swearing and immigrant-beating, the most popular activity of the evening was glass-smashing. One of the walls was used as a sort of dartboard, with tumblers being thrown at the target instead of darts. Another destructive game was a beer race, in which a circle of men all started drinking together with full schooners which they hurled to the floor as soon as they had drained the last drop. The last man to have an intact glass in his hand bought the next round of drinks. The publicans made no attempt to check or change these activities, and all night long glasses were being freely shattered by individual drinkers as well as those in racing and dart-playing circles. Breaking a glass in the north-west is rather like belching in Arabia, for it appears to be done as a mark of appreciation or elation. In Port Hedland, happiness comes smithereen-shaped.

In a quieter part of the beer garden there was much talk of mineral finds, gouging and prospecting. It was interesting to find that the real 'miners' nowadays tend to be rather studious types of boffin-like appearance, whose work underground involves handling complicated electronic equipment, and whose above-ground behaviour is appropriately staid. The saloon-bar 'characters' with big muscles and bigger mouths, who perhaps subconsciously model themselves on the Dangerous Dan McGrew prototype, are construction workers and port labourers. As always, the biggest line-shooters are the prospectors. In the pub, a drunken Englishman offered me 50 per cent of his claim for $1,000, which he said he desperately needed for prospecting equipment. Later on, a bearded character said he would let me in on 'his secret'—the whereabouts of the world's richest uranium deposits, if I would buy him a middy (10 oz) of beer, price 20 cents. I bought him the beer but have remained a reporter.

In another corner two policeman were getting into an argument which looked as though it would end in several spectacular arrests. On closer observation it appeared the cause of the dispute was not an attempt on the part of the police to maintain law and order, but rather a complaint by the drinkers that the constabulary had been over-zealous in their duties by running two popular local prostitutes out of Port Hedland since last week-end. 'You keep women out of this town so that all you cops and white socks (office workers) can play fairies. Real men won't stay here without girls,' snarled one angry boozer.

The woman shortage may well be a reason for so much fluidity of personnel in the North, for it is still true to say that the new mining towns are places to work and get rich in, rather than places to live in. But they are fast changing this aspect of their frontier image. When I first visited Port Hedland in 1967, my hotel accommodation (the best in town costing $12 a night) consisted of a barrack-like cell which I shared with four other guests (presumably also paying $12 apiece). There were only four beds among the five of us, so the last arrival had to sleep on the floor— a particularly distasteful experience as the alcoholic excesses of pay-day night were taking a heavy toll in vomit. The menu at all meal-times was steak and chips, beer was the only drink, flies and dust covered everything and the water from the cold tap trickled out at temperatures a few degrees short of boiling point. Three years later, Port Hedland's regular accommodation for visitors was a sleek and luxurious air-conditioned Spanish-style hotel, complete with swimming pool, Muzak, mini-skirted waitresses bearing daiquiris, and midnight dining off a gourmet's menu that included oysters, lobster Thermidor, Châteaubriant and strawberries.

This pattern of improving sophistication is being repeated

throughout the north-west. At the mighty 2,000-million-ton iron-
ore mountain of Tom Price, where Marion shovels costing $1 mil-
lion each work night and day taking 25-ton gulps of the precious
metal and disgorging them via three mammoth crushers with much
dust and thunder into 100-ton transport trucks that would dwarf a
London bus, it seems impossible to imagine anything other than
the cacophony and grime of heavy industry existing in the neighbourhood. Yet only a few miles away the township of Tom Price
is a cocooned oasis of air-conditioned comfort. 'Growing Town,
Growing Children, Drive Slowly,' says a sign on the edge of the
housing area, which I first saw when it was a scruffy collection of
caravans and wooden sheds. Now Tom Price has some 400
company-owned three-bedroom houses, each costing $30,000,
complete with four-piece suite furnishings, washing machines,
deep-freeze, crockery, kitchen equipment, television, radio, re-
frigerator, air-conditioning and all the most mod of mod cons.
A Tom Price employee can rent this gracious living unit for $6 a
week—a subsidised price to induce families to put their roots
down there—and the bait seems to be working well. Although
single men rarely stay for longer than six months, thereby pre-
senting the mine with a heavy labour turnover and high re-training
costs, Tom Price town now has a permanent population of about
300 families, enjoying the community centre, supermarket, tennis
courts, swimming pool, schools and motel which the benevolent
mining companies have created in the desert. Community spirit is
developing, lawns and gardens are springing up all over the town
and clubs are forming in profusion. Over the next ten years, Tom
Price looks set fair to become another Mt Isa.

   The ore from Tom Price travels 182 miles along a specially
built railway to the bay of Dampier, named after the Somerset-
born British explorer-pirate who discovered this coastline in 1688.
Until six years ago the district was virtually unchanged from the
time William Dampier first set foot on it, but in 1964 Hamersley
Iron signed a contract with seven Japanese steel mills to deliver
65 million tons of iron during the following decade. The contract
specified that 21 months from the date of the signing a Japanese
ore-carrier would tie up at a fully mechanized harbour terminal,
complete with automatic crushing plant and conveyer loaders. As
a result of this agreement, the railway and town of Dampier were
speedily created out of a wasteland of bleak and uninhabited rocks.

   Building the railway involved strains and obstacles whose
immensity cannot be appreciated until a visit has been paid to the

burial ground of an early train. Soon after the prodigiously energetic Thursday Islander plate-laying team (renamed the Thirsty Islanders on account of their legendary beer consumption) had finished the 182-mile track at a rate of over 2 miles a day despite the boiling sun, the monsoonal rains came down with a vengeance. Experts thought the line would take the strain of such climatic vicissitudes, but the experts were wrong. One morning a 700-yard train consisting of 200 trucks filled with 20,000 tons of ore drawn by two 2,750-horsepower diesel locomotives collapsed into the soggy earth only a few miles from Dampier, battering forward into subterranean depths for several horrifying minutes until the entire monster was mangled to pieces. The train now lies rotting and rusting in its gargantuan graveyard, looking like a victim of a giant who suddenly lost his temper with his toy and smashed it to pieces. Seen today, it is an awe-inspiring monument to the hazards that had to be conquered before men could tame the Pilbara.

The taming seems worthwhile at the rail-head, which now boasts the fastest conveyor loading system in the world, and a $50 million ore-pelletizing plant. Nearby is the township of Dampier, which now has some 500 $30,000 houses, laid out in neat terraces overlooking the sea. As at Tom Price, these homes are let fully furnished at peppercorn rents of $6 per week, and when a new family moves in they even find enough food for a week in the refrigerator. Another innovation at Dampier is Australia's largest desalination plant, sucking some 400,000 gallons of water a day from the Indian Ocean and processing it into sweet and potable liquid that gives residents the best free drink in the entire North (where bore water is all too apt to become brackish). Moving around in Dampier from an air-conditioned office block complete with fountains, to a gleaming new supermarket, to the shark-free swimming enclosure on the beach, to the nine-hole golf course, and finally to the sumptuous luxury of the Mermaid Hotel, one is tempted to reflect that life in one of Australia's pioneer mining towns is agreeably comfortable.

Not everyone concurs with this assessment, for there are many disadvantages to life in communities such as Dampier, Port Hedland and Tom Price. The isolation can become at worst psychologically disturbing and at best highly inconvenient (at the time of writing, one cannot get a suit cleaned in Port Hedland except by sending it 1,400 miles to Perth). The climate, too, can break people, for even with air-conditioning the summer heat of

110° can seem murderously oppressive, as can the tropical storms and occasional 100 m.p.h. cyclones that occur before the wet. But those who stress these disadvantages are out of tune with the spirit of the Pilbara, a region where the eccentricities of God are dwarfed by the miracles of man.

Six years ago there was virtually nothing in this region. Now thanks to human ingenuity, it is the Aladdin's Cave of Australia and the powerhouse of Japan. Three colossal iron-ore deposits have so far been tapped—Mt Tom Price, Mt Newman (for some reason Mt Newman's deposits are actually in Mt Whaleback, but what's in a name?) and Robe River (only just in production). No one knows exactly how much mineral wealth these colossi contain, for the estimates and forecasts overtake themselves at every new geological survey. Tom Price, for example, was originally thought to contain 900 million tons of ore. By late 1968, the countryside immediately surrounding the mountain was declared to contain a further 30,000 million tons. In March 1969 Sir Maurice Mawby of Rio Tinto Zinc announced that Tom Price probably contained more than 100,000 million tons, most of it equal to or better in grade than the average North American ores. Several experts argue that Mt Newman and Robe River exceed Tom Price in size, and no doubt all their predictions will be revised upwards yet again before this book is off the presses. All one can say is that at a conservative estimate the three biggest Pilbara mines between them contain at least five billion tons of the highest quality hematite ore, and more than two hundred billion tons of lower-grade ores, worth in approximate cash value well over $100 trillion to Japan's hungry steel mills (which now take 88 per cent of Australia's iron-ore exports and have to date signed contracts worth more than $1,500 million with Australian-based mining companies).

There are several other large and profitable mines in the Pilbara particularly at Mt Goldsworthy, Paraburdoo and Mt Wittenoom, while the search for more varied minerals in the region—from anthracite to zinc—is continuing apace with many encouraging pointers to commercially viable deposits.

Even more exciting to the eye than the mines are the new roads, railways and population centres. Until the mid-1960s the Pilbara's 1,000 square miles were just about the most God-forsaken of the continent's three million square miles, for less than 2,000 people eked out a wretched existence there. By 1980, the Pilbara is expected to have 100,000 residents, living in prosperity and comfort and served by a network of good communications. By then, the country that William Dampier accurately described as 'past belief wretched', will in little more than a decade have become 'past belief rich'.

SALE AND RED ADAIR

Although the iron-ore centres are the most sensational examples of Australia's mineral developments, there are, of course, many other settlements throughout the continent which are experiencing similar transformations to those in the Pilbara. Sometimes brand-new towns have to be created out of nothing, as in the case of the bauxite deposits near Gove in the Northern Territory. Sometimes a declining population centre gets a transfusion of frenzied development, as happened to Kalgoorlie in Western Australia when amateur prospectors led Western Mining Corporation to nickel deposits with over 10 million tons of reserves averaging 3·8 per cent nickel. At other heartbreaking moments, substantial mineral strikes are made in regions so remote and isolated that it is not commercially worthwhile to extract them. Most frequently, large and unsung increases in production are made from existing mines. It is not generally realized, for instance, that Australia's revamped nineteenth-century coal fields are providing Japan with coal in vast quantities that almost equal iron-ore sales in export value.

With so much prominence being given to the shining new physical developments that the mineral boom has brought in its wake, it is worth looking at the psychological and social benefits that mineral strikes bring to established communities. One older town in another part of the continent which has had its character fundamentally changed by mineral discoveries is Sale (population 12,000), which stands in the southernmost part of Victoria just a few miles from the shores of the Bass Strait. Sale has existed for a century and a quarter, having been named in honour of an Anglo-Indian military hero, Sir Robert (Fighting Bob) Sale, who was killed on the North-West Frontier in 1845. For the 120 years following his death, the town remained a sleepy, rather colonial village, with two principal activities—agriculture, which was supported by prosperous farmers in the surrounding Gippsland basin, and religion, which was supported by devout attenders of Sale's two cathedrals and eleven churches.

In 1965 Lewis Weeks' offshore oil and gas discoveries shook Sale out of its stupor. A notice was put up on the outskirts of the town, saying 'Welcome to the centre of Australia's Oil and Gas Development', and during the next four years 4,000 new inhabitants moved into the area, many of them American oil-industry technicians. This population growth triggered off a building boom in shops, offices and houses. Accommodation became highly expensive. Three-bedroomed homes which had rented at $20 a week before the oil strike were, by 1970, renting for up to $80 a week. Blocks of land which had been worth $500 before 1965 were changing hands five years later for $5,000. Retailers reported 20 per cent annual increases in their turnovers, and Woolworths started building a supermarket. A $10 million refining plant, helicopter base and office headquarters for the BHP-Esso consortium were constructed just outside the town at Longford. New hotels, pubs and restaurants opened up, of which the most ambitious was an establishment appositely named 'The Platform'. Although it introduced certain diverting gastronomic innovations, such as serving claret chilled in an ice bucket and spelling Châteaubriant beginning with 'Sh' on the menu, the restaurant, with its high prices and exotic bill of fare, was the town's premier statussymbol of its own growing sophistication. Its creation marked a new era of self-confidence and optimism about Sale's future.

Sale sprang to international prominence in December 1968 when the Marlin Oil Rig just 28 miles offshore suddenly suffered a 'blowout'. A blowout is perhaps the most dangerous thing that can happen to an oil well, and in this case it meant that thousands of cubic feet of natural methane gas were bursting out of a hole underneath the sea-bed, churning up the waves into white foam for hundreds of yards around the rig, and exposing the oil-field to a severe fire risk.

Many people in Sale were alarmed when they first heard the news of this disaster, fearing that they might be poisoned by noxious gas fumes if the wind changed, or that the new prosperity of the town might vanish if a bad fire swept through the oil-field. But such fears proved unjustified, and in fact the immediate shortterm prosperity of the town increased considerably, for BHP and Esso mounted a massive five-million-dollar repair operation based on Sale which mobilized over a thousand men, three giant barges, a squadron of helicopters and light aircraft, 30,000 tons of pumping machinery and ten million dollars worth of special equipment (much of which had to be flown in to Sale's RAAF base from Texas by chartered Boeing 707s).

Also flown in from Texas was the celebrated oil industry troubleshooter, 53-year-old Paul 'Red' Adair. Complete with red asbestos underwear, red helmet, red uniform emblazoned 'Wild Well Control Company', and red hair, the blowout and fire-fighting expert created a sensation in Australia. In some ways, Adair's arrival woke the Australian public up to the true global importance of their mineral wealth. For during the 29 days it took to suppress the blowout, media coverage of the saga was world-wide, tension kept at fever pitch and foreign currency was spent like water to cope with the emergency. Certainly the people of Sale were stunned by the international oil tycoons, technical experts, celebrities, reporters, TV crews and observers who arrived to play their respective parts in the drama. At Sale's Wurruk Motel, where most of the big names were based, the telephonist (who had hitherto always closed her switchboard at 9 p.m.) could hardly adjust to the sudden rush of intercontinental calls, and was for ever ringing the numbers of sleepy farmers in Portland, Victoria, instead of drilling companies in Portland, Oregon. But despite such little local difficulties, and the much more serious bad weather conditions in the Bass Strait, Red Adair sealed the blowout on January 1st, 1969. He edged his repair barges up to the rig, checking the atmosphere for safety every few yards with explosion meters and then pumped 200,000 tons of chemically treated mud onto the leak. Soon after midnight he sent a radio message back to the shore: 'The well is killed.' It made a welcome New Year's Day present for the oil companies, who had been losing around half a million dollars a day in escaping gas reserves and repair expenses. Red Adair flew triumphantly to Melbourne, where he had to suffer the indignity of being turned out of a bar in the Southern Cross Hotel for not wearing a tie, and then home to Texas. The Marlin operation, he said, was 'one of the greatest achievements of my career'.

It is not too far-fetched to say that the Marlin blowout episode marked an important milestone in Australia's appreciation of its own importance as a great mineral-rich nation. Statistics of iron-ore output from the Pilbara, or nickel reserves at Kambalda, or beach mineral yields in Southern Queensland, are apt to be dry recitations which mean little to the man in the street. But Marlin was a big drama, with big stars and big money. There will be plenty more of all three if the boom continues with still more of the new discoveries that most experts now predict, for despite the temporary stock-market setbacks the story of Australia's mineral wealth at this moment in time looks like being a story without an end.

3

TALES OF TEN CITIES

Australia's heart beats loudest in her cities. Forget the myth of the bush-loving millions, scattered all across the continent, engaged in sheep-shearing and other rural pursuits. In fact, despite the new mineral developments, 85 per cent of the country's 13 million people are concentrated in metropolitan areas doing office or industrial work.

This concentration of people happened naturally, for Australia was born as a suburban nation. Its city centres have had no ghettoes to drive people out, and there has been no large-scale exodus from the countryside to drive people in. Average Man came to Average Suburb simply because he liked it. His aspirations were satisfied by a quarter-acre block of land on which he could build his own house and cultivate his own garden. The process was continuous, egalitarian, and still goes steadily on today. That is why a city like Melbourne, with 2 million people, sprawls across half a million acres, or Brisbane, with 750,000 inhabitants, sprawls over 474 square miles. Because of the space, and the superlative facilities for recreation all around the population centres, Australia has few of the pent-up emotions, tensions, or inhibitions whose tightening or relaxation gives other world cities their special characters. Whether it is the neurotic crumbling tautness of New York, or the foot-loose swinging tolerance of London, or the humming hysterical industriousness of Tokyo, one has the feeling that the tone of these cities is being set by the mass of their citizens. In Australia, the masses are happily separate from the cares of their conurbations, and so the tone of the cities is set by the few.

Everyone agrees that Australia's cities are different in tone from one another. There is an old anecdote, said to be illustrative of the character of the various State capitals, which tells of an immigrant-carrying ship landing at each of the main population centres. When the ship docks at Perth, the first question to the immigrants on landing is: 'What will you have to drink?' At Adelaide, the question is: 'What church do you belong to?' At Melbourne: 'What school did you go to?' At Sydney: 'How much money are you worth?' And at Brisbane, again: 'What will you have to drink?' There is still a surprising amount of truth about each city in the implications of these questions, but the changes in Australia during the 1960s have inevitably had so much effect that the old urban behaviour patterns among the few pace-setters, like religious feuds, snobbery and drunkenness, are fast being replaced by new attitudes and activities.

One way of updating the capsule summary of the big cities would perhaps be to compare them to rooms. One could say that Sydney is the showroom of Australia; Melbourne the boardroom; Adelaide the library; Perth the laboratory; and Brisbane the dormitory. But such labels cannot be understood until a closer look has been taken at each individual metropolis.

SYDNEY

To many visitors, the first impression of Sydney is a bad smell. It comes from a bones-into-glue factory near Mascot Airport whose chimneys pour an oderiferous aroma of sulphur and sheep offal straight across the tarmac area designated for arriving air travellers·

The owner of this pungent enterprise is a wealthy Sydney businessman, Mr Walt McGrath. At the time of the Queen's last visit to Australia he was asked if he would mind closing down his production line for one day, so that the stench would not wrinkle the Royal nostrils. Walt McGrath refused, saying indignantly, 'Her Majesty says she wants to meet the people. She might as well smell 'em.'

When this story is told in certain parts of Melbourne and Adelaide, monocles are apt to start falling out of the eyes of horrified listeners, aghast at such *lèse-majesté*. Sydneysiders just roar with laughter, saying proudly, 'That's typical Sinny.' A fair comment, for if anything is typical of Sydney it's a certain brash vitality, an irreverence for tradition, a worship of money-making and a love of flamboyant ostentation. Because of these qualities this 2½ million metropolis, built on a harbour site of breath-taking beauty, has a pace, a style and a way of life all of its own.

The pace is international, for Sydney, alone of Australia's population centres, really does have the atmosphere of a world city. It could be described as a San Francisco running at a Los

Angeles tempo. A good place to start justifying that label is 'Up the Cross'.

Kings Cross is where Australia swings. This pulsating square-mile suburb of 100,000 people and almost as many places of entertainment has, in its time, been called the Soho, the Montmartre, the Greenwich Village, the Sunset Strip and the Haight-Ashbury of the Southern Hemisphere. There is a hollow ring to most of these comparisons, for the prevailing atmosphere of the Cross is one of flashy ersatz artificiality. Nevertheless, it is a bubbling melting pot for innumerable nationalities, cultures, generations, professions and pastimes, and in this role the Cross today reflects more than a touch of Americanization.

Provided one can get through its streets without being mugged (the Cross has the highest rate of violent crime in Australia), a stroll through the golden square mile will take in a wide variety of scenes. Restaurateurs gratifying the caviare palates of bon viveurs; street walkers competing successfully with street preachers; junkies peddling pot and potters peddling junk; uxorious night-owls dancing into the small hours in luxurious nightclubs; over-land tourists buying underground newspapers; neon-lipped teenie-boppers jostling with neon-lit souvenir shoppers; theatre-going trippers and show-stopping strippers; go-go dancers and stop-stop traffic jams, all are found 25 hours a day in the pocket cosmopolis of Kings Cross.

The most recent innovation to quicken Sydney's international heartbeat has been the flow of US servicemen on 5 days Rest and Recreation leave from Vietnam. Since October 1967 R and R boys have been arriving in Sydney at the rate of 1,000 a week. They come with anything up to $250 of spending money in their pockets, and for such visitors the business community of Kings Cross un-rolls a red carpet—or rather a golden fleece. Merchant adventurers of every imaginable type fight for the R and R custom, said to be worth $50 million annually. Even the scruffiest of Italian pizza houses has now had a facelift and displays the proud insignia of American Express and Diners Club; names have been changed to such homesickness-curing titles as 'Hamburger Heaven', 'Texan Table' and 'Lazy Y Ranch House'. Hotel standards have improved beyond recognition. There are endless stories about the standards of service in Australian hotels before the time of this American transfusion, such as the one about the departing English company chairman who asked the reception desk of a large Sydney hotel if someone would fetch his suitcases down from his room. 'You look healthy enough. Carry your own bloody bags,' came the sharp retort. But such incidents belong to the past. Thanks to the dramatic growth of international tourist traffic (increasing by around 25 per cent a year) particularly from the USA, the quality of Sydney's accommodation, restaurants and night life has risen to the best international levels—particularly at Kings Cross.

Because Australian hospitality is every bit as warm-hearted and generous as its practitioners claim, R and R boys do not, on the whole, get left stranded in the bright and red-light zones. With luck they will get taken in by a family, preferably a rich one living in the eastern suburbs, and there they will get a good glimpse of the life style of Sydney's plutocracy.

The eastern suburbs epitomize Sydney's faith in Oscar Wilde's famous dictum that 'it is only shallow people who do not judge by appearances'. Eastwards from Rushcutters Bay status is measured by the size of the swimming pool, the chromium on the motor car, and most important of all, by the number of windows giving a harbour view. Sydneysiders want to live in the eastern suburbs because they're built on a series of rocky bays and inlets overhanging the celebrated harbour, whose panorama must be a leading contender in any competition for the most beautiful view in the world. Seen across the translucent turquoise waters of the harbour, from some eastern suburbs vantage point such as Vaucluse or Watson's Bay, the Sydney skyline looks like a Constantinople and Manhattan rolled into one, set as a coronet on a backcloth of blue velvet, shimmering in the brilliance of the Pacific sunlight.

It is this view, together with the delights of living beside so many famous neighbours, which pushes up the real-estate values to astronomical heights. Eastern suburbs land costs an average of $11 per square foot. A one bedroom 'home unit' (apartment) will cost up to $25,000. A three-bedroomed house can easily run to $70,000. On Darling Point, which is to Sydney what Bel Air is to Los Angeles, a luxury penthouse changes hands at $200,000. It all comes as a bit of a shock to those innocents who calculate that land in Australia must be cheap because there is so much space, but the beautiful Eastern suburbanites just dig those crazy prices. The Sydney ethos insists that looking rich is far more important than being rich, so no matter that the house is mortgaged to the hilt, or that the bailiffs are threatening to remove the vinyl and imitation mahogany four-piece suite because the HP payments are six months overdue. Whether the stock market soars or slumps, the eastern suburbs show goes on—and a great show it is, with champagne parties, motor launches, private swimming pools and much boasting about share and property prices—provided you're not the one who's got to face the bank manager in the morning.

But showmanship and living to the precipice of income are habits not confined to the glossier shores of Darling Point. For Sydney is a Canaan for the common man, and the places where the modern equivalents of milk and honey flow fastest are the Leagues Clubs. No communist or socialist community can ever hope to emulate the luxurious facilities that Sydney's working men have created for themselves in these proletarian palaces. The doyen of them all is the South Sydney Junior Leagues Club. Behind its vast but rather dowdy exterior in Anzac Parade lies a spectacular paradise of billiard rooms, squash courts, bowling alleys, libraries, nurseries, tennis courts, gymnasia, sauna baths, lounges, cabaret floors, roof gardens, bars and restaurants with superb menus at subsidised prices. Air-conditioned throughout, and decorated in cinema-foyer luxury, the South Sydney Junior Leagues Club is probably the grandest establishment of its kind in the world. Its 50,000 members are all working men and women, earning average wages. The secret of how they collectively manage to acquire such splendid surroundings lies in the gleaming rows of pokies (poker machines) which made a net profit for the South Sydney of $1,390,325 in 1968–69. It's a Las Vegas-style spectacle when the members are 'bobbertooing' (putting a bob or two in) the pokies. Clad mainly in slacks and shirtsleeves, lines and lines of muscular working men front up to the one-armed bandits of their choice early in the evening and are apt to enter what appears to be a handle-pulling trance for anything up to several hours. Often they play two or three machines at once, feeding in 5 cent, 10 cent and 20 cent coins with a routine so mechanical that it makes the players look like robots. There is a lot of mystique surrounding the pokies. Any one wishing to make a temporary break for dinner or a drink usually reserves his personal machines by moving a small metal tab across the coin slot, thereby making it impossible for any intruder to break the lucky, or more usually unlucky, spell. Also, players talk to their pokies as if they were animals or wives (it's a long-standing joke that New South Welshmen do talk more to the fruit machines than they do to their families). As one walks down the lines of players sweating with concentration, many weird and wonderful expressions are to be heard, such as 'Wouldn't it rot yer socks' (Can you believe I'm so unlucky); 'Sweet as a nut yer beaut' (Everything's wonderful, my beauty); 'So stiff, she's crook' (So unlucky, the machine must be broken) or 'C'mittee must be building another wing' (the traditional reason for rigging the machines' odds to the greater profit of the Club).

Leagues Clubs' poker machines have a considerable effect on the local economy (New South Wales is the only State in which they are legal) for although they usually pay out 90 per cent of their takings in winnings, nevertheless many a family budget is left short because Dad's been out of luck bobbertooing. This doesn't stop Dad from coming back to try his luck again after the next wage packet, because there's something in the Sydney atmosphere that encourages a 'gather ye rosebuds while ye may' spirit. As long as the sunshine is free and the Leagues Club subscription is low, the attitude is 'She'll be right' (it will be OK), so everyone in Sydney gambles hard—from shiftworkers to stockbrokers.

One of the most attractive aspects of Sydney is the immense civic pride of its citizens, although again it's appearances that count most with them. That must be the reason why everyone is so proud of the now legendary Opera House, which a Sydney Member of Parliament and Government Minister, Mr Billy Wentworth, felicitously described to me as 'The greatest public-relations building since the pyramids.' The first performance at the Sydney Opera House (if it ever gets completed) must surely be a musical comedy based on the story of its own building. Commissioned in 1962 at an estimated cost of $6 million from a shell and wing design by the Danish architect, Joern Utzon, the Opera House—amidst a storm of tantrums, flashes of genius, rows and walk-outs—has so far cost $60 million and is estimated to cost at least $25 million more before it is finished. When I first saw it in April 1967, the last of its 1,555,941 white ceramic tiles was being put on the roof, but simultaneously the interior was being torn out as it had been discovered that no space was left for the stage and orchestra stalls!

Yet as the estimates soar and the lunacies increase, the pride of Sydneysiders in their new cultural monument increases also. The lotteries and fund-raising drives for the project reach their targets with ease, and almost everyone you ask seems genuinely excited about the scope and design of the conception, some even by the extravagance of its execution.

Undoubtedly the Opera House is madness, and on a gigantic scale. But as one looks at Utzon's exotic shells, seemingly floating over the harbour from that superb site, an amended version of George II's remark on Wolfe springs to mind: 'The Sydney civic authorities are mad, are they? Then I wish they would bite some of the world's other civic authorities.'

Madness of a less laudable kind has been shown by the authorities' neglect of environmental planning, particularly over the inland suburbs. In some of these, decay is as depressing as in the seedier ethnic districts of Chicago or Manchester. Astonishingly, only 140,000 of Sydney's 670,000 homes have proper sewerage (no wonder the harbour is unsafe for bathing), and the atmosphere of peeling stucco, jerry-built brick and corrugated-iron cubicles unworthy to be called houses, narrow streets with chronic traffic jams, honky-tonk neon-lit garishness, and continual noise and smells all add up to a metropolitan version of Dante's Inferno. The trouble has arisen because Sydney is always too much on the make for the immediate present to worry unduly about long-term planning for the future. Also, the people who live in Sydney's slums are new Australian migrants who make the least fuss about living conditions. But now that Australia as a whole, and Sydney in particular, has 'come good', more thought is being given to the layout of streets, houses and other amenities. Yet as Sydney marches towards a projected population of 7 million by the year 2000, some experts fear an urban chaos as bad as New York's.

Not long ago, a distinguished town planner from Britain was given a VIP view of the entire city by special helicopter flight. After landing, his hosts asked for his comments. 'It's the finest site of any city in the world', he observed diplomatically, then added with a sigh of hopelessness, 'It must have been a great place before the whites arrived.'

Yet despite the many shortcomings of parts of Sydney's man-made environment, the quality of life in Australia's premier city remains extraordinarily high, largely because the climatic God-made environment is so marvellous.

Enjoying an average of 320 days sunlight a year, Sydney is a city which really makes you want to bounce out of bed at 7 in the morning and rush off to the beaches, the tennis courts or the boats. The surf is so important that even the news bulletins are apt to end with the words 'And they're rolling at Bondi'.

Ah, Bondi! Merely thinking about this magnificent half-mile crescent of golden sand and pounding surf during the depths of an

English winter makes one yearn to be 12,000 miles away in Sydney. For riding Bondi's early-morning rollers adds a new dimension to human experience. This spectacular beach, which will attract anything up to 100,000 swimmers and sunbathers on a hot afternoon, is almost deserted before breakfast, apart from the dutiful lifeguards and perhaps fifty energetic surfing enthusiasts, yet in this matutinal scene is distilled the real meaning of Sydney's way of life. For if you ask any of these dawn swimmers as they emerge from the waves just how they feel, the answer will almost certainly be a variation on the theme that they feel 'beaut stoked' (magnificently super-stimulated). What this phrase really conveys is that living on a seaboard of Pacific surf-breakers creates a euphoria of mental and sensual enjoyment all of its own. Half an hour of catching waves sends jaded executives off to their desks in a mood of vigorous vitality; it relaxes tense mothers who come with squawking infants to spend the afternoon on the beach; it increases the bliss of young lovers and teenage hedonists; even the turned-on and dropped-out layabout brigade in Australia, 'the surfies', seem infinitely more attractive than their international equivalents, because they're hooked first and foremost on sand, sun and sea.

'Life begins on Friday arvo' (afternoon) in Sydney, the leisure capital of the world. Its wonderful opportunities to have a good life in the open air recharge the human batteries, dissolve environmental and social resentments (as John Pringle has written in *Australian Accent*—'you cannot tell a man's income from his bathing suit'), and stimulate the receptive individual into a mood of euphoric optimism about the future. Add to these heady feelings the realities of limitless financial opportunities, the visual delights of the harbour site, and the boom and bustle of a big international city on the move, and it's easy to understand why Sydneysiders love their town in the same way that a warm-blooded male loves a beautiful and explosively exciting mistress.

MELBOURNE

If Queen Victoria were still alive, not only would she approve of Melbourne, she would probably feel more at home there than in any other city of her former Empire. For Melbourne doesn't move with the times, rather it does its best to stop the times from moving. Rare indeed are the concessions made by the City Fathers to the winds of twentieth-century change. As Robin Boyd, Melbourne's leading environmental expert put it: 'No one could blame a visitor for judging from the usual official attitude towards anything remotely progressive that the city has a mind like a buttoned-up raincoat. It will be, without question, the last capital city in Australia to change the rules on censorship, capital punishment and ceremonies performed in uniform.'

Melbourne's 1870 façade of Victorian architecture, antique trams and anachronistic rituals, together with its 1670 façade of puritanism, Sunday observance and churchgoing, deceives many 1970 observers into thinking that there is nothing much else behind these formidable fronts. Ava Gardner, when filming *On the Beach* damned Melbourne as 'a fine place to make a film about the end of the world'. Billy Graham praised it as 'one of the most moral cities I have ever seen'. Both comments are continuously re-echoed by visitors from overseas. But although every joke at the expense of Melbourne's inherent stuffiness is probably true, it is a short-sighted observer who misses the more exciting aspects of this powerful city.

The power comes from the fact that Melbourne is Australia's financial capital, and in this role its leaders have recently performed many highly original and complex manoeuvres to cope with the lucrative new industrial and mineral expansion. The leading financier in this field is Sir Ian Potter, founder of the stockbroking firm that bears his name. A handsome, snowy-haired 65-year-old, Potter has done more than any other individual to ensure that Australians get a decent share in their own mineral boom. He floated the first of the new mineral issues—Hamersley Iron—at $2.50 a share. Eighteen months later these same shares stood at $12, and have climbed steadily ever since with the rising output of iron ore from Mt Tom Price. This was a crucial turning-point in the nation's financial history, because for the first time it gave the Australian public sufficient confidence to invest in their own equities. Potter and his equivalents have since been able to raise domestic capital for many other successful ventures, and the idea of owning shares is now so widespread that there are today more Australian shareholders per head of population than there are in Britain or America. Potter's greatest triumph has been the Mt Newman iron ore project, for which he privately obtained over $100 million of local Australian investment, thus making it the first of the nation's major mineral developments to be entirely Australian-owned.

Sir Ian Potter is important because he represents a breed of financial giants found only in Melbourne—or to be even more precise, found only in Collins Street. This is the Wall Street of Australia, centre for stockbroking firms, insurance companies, and headquarters for many of the mightiest corporations such as Broken Hill Proprietary and Conzinc Rio Tinto of Australia. It has long been fashionable to say that Collins Street money, though big, is frozen solid, and that the only place to raise capital for entrepreneurial initiatives is in Sydney. Certainly a good many members of the Melbourne financial community are arch-conservatives. I once met a stockbroker who spent most of lunch lamenting the recent 700 per cent rise in BHP shares (now yielding around 1 per cent) because two years ago he had put some of his biggest clients into this stock on the ground that it was the safest 8 per cent yield he could find. 'Terrifying' was the word he kept using about the handsome profits he had made for his no doubt delighted customers. But this degree of ice-age caution is being thawed away by the sunshine of mineral-induced national self-confidence. Sir Ian Potter, for example, has not just confined his investment exploits to iron ore. His money recently pioneered the creation of a new fleet of containerized cargo ships, played a large part in the Bass Strait oil development, helps support the Elizabethan Theatre Trust and finances a foundation for educational research. There is perhaps nothing startling about this type of profitable investment combined with public-spirited philanthropy by American standards, but in Australia the really big fortunes are only just beginning to be made, and so the world of high finance is now starting to spread its wings. Like the rest of the continent, Collins Street is waking up.

Architecturally, Collins Street is a gem, particularly at the top end where the big bluestone office buildings send Betjemanesque connoisseurs of Victoriana into ecstasies of appreciation. But for those in search of human vitality, it's better to visit the lower extremity of this great boulevard, which is always known as the 'Paris End' of Collins Street on account of its numerous restaurants and outdoor cafés. Although Melbourne's laws characteristically prohibit the consumption of alcohol in these pavement hostelries, nevertheless the atmosphere in this area is as gay and colourful as in the Champs Elysées, even if the staple diet does have to be pizza rather than Pernod.

There must now be a good case for including a pizza in the heraldic design of Melbourne's coat of arms, for there are over 200,000 Italians living in the city (10 per cent of the total population), and between them they run most of the service, some of the manufacturing and just about all of the catering industries.

It is a sociological mystery why Melbourne should have become the Naples of Australia. It is assumed that the Italians just emigrated, multiplied, and happened to pick the capital of Victoria for settlement because they had most friends there and because jobs were always available. Italian labour in Melbourne today makes up over 60 per cent of the building industry's work force, 24 per cent of Ford's manpower, and more than 20 per cent of the staff at General Motors-Holden. They are also prolific in hairdressing, newsagents, shops, and above all in hotels, restaurants and wine-making. The Italians' great achievement is that they have set the pace in Melbourne for the good life. For an urban civilization, like Napoleon's army, marches on its stomach, and thanks to over 500 continental delicatessens, two million gallons of locally-made wine, and over two hundred good restaurants, Italian-inspired Melbourne marches on as a very civilized gastronomic city.

Anglo-Saxons are doing their bit for civilization too. There are two good permanent repertory companies in Melbourne, more cinemas than in any other city in the Southern Hemisphere, a world-class concert auditorium in the shape of the Meyer Music Bowl, the headquarters of the Australian Ballet Company and a brand new Arts Centre. This was started about the same time as the Sydney Opera House, but unlike that ill-fated Danish dream, Melbourne's Arts Centre is being completed on time and under budget. Its proud father is a local architect, Roy Grounds, who has designed for his city on the elegant seven-and-a half-acre site on tree-lined St Kilda Road a spectacular series of rectangular courts which house six miles of art gallery, a concert hall, a theatre, an auditorium for ballet, experimental theatre and film studios, restaurants, cafeteria and a display hall. Despite minor criticisms of the motel-lobby type entrance, and the monotonous lighting effects of the art gallery, the Arts Centre is judged a triumphant success by the people of Victoria (who paid for it one quarter of the cost of the still unfinished $85 million Sydney Opera House) and a delighted Victoria State Government recommended a knighthood for its creator.

Melbourne's world of cultural centres, expensive restaurants and financial institutions, together with the underlying conservatism and puritanism, does not perhaps sound the most attractive of environments for young people. This is indeed the case, for to judge from the comments of the large number of young Melbournian expatriates in other Australian cities, Melbourne is a great place to be away from—at least temporarily. In Sydney, the surf beaches are nearer, the parties wilder, the morality more lenient, so go north young man to sow your wild oats. But Melbourne is really a city for doers rather than for swingers. It offers more stable careers, and more tangible opportunities, and the result is that many young rebels who storm out of Billy Graham's favourite city in their late teens return a year or two later to settle down to work. The tone of Young Melbourne thus tends to be set by an interesting milieu of 25- to 35-year-olds working in fields like television, advertising, stockbroking, mining, commerce and real estate. They appear as a rather tough go-go crowd with few of the polished superiorities or gnawing self-neuroses which are apt to characterize respectively their British and American equivalents. But for all their hard-headedness, they certainly know how to enjoy life. A good place to see the young Melbourne professionals letting their hair down is inside the palatial pleasure-dome of Captain Peter Janson.

Captain Janson—the military title was awarded him by the King of Bhutan after a few days of courageous partridge-shooting on the Tibet border—is a 32-year-old self-employed public relations man, who singlehandedly tries to make up for all the swinging the other 1,999,999 citizens of Melbourne don't get round to doing. He lives in a spectacular and sumptuously furnished four-storey circular tower which is perched on top of the antiquely dignified Federal Hotel in Collins Street. Antiquity and dignity end in the Federal Hotel once you reach the 7th floor and ring Janson's bell. Inside, it's Paris to peanuts (to use a local racing expression) that mine host will be in the midst of one of his regular 24-hour-a-day rave-ups. Provided a guest can dodge the exploding champagne corks and avoid having his toes chewed off by the resident foot fetishist—a giant Dobermann Pinscher named Max, he will climb skywards through exotically-named parlours, such as the music gallery (gold carpets, red silk trumpet banners on the walls, and an acoustically perfect stereo apparatus), and the seduction suite (complete with four-poster bed, sunken bath, self-dimming candelabra, porthole windows and an overhead mirror), until somewhere in this hedonistic labyrinth he confronts the black-bearded Rabelaisian-chuckling visage of the proprietor.

Peter Janson will probably be too busy for civilities, as he will just be securing from some Oriental airline representative a deal

whereby sixteen free first-class tickets from Melbourne to Hong
Kong via Paris will be issued to Janson Associates in return for
two favourable paragraphs in the nature-spotters' diary of the
Ballarat Echo. However, should he be free from such wheels and
deals, Janson will bathe the new arrival in champagne, rattle
through a brisk self-portrait mentioning his exploits as a bull-
fighter in Mexico, a racing driver in Europe, an elephant-hunter
in Africa, and a tiger-shooter in Tibet, and then introduce his new
guest in flatteringly hyperbolic terms to the assembled company.
This company, provided the hour is early enough in the day for its
members not to be horizontal, consists of lively young businessmen, full of enthusiasm for the new film they're making, the great
share they've just bought, the property deal they're just putting
through, or the improved sales figures they're just releasing. It
may not add up to great intellectual conversation, but these kind
of gatherings certainly give the visitor an insight into the get-up-
and-go spirit of the younger Australian commercial adventurers,
and belies the myth about the tedium of Melbourne. For all his
froth and bubbly, New Zealand-born Peter Janson is very much
one of this new professional breed. An entrepreneur extraordinary,
he can put together almost any middle-level deal in Victoria within
hours. Need a fleet of trade-price cars to start a rental business?
Land for a new casino? Landing rights for an airline? A promotion
campaign for Gippsland Tourism? Janson can fix it. Last time I
was in Melbourne, I arrived on Christmas Eve desperate to raise
a first-class crew of TV film technicians, extensive editing
facilities, and an interviewing studio all for immediate use on
Christmas Day, Boxing Day through to the New Year—the one
period when all Australia goes into a beery coma of holiday
relaxation. Janson arranged everything within half an hour.

Such a flamboyant extrovert might be thought more at home in
the South Sea bubble atmosphere of Sydney rather than in the
constricting staidness of traditional Melbourne, but Janson pooh-
poohs such a suggestion with a nice compliment to the commercial
character of his adopted city. 'Here the money's real, the people
are real, and you know exactly where you stand. In Sydney,
everyone's living to the credit limit, everyone's putting on an act,
and you never know who's going to be in the bankruptcy court
tomorrow.'

Peter Janson and his contemporary equivalents tend to look
down on, and in turn are looked down on by, two other segments
of Melbourne that deserve a mention—suburbia and snobsville.

The suburbs are what's wrong with Melbourne. Once a visitor has moved beyond the city limits, he finds himself in a visual and spiritual environment of unequalled parochial ennui. The only thing that's more boring than the endless rows of red brick matchboxes in places like Moonee Ponds (the suburb reserved for the deadliest shafts of wit from local satirist Barry Humphries) are the people who live inside them. The flag-wavingly patriotic Edna Everage, her husband Norm, and the pathetic bore Sandy Stone —all Humphries' creations—are not just stage characters, they are archetypal figures straight from Melbourne suburbia. Banalities and clichés pour out of their mouths in strips of heavy leaden type. Their prejudices and platitudes come in mass-produced uniformity. Their recreations will start and end with the dedicated following of Australian Rules football. Their tastes are invariably in the category defined by Sir Kenneth Clark as 'ghastly-good'. A typical suburban sitting-room might be decorated with lace curtains, a vinyl-covered settee, wallpaper depicting koala bears, four plaster ducks in flight above the piano (which is never played or tuned) and beneath crossed Union Jacks a large reproduction portrait of the Royal Family and their corgis—and make sure you don't trip over the plastic gnome as you go out into the garden.

The keynote of these districts is their complacency about the status quo. Most suburbanites are madly proud to have been born in Australia, to be living in Australia and to be going to die in Australia—and they have precious few other ambitions.

Fortunately, Australian life is much more exciting and diverse than the stagnant cultural waters of Moonee Ponds. But what keeps Melbourne in its outwardly frozen state of puritanical conservatism is the holier-than-thou alliance of the suburban squares and the society snobs. The citadel of Melbournian stuffiness is Toorak, a perfumed stockade of a suburb in which men put on a suit and tie to dig their gardens, and women attire themselves in long white gloves to go out to cocktails. Created by the need of the insecure Australian rich to live as near to one another as possible, Toorak contains the greatest concentration of wealth, titles and exclusivity to be found south of the Equator. At the last count 'the village' as it is always called contained 42 Rolls Royces and 31 knights in its four square-mile area, and house prices top even the extortionate rates of Sydney's harbour-view home units. The style of Toorak is definitely 'Outsiders—keep off the grass.' In the 1930s traders had to build their shop-fronts in mock Tudor to attract business, and even as late as 1968 the Toorak planning authorities would only permit the construction of the area's first service station after the owners had agreed to limit themselves to one petrol sign and to create the entire building in the style of a country ranch. The feeling of being on a synthetic Hollywood film set is further encouraged by Toorak's houses, which tend to be palatial edifices in spotless condition with lawns and large swimming pools, although now, amidst much horrified squawking from local magnates and matrons, high-rise apartment buildings are starting to show their unbeautiful heads. 'These silly parvenus will not be accepted. There'll be many a social climbing accident in all those skyscrapers,' one local society queen told me. She knew what she was talking about, for social mountaineering is largely Toorak's *raison d'être*. Its physical surroundings are not so agreeably as one or two other Melbourne suburbs, and even the much-eulogized view over the insalubrious Yarra River is vastly overrated. But in a country full of uncertainties about its social hierarchy, it's real one-upmanship to live alongside the great families like the Baillieus, the Myers, the Clarkes, the Nathans and the Holts; it's a boost for the morale to be able to nod to a knight's lady while doing the shopping; it's sometimes lucrative to hear a Rolls Royce owner tipping mining shares over the evening cocktail; it's exciting to know a neighbour who gets invited to the Government House garden party on the Queen's Birthday, and very heaven to be invited there oneself; and best of all it's great being envied for living in Toorak by all those outsiders in the ordinary suburbs. Cocooned by money, and by the adulation of those who don't know that Toorak's really a very ordinary place, Melbourne's social establishment has become, at least outwardly, interested chiefly in consolidating its present and is not too much concerned with experiments for the future. A quarter of a century ago, a former Vice-Chancellor of Melbourne University composed a somewhat disrespectful ditty about the city's pace-setting suburb:

> Sing a song of Melbourne
> Money by the sack
> Twenty thousand squatters
> Squatting in Toorak
>
> Heaven all around them
> Hear the angels sing
> Strictly no admittance here
> God Save The King!

As a summary of the present tone of high-society Melbourne, these lines are still painfully accurate. The neo-colonial Olde Worlde atmosphere that is still the hallmark of Victoria's capital is slowly crumbling away, but the change is coming not from the top but from migrants and energetic young professionals working their way up from the bottom.

CANBERRA

President Kennedy used to say of Washington DC that it was a city 'of southern efficiency and northern charm'. Canberra, Australia's political and administrative capital, is a similarly schizophrenic hybrid. As a city it seems to combine the sedateness and conservatism of Victoria with the ostentatious arrogance of New South Wales. It displeases everyone, but it works.

Canberra was born out of jealousy. Because Sydney and Melbourne both wanted the Australian Parliament to be within their own city limits, a compromise had to be reached, and in March 1913 one thousand square miles of deserted scrubland mid-way between the two big cities was officially designated 'Australian Capital Territory'. Named Canberra after the aboriginal word 'Canberry'—a meeting place—the new 'bush capital' was slow to develop because of the understandable reluctance of civil servants to move from their comfortable homes in Melbourne to a pioneer existence in the wilderness of the Molonglo valley. But thanks to a visionary city plan designed by a young Chicago architect, Walter Burley Griffin (who had won a $3,500 competition to get the commission) Australia's new capital gradually developed into one of the most spectacular aesthetic environments in the world.

The focal point of the design is a vast artificial lake, named after its creator, which bisects Canberra and gives it the feel of being an inland marine city. Costing multi-millions, Lake Burley Griffin has not been without its critics, but it was defended at the time of its creation by the then Prime Minister, Sir Robert Menzies, with the words 'What would London be without the Thames? Paris without the Seine? Or Vienna without the Danube?' The oratorical comparisons are not all that ridiculous, for the azure waters of the lake do endow Canberra with a showpiece image of sparkling sequins, as well as providing a magnificent extra dimension to panoramic views of the city. On the perimeter of this expanse of water (which was flooded in 1958) a network of restaurants, concert halls, parks, piers, yachting marinas, animal sanctuaries and gardens will soon be constructed, thereby enhancing the capital's amenities still further.

Second only to the lake as a visual attraction are Canberra's three million trees, planted by expert silviculturists half a century ago in order to give the maximum colour contrasts to the parks, avenues and boulevards.

Walking through Canberra in autumn, one sees Canadian maples, British elms, Lombardy poplars, Japanese cherries and African jacarandas together with Australian mimosas, casuarinas, kurrajongs, eucalypti and willows all melting their multi-coloured hues into a kaleidoscopic mosaic of ambers, golds, ochres, russets, deep browns and imperial purples.

The lake, the trees, the national buildings and monuments, and the clean and broad circular lines of the main streets all make Canberra a memorable place to visit, and it comes as no surprise to find that 600,000 tourists come to the capital each year. But a city exists for people rather than for sights, and here opinion on the merits of Canberra is divided.

Canberra has a population of 130,000, growing at a steady rate of 10·3 per cent a year. Over half the inhabitants are under 21, and of the work force, one-third are civil servants. It's very much an administrators' town, for although Canberra's *raison d'être* was to be the nation's political centre, in fact Parliament only sits for 88 days a year, or to be more precise, for twenty-two weeks a year from Tuesdays to Fridays. Because of this relaxed timetable, although politicians are frequently in Canberra, they are rarely of Canberra. Few of them have ever spent a week-end there, and the four-day exodus does much to explain the oft-repeated criticism that the capital is a 'soulless' place.

But it can be argued that the alleged soullessness comes more from the oppressive presence of the administrators than from the prolonged absences of the politicians. Canberra is an exceptionally well-run town. The roads are excellent, the housing facilities are the best in Australia (all homes on ACT are individually styled and designed, the freeholds are owned by the government, and tenants take 99-year leases). The schools are outstanding (early in 1969 the Federal Government rejected a New South Wales request for a $5 million educational grant for its schools, which serve a 4 million population, but a week later gave a $3.6 million educational grant to Canberra's schools serving a population of 130,000). There are no slums, little traffic congestion and few social problems. There is great architectural charm in the public buildings, particularly the embassies, which are built in the style of the nation concerned—for example, the American Embassy is a replica of some colonial mansion in Williamsburg, Virginia. The streets are neat and are kept spotlessly clean. Even the lawns of private houses look as though they have been individually trimmed with nail scissors. It all adds up to an Urban District Councillor's Utopia.

Yet many of Canberra's permanent residents winge (grumble) about their environment just because it is so immaculate. One senior civil servant summed up his grievances: 'The Department of the Interior is the Great White Father of Canberra. You can't do anything without its approval. You even have to buy your Christmas trees from the Department—at the regulation price of 70 cents for a regulation 8-foot tree. At one time you had to have your hedge clipped by the Department's gardeners. Personally, I'd just love to be able to go down to a messy old market, get my hands dirty, and buy my shrubs and garden plants the way everyone else in Australia does. But that's not the only disadvantage of Canberra. The cost of living is sky-high, because everything comes from so far away. You have to pay the earth for oil central heating because at 2,000 feet above sea level this is the only Australian city where you regularly get freezing in winter. There are some preposterous taxes here, like the tax on windows and the new tax they've just imposed on lavatory pans. There's nowhere to go in the evenings. Conversation here is usually very out of touch and provincial and everyone with a bit of life in them hoofs off to Sydney and Melbourne at week-ends. This is a dead town.'

But even if it is temporarily true that Canberra is still a town without a soul, it is nevertheless very much a city with a future. By 1984 a quarter of a million people will be living there. The cosmopolitan beau monde of embassy staffs is steadily increasing, as are the number of Australian civil servants who return from overseas (often with a duty-free Mercedes or Volkswagen—the most popular cars in Canberra) and demand an extra touch of sophistication from their home town. To meet these demands, Canberra has developed six first-class hotels, several cinemas, a theatre, and a large immigrant population is steadily moving in (one-sixth of Canberra's population was born outside Australia) bringing with it the usual New Australian benefits of restaurants and international good taste. Light industry is being established in the Fyshwick area, national companies now find it more or less obligatory to have an office in Canberra, often for lobbying purposes, and the construction industry (building-company employees at present account for 15 per cent of the capital's work force) is shooting ahead with work on new roads, 1,000 new houses a year, and several national buildings of importance including a National Gallery and a new Parliament Building. As Prime Ministers, Ministers and even Governors-General impinge more on Australia's national consciousness through the growing powers of central government and the mass media, Canberra's future importance is certain to increase.

I once asked the uncrowned Queen of Washington DC, 87-year-old Mrs Alice Roosevelt Longworth, the daughter of President Theodore Roosevelt, what America's capital had been like when she went to the White House 69 years ago. 'Washington in those days was a perfectly ghastly hick town,' she recalled, 'very dreary and provincial, and always being accused by New Yorkers of being out of touch.' This, of course, is precisely what Melbournians and Sydneysiders now say of Canberra. Just as Washington DC is today regarded by many as one of the most interesting and agreeable of American cities on account of its political excitements and well-planned, tree-lined physical environment, the same will surely be true of Canberra in two or three generations' time.

Canberra then is in a transitional phase from bush capital to 'Australia's greatest inland city' (as the tourist guides like to call it), and its residents are, in their way, pioneers just as much as the inhabitants of Port Hedland and other frontier towns in the north-west, even if the style of pioneering is vastly different. At the moment, it is easy to have sympathy with those who complain that the sedate provincialism does make capital life a trifle tedious. One evening I was introduced to a rather venerable-looking gentleman whom I asked why he lived in Canberra. 'Because of the death taxes,' he replied. 'As I am a resident here my heirs will only have to pay Federal duty, and will be exempt from State death duties.' Even if it's not yet too good for high living, Canberra, it seems, is literally a great place to die in.

ADELAIDE

At Adelaide's airport, hares and rabbits comfortably outnumber planes and passengers. Apparently unperturbed by the roar of jet take-offs and landings, these phlegmatic rodents gambol in the grassland areas around the runways, symbolically announcing to the traveller that he has left Australia's big cities behind and is now arriving in a peaceful country town.

It is possible to spend several days in Adelaide and preserve a mythical belief in its pastoral tranquillity. For the city (population 750,000) is a planner's dream, with its wide streets and avenues all running in immaculate parallelograms; its grass squares and leafy parks; its stone colonial façades and proliferating churches; and its 17 miles of surf beaches within the metropolitan area. The visual impression of semi-rural somnolence is supported by the behaviour-pattern of certain types of Adelaideans who create an atmosphere of provincial complacency rising at times to a self-congratulatory smugness about the fact that Adelaide is a city in which nothing ever happens. Sir Thomas Playford, former Premier of South Australia, explained: 'Adelaide takes a lot of pride in the purity of its origins. This was not a penal settlement, so there were never any convicts here. No Irish settlers ever came here and there was no invasion of American servicemen to corrupt us here during the war. You see, Adelaide was founded by, and is still run by, a lot of religious Scotsmen—when I said that to an American visitor the other day he interrupted me with "Good God—not as bad as that!"'

It's still very nearly as bad as that, for Adelaide relishes its self-imposed labels of 'The Edinburgh of the South', and 'The City of Churches', and does its best to live up to them. For this was the last town in Australia to ease the drinking hours (in 1968) from the rigidly imposed 6 p.m. curfew; it has an easily identifiable establishment of city elders who, from the depths of their club armchairs, set a high moral tone of social, ethical and religious superiority; Catholic and Protestant feuding is an ingrained habit throughout the city, and there are many preachers in the John Knox-Ian Paisley mould; and the local Government House protocol of bowings and scrapings is so elaborate that it makes Holyrood Palace look distinctly bourgeois by comparison.

Yet all this stuffiness is but one aspect of Adelaide, which some younger residents prefer to call 'The City of Culture'. This grandiose title derives from the success of Adelaide's biennial Festival of the Arts, currently under the directorship of Sir Robert Helpmann, the Australian-born world-famous ballet choreo-grapher. The Adelaide Festival is streets ahead of any comparable project in Australia. Its 1970 programme included highlights such as Rudolf Nureyev dancing with the Australian Ballet Company, the English Opera Group with Peter Pears and Benjamin Britten, the Royal Shakespeare Company, the Warsaw Philharmonic Orchestra, the Georgian Dance Ensemble, the Bunraku Puppets, the Pompeii Collection, and several specially commissioned local productions.

But culture does not end with the Festival. Adelaide's streets are liberally sprinkled with bookshops, all apparently doing a roaring trade. The best of these (and probably the best book-shop in Australia, too) is owned by a literary maverick called Max Harris, who sells a quarter of a million titles a year from his unpretentious store. A good proportion of these are bought by readers of Harris' entertaining column 'Browsing', which is published weekly in *The Australian*, and also by sub-scribers to the bookshop catalogue which is a good read in itself on account of the jokes and hoaxes Harris includes. Recently he advertised *The Sex Fiend's Lunar Monthly* at subscription rates of $400 a year, and actually got one customer—an earthly sex fiend who sent him $100 for three months worth of copies and said he was saving up his overtime in order to be able to afford the full annual cost of outer-space pornography.

Adelaide contains the headquarter of several book publishing firms including Rigby's, which is one of the largest and last all-Australian houses. It specializes not in fantasies such as *The Sex Fiend's Lunar Monthly* (although Rigby's did break a Southern Hemisphere and possibly a world publishing record by getting its version of the *Kama Sutra* onto the bookstalls only nine days after the Australian censors lifted their 10-year yoni-ban) but rather in 'Australiana' books. Rigby's general manager, Mr Lance Tainton, told me: 'You can publish almost any non-fiction work on Australia in Australia and it will be a huge success. There's a tremendous curiosity about the unreported parts of this country and a real thirst for knowledge about our history and our origins. We sold 30,000 copies of Douglas Lockwood's book *I, the Abori-ginal*, and 20,000 copies of this little book *The Dreamtime*, about Aboriginal myths and legends. Our greatest best-seller of all time, which broke all records in Australia, is *The Australians* (a 360-page coffee-table book selling for $8.95). Our first 35,000 copies sold out in four days, the next 20,000 copies went in two weeks, and seven weeks later we sold out another 20,000 printing. So far, over 120,000 copies have been bought, and it's still going strong. To give you the other side of the picture, we do our bit by publishing new Australian novelists, but these are very disappointing. If we get a sale of 2,000 we consider ourselves very lucky, even with the Adelaide public who are generally speaking great book buyers.'

Besides books and festivals, Adelaide is also a fine city for drinking. For once in Australia, the local tipple is not exclusively beer-orientated, because Adelaide is but a short drive away from some of the world's finest vineyards, particularly those in the Barossa Valley where the descendants of early German migrants practise viniculture with the same dedication and almost as good results as their Teutonic cousins on the banks of the Rhine. As a result of the city's proximity to the grape-producing areas, an invitation to have a drink in Adelaide can well mean a few delectable sips of Seppelts' or Penfold's latest vintage, rather than the usual swills of ice-cold ale.

One man who bridges the gap between Adelaide's worlds of Bacchus and Solomon is a 42-year-old bachelor, Derek Jolly, who could be said to personify the new wave of cultural innovation that characterizes modern Adelaide. 'Decca', as Jolly's friends always call him, is the wealthy great great great grandson of Dr Penfold, founder of the famous Australian wine-making company that bears his name. After an education at Geelong Grammar (known as the Eton of Australia long before Prince Charles went there), Decca spent his salad days indulging various whims and hobbies such as amateur photography, sound recording, motor racing (he was Graham Hill's co-driver at Le Mans in 1959) and globe trotting (six round-the-world trips in ten years). Returning to his native city in 1964, Decca bought a cluster of terrace houses in a run-down part of North Adelaide and announced his intention of turning them into a cultural centre. At first, everyone guffawed at the absurdity of such an idea, but having acquired a two-and-a-half acre site with 110 yards of street frontage, Jolly knocked down the houses, built a high-class restaurant named Decca's Place and started to implement his master plan. Announcing 'As soon as you feed people you've got them trapped,' he proceeded to open an art gallery, a sound recording studio, an antique shop, a photographic studio, a wine store, two boutiques, a hairdresser, a printing and design studio and several select small shops on leases. All are housed on the Melbourne Street site which he has built in white Spanish-style stone, complete with shaded verandahs and twirling vines. Another restaurant, an hotel, and more studios and galleries are being planned, and work has now started on the *pièce de résistance* of Decca's scheme, a $1 million arts centre to be named after the late Professor John Bishop, who founded the Adelaide Festival of the Arts. Says Derek Jolly of his empire: 'I'm creating an exciting environment here to electrify the whole culture and way of life of Adelaide. It's my mission to give the enormous amount of talent here a real opportunity to develop its potential. I've been all over the world and I really do know what I'm talking about when I say that here in this city there's a mass of world-class talent just going to waste. For example, I know we have the people here who can make Adelaide lead the world in the audio-visual arts. We can set new standards for artistic appreciation, and for the appreciation of the good things in life like food and wine, and colourful clothes. I want my centre to attract people from all over Australia and the world by its excellence. There's no reason why we can't set completely new trends here. Money? I'm not interested in it any more. My mining shares have gone up ten times over the last few years, so now I'm spending my money on something I really believe in. I want to make Adelaide the Florence of the modern world.'

Even making allowances for dreams and exaggeration, it's difficult not to admire the manic enthusiasm of Derek Jolly, particularly as so many of his apparently crazy schemes have already been translated into reality. On my last evening in Adelaide I dined (superbly) at Decca's Place with the proprietor and a group of his friends ('they're all setting the pace in this city'). After listening to their descriptions of new industries moving into the town, new real-estate developments, new nightclubs and new eating places opening up, and new cultural projects being formed, I came away impressed, inclined to agree with Donald Horne's compliment to Adelaide (written five years ago in *The Lucky Country*): 'Compared with their own past relations to each other Brisbane falls backwards, Sydney falls apart, Melbourne moves forward to stay where it is, Adelaide goes ahead.'

PERTH

Perth is where the Australian dream comes true. Once regarded as 'The Cinderella Capital', it seems to have used its slower growth and greater isolation to pick out and implement the best ideas from all the other Australian cities. Now, like a suddenly created beauty outshining her ugly sisters, Perth is surging ahead of all rivals. The informal friendliness of Brisbane; the surf-soaked leisure of Sydney; the financial enterprise of Melbourne; the horticultural beauty of Canberra; the environmental and cultural grace of Adelaide; all are distilled in the capital of Western Australia.

The visual delights of Perth make it one of the world's most beautiful cities. Centrepiece is the Swan River which meanders with a mazy motion round the urban perimeter, sparkling cheerfully in the sunlight. It broadens out into the estuary-sized dimensions of 'Perth Water', always bobbing with small sail boats, then pinches itself together to allow a crossing from South Perth by the Narrows Bridge—a structure of featherlight architectural excellence—and sweeps out again towards the great port of Fremantle. The Swan lives up to its name in grace and beauty. Gliding along its banks, one passes newly-risen skyscrapers; a thousand acres of botanical parks; the dignified stone faculty buildings—complete with Doric colonnades—of the University of Western Australia; the velvet lawns and ornate homes of the wealthy suburb of Dalkeith; numerous sandy coves and beaches; ribbons of picturesquely-lighted freeways and expressways now being decorated at their interchanges with ornamental lakes, waterfalls, picnic spots and myriad trees and plants; and above all tens of thousands of private gardens, exploding with a blaze of colour created by beds full of bougainvillea, azaleas, dahlias, hydrangeas, roses and a multitude of tropical shrubs.

So magnificent are these flowers that one feels one must have dropped in on a model senior citizens' village, populated exclusively by retired professional gardeners. Yet despite its comparatively small size (505,000 people), Perth is very much an active man's city, now booming with the new riches of Western Australia's great mineral discoveries, and becoming increasingly cosmopolitan as migrants and overseas businessmen (there are now 2,800 Americans living in the city) move in. Perth would be a good place to take the temperature of Australia's current mineral fever, if only the mercury would stop shooting out of the top of the thermometer. For if you ask any Perth expert about the boom you won't get a word in edgeways for the next two hours. Impressive statistics are rapped out like machine-gun fire, typists and tea-boys tip you the form on mining shares the way their British equivalents tip race-horses, and even senior civil servants and State ministers describe the activities of the mining and industrial companies in an ultra-optimistic jargon more usually associated with TV commercials than government offices.

The boom, which officials now like to call 'The Everything Rush', because so many non-mining projects are at the fore, has undoubtedly brought massive prosperity to Perth. At the bustling PR-conscious Department of Industrial Development, they tell you that overseas capital investment in Western Australia during the sixties totalled over $1,000 million—more than Australia's entire gold and foreign exchange reserves. Mining experts report that there are now some 300 companies searching the State for minerals and that claims have risen by 12,000 per cent in the last three years. Real-estate men say that land prices in the city centre have quadrupled during the decade, and that there will be five new hotels and twenty-four new skyscraper blocks in the central area by the end of 1970. Yet everyone agrees that the treasure hunt is in the most premature of stages, and that the early benefits to Perth in the already visible shape of new offices, factories and industrial projects are but the first drops in the flood of developments to come. Perth expects to be a city of a million people by 1985, and the way they talk, just about every member of the present adult population expects to be a millionaire around the same time.

One young man who has already deposited several million dollars in his bank account is Garrick Agnew, a 38-year-old mining tycoon well on his way to moving into the Kaiser–Getty class of fortune. Coming from a modestly affluent Perth family, Agnew got a degree in engineering from the University of Western Australia, and then won his way to the Harvard School of Business. 'When I graduated from the Harvard Business School in 1954 there were no real opportunities for quick advancement being offered by big Australian companies to people with good qualifications. As a result, I thought I'd have a go at working for myself. I haven't regretted it,' he says. That last sentence must be one of the most remarkable understatements ever to fall from the lips of an Australian industrialist for Garrick Agnew has recently emerged as one of the most important figures in his country's mineral world. At the age of 32 he discovered and pegged the limonite deposits at Robe River in the north-west (still unestimated accurately, but known to approximate in size to the Mt Newman and Mt Tom Price fields), which will be mined from 1971 onwards by a consortium consisting principally of Mitsui of Japan and Cleveland Cliffs of the USA. Agnew controls 5 per cent of the equity of this $1,260 million project, and will in addition receive a substantial royalty on the f.o.b. value of the exported ore. Agnew was also the pioneer of the Western Australia solar salt industry (he holds a 20 per cent stake in Shark Bay Salt), and has a major share in several other new mining ventures. Perth businessmen speak with awe about this shy, tight-lipped, professional financier and say that during the 1970s Garrick Agnew's deals will make him worth 'literally hundreds of millions of dollars'.

Yet while all the frenzy of big developments and deals goes on, Perth has not got so immersed in the scrabble for dollars that it has repeated Sydney's mistake of neglecting its physical environment. Under the watchful championship of Lord Mayor Thomas Wardle (universally known as 'Tom the Cheap' on account of his chain of cut-price grocery stores) the city's already superlative design and layout is likely to be still further improved as the Council gradually implements a master plan that was originally drawn up by Paul Ritter—an effervescent architect who could be described as the Walter Burley Griffin of Perth. Ritter is a Czechoslovakian-born specialist in town planning, and author of several books on the subject, who emigrated from England nine years ago. He was appointed City Architect and City Planner of Perth and in these roles proved himself to be the livest of live wires, making brilliant use of TV to get the population excited about his extensive schemes for redevelopment areas, freeway systems, water garden and fountain complexes, picnic spots, gardens and beautified car parks. Many of these plans have been or are being fully implemented, but somewhere along the line, Ritter had a comic-opera quarrel with his employers, the Perth City Council, and was dismissed for alleged disobedience. Encouraged by the substantial public support for his side of the argument which came his way as a result of the lengthy television coverage given to the dispute, Ritter, although theoretically disgraced, promptly got himself elected to the City Council and now plays the role of gadfly and people's tribune among the civic dignitaries who sacked him. From his hillside home in East Perth ('where else in the world can one get a 7-bedroom house, a swimming pool, 200 mandarin trees and $3\frac{1}{2}$ acres of garden with a river containing fresh lobsters at the bottom of it, all for $4,000 down?'), Ritter now operates as a freelance planning and architectural consultant, author and inventor of gadgets. 'Here I am a big fish without being in the rat race,' he says. 'I make all the money I want and I feel my ideas are helping to change the face of Australia, perhaps even more so now that I do not hold an official

post. I love Perth. It has an immensely stimulating atmosphere
because it is both a Wild West frontier town and at the same time
a highly sophisticated city. The result is that ideas which would
take 20 years to get through in Europe, get through in 2 years here.'

Perth is a great place to peddle dreams, for in the current mood
of optimism there are always ready public and private backers of
bright new ideas. Chief among these on an official level is the
Department of Industrial Development, which will give a sympathetic hearing to almost any scheme, and has backed, at least
in the early stages, innumerable visionary projects from blowing
harbours out of coastal rocks by nuclear explosions to building
the world's first-ever polystyrene houses of plastic bricks. 'We're
a laboratory for experiments in development,' one DID official
said. 'We believe that anything is possible for those who think big.'

But the new ideas are not just confined to the industrial and
financial worlds. Perth works hard to create its own cultural
milieu, and on the whole succeeds in reaching a surprisingly high
level of quality. Every year the city mounts a five-week arts
festival run on a meagre subsidy of $40,000. Considering the
massive distances that most performers have to travel, the programme of this festival is ambitious and successful. For example,
the Melbourne Theatre Company's Perth production of *Henry IV,
Part I*, which I saw, would be a worthy rival to the Royal
Shakespeare version in London, and several of the concerts and
art films would also rate high by international standards. Local
pride demands that a fair go is given to Western Australian
performers at this festival, and inevitably this leads to a falling
off in quality. As a friendly reviewer in *The Bulletin* said of the
1969 festival, 'Just about every bloke with a fiddle seems to have
been accommodated this year.'

Yet for all the much-resented jibes from sophisticated reviewers
who come over from the eastern states, Perth deserves considerable cultural credit for sheer effort. In addition to the festival
activities, the city runs to five theatres, two concert halls, three art
cinemas, and a well-written monthly critical journal, *The Critic*,
covering the arts, while construction of a government-sponsored
$23 million cultural centre along the lines of Melbourne's is to
start next year on a King William Street site.

Perhaps this doesn't add up to all that much by the standards
of Broadway, or London's West End, but few residents of Perth
now complain that they are living in a culturally deprived city.

But both in culture and commerce Perth's greatest problem—

which may yet turn out to be a benefit—is its tremendous isolation. Mention this word in the West, and you get hit over the head with a barrage of statistics about the size of Perth's $85 million airport (at 10,500 ft the longest runway in Australia), the new Indian Pacific rail gauge link-up which is making Sydney a mere 60 hours away, and a flood of information about prospective new express air and cargo services. Yet all these cannot remove the fact that Perth is the world's loneliest city, its nearest large metropolitan neighbour being Djakarta, some 1,800 miles away (Sydney is 300 miles more distant). Remoteness on this scale means that Perth, for all its California-sized boom and beauty, still lacks self-confidence, because it does not know how others judge it. The people have a decided inferiority complex about 'Wise Men from the East', as they defensively call visiting firemen from Melbourne and Sydney, and they worry more than anywhere else in Australia about their city's national and international image. Yet if the West's gold rush continues, the uncertainty and insecurity gap will soon be filled, for on all counts Perth seems set fair to outpace all her sister cities in Australia by the end of the century.

DARWIN

The best way to see Darwin is from the front seat of Mick the Greek's Rolls Royce. For as they tell you in cities like Melbourne and Sydney 2,000 miles away, Mick the Greek is Darwin. He built most of it, owns most of it and now runs most of it.

Mick's life story is the Cinderella immigrant dream come true. Born Michael Paspalis 57 years ago in the Dodecanese Islands, he came to Australia at the age of six and went to state school in Port Hedland. His tobacconist father died almost immediately after arriving and times were hard for the family. Young Michael had to leave school at 13 and start work in Darwin as a butcher's boy. He supplemented his wages by night work at an ice works and by walking 60 miles each week-end to the Northern Territory cattle station picturesquely named Humpty Doo to cart buffalo hides at five cents a time. By the age of 17 he had saved up enough money to buy two run-down houses at an auction sale for $1,500, and from that moment on he was in the real-estate business.

At this time (the 1930s) Darwin was a sweltering shanty town of about 6,000 people with no apparent future. There wasn't a single eating place in the area, so Paspalis and his wife started a cafe called 'The Rendezvous' which boomed with wartime trade provided by US servicemen. When Darwin suffered a Japanese air-raid in 1940, local wits say that only two noises could be heard. One was the falling of the bombs, the other was Mick the Greek digging up his savings chest buried in his back garden.

After the war, Paspalis bought the town's sole pub, the Hotel Darwin. It was the biggest rough-house in the Northern Territory, and its proprietor became known as 'The Greek with Guts' because of his willingness to leap over the bar and settle trouble-makers with his own fists. But pulling no punches and much beer brought its rewards, and with them Paspalis was able to lay the foundations of his fortune by purchasing blocks of land, flats, a fleet of pearling boats and putting up another hotel.

Driving around the town with Michael Paspalis today is an eye-opening experience. Sneered at in the South for decades as 'the ass-hole of Australia', modern Darwin is a booming mini-city thanks to the mineral and agricultural developments around the north. It now has a population of 30,000 growing by 12 per cent a year, and enjoys the most racially relaxed atmosphere of any town in Australia. 5,000 Greeks are the dominant community, but some 3,000 Australian Chinese run many of the cafés and shops and provided the late Mayor, Mr Harry Chan; 2,000 Aborigines float in and out with indeterminate occupations usually connected with agriculture; and the rest of the population is a mixture of Anglo-Saxons (7,000 of them civil servants), Italians, Central Europeans, and the occasional Americans, together with an inter-married hotch-potch of Asian immigrants (who got in before the White Australian policy reared its head) from Japan, Indonesia, Malaya, West Irian, Papua and the islands of Micronesia. Although drunken brawls between members of these various ethnic groups break out fairly frequently, especially in one hotel bar unofficially known as 'The Bloodhouse', the sober majority live together harmoniously, keeping the temperature of the Darwin racial melting-pot agreeably cool.

This is more than can be said for Darwin's weather. On the rare occasions when the thermometer reading falls below 75° F., the local people talk about it for a week, and a visitor frequently gets told about that historic day many years ago when the tempera-ture dropped to the marrow-freezing level of 50 degrees—so cold that the workmen actually had to put on shirts!

As a result of its oppressive climate, Darwin has a tropical languor about it, and the inhabitants have a relaxed siesta-taking 'she'll be right tomorrow' attitude to life. Enquiring about political problems in the Northern Territory, one gets the firm answer in Darwin that there aren't any, apart from those thought up by a ratbag (eccentric) on the Legislative Council called Tiger Brennan, who specializes in needling Canberra. Certainly there's no political controversy. A geologist from the Minerals Bureau who had emigrated from Nairobi told me that the most inflammatory election slogan he had ever seen chalked up on a wall in Darwin was the exhortation 'Ask Menzies!' It seemed a very different tempo from the Mau Mau dramas he had lived through in Kenya.

Yet Darwin's new affluence is changing its traditional indolence. Dick Ward, a local lawyer and aspiring Labor Party politician, said of the boom, 'We're getting our share of the action here all right. Foreign companies have moved in here with registered offices in vast quantities. Law work has quadrupled in the last five years. We've seen a good establishment of new primary schools and high schools, and an increase in teachers. There's now a graduates association, three dramatic societies, a music society and a theatre. Business is booming. We're not rivalling Sydney yet, but we're trying.'

Michael Paspalis is the one man in Darwin who actually has outrivalled Sydney. Until the mining boom made fortunes and vast royalty incomes for men like Lang Hancock, Paspalis was the nation's biggest individual taxpayer and is still the largest individual shareholder in Australian Government bonds. My tour of Darwin in his Rolls had a distinctly feudal flavour to it, as the great tycoon casually acknowledged the salutations of humble pedestrians and concentrated on pointing out the extent of his territorial empire.

'This is the Paspalis building . . . in fact, there are quite a few Paspalis buildings here—about six, I think. Now these are my shops . . . I have about thirty altogether. There are two beaut little blocks of land of mine. I picked them up for $2,000 and they're now worth all of $100,000. That's the Darwin Hotel, where my wife and I started. I'll just show you the Fanny Bay Hotel, which is mine too. They're both leased on very favourable terms to the Brewery, but I'm going to build myself a new one out at Nightcliff, which is going to be the coming area of Darwin. I've got quite a bit of land there. Now these are my three film theatres—I have a monopoly for Darwin—there's the Pratt which seats 1,100 . . . here's the Star which holds 1,200 . . . and now

here's my Drive-in . . . the best in Australia, it cost me $500,000
and holds 900 cars—coins the money too. I've got about 27 acres
around the drive-in, and it's a good area for the future.'

Despite all this big talk, Paspalis remains a shy man, and
as he himself says, an essentially simple one. He reckons his
proudest achievement, outside his own family, is that he has never
borrowed a cent to finance his various enterprises. Each new
venture has been bought with the profits of the last one, and never
has a bank manager had to be asked even for a bridging loan. It
makes one wonder how much larger the Paspalis fortune would
be if its owner applied the intricacies of tax-allowable loan
financing, and put his millions into glamour equities rather than
Government bonds. But Mick the Greek has made his pile by a
simple creed: 'I have always been a hard worker and so has my
wife. Beyond that our secret is that we've had faith in Darwin and
its future for a long time. This is going to be a very big and rich
city. Even in the next few years, everything here will shoot ahead.
I don't sell much—I just sit and wait for Darwin to double my
money.'

I later encountered Michael Paspalis in England. He and his
family were on a grand tour of Europe, the highlight of which
was an invitation to a Royal Garden Party at Buckingham Palace.
I asked the King of Darwin to lunch, to which he came one hour
late with the unique apology 'I'm sorry I was held up, but I just
had to buy another Rolls Royce.' Darwin's evidently a place where
the money doubles pretty quickly.

TOWNSVILLE, ROCKHAMPTON AND GLADSTONE

'Townsville? Well, to be quite candid, I wouldn't go there if I
was you. The hotels are bloody awful, the people are a pretty
lazy lot of ratbags, and though the beaches are beaut there are
too many jellyfish around for my liking. They've had a shark
attack up there recently. Some poor bloke who was paddling in
just two feet of water got himself taken. Of course, if you do go
there, they'll tell you differently, but then everyone up in Townsville has bloody well gone Troppo.'

This advice was given to me by a desk-bound official in
Brisbane, whose office door plaque announced his occupation to
be Queensland's Tourist Promotion Officer. Perversely encouraged
by his unusual methods of promoting tourism I included Townsville on my itinerary.

I began to see what was meant by 'going Troppo' (going mad because of living too long in the Tropics) when my Trans-Australia Airlines Fokker Friendship flight between Mt Isa and Townsville got up to some strange aeronautical jinks. Shortly after take-off, instead of climbing steadily, we plummeted earthwards, levelling up only at hedge-hopping height. Anxiety among the half-dozen passengers increased still further when the stewardess was seen going up to the cockpit with a small black box in her hand, just as the plane's wings were doing much tortuous tilting and angle-changing while we swooped low over the Mary Kathleen uranium mine. Eventually we ascended from these perilous low-level swoops, and the stewardess emerged from her session with the pilot. 'What's the trouble?' enquired six nervous voices. 'No trouble at all,' she said with a ringing laugh, 'I just thought I'd get some snaps of Mary Kay with my Brownie.' This level of airsick humour was kept going throughout the flight, with the pilot announcing on his intercom, 'Liz Taylor back there will shortly be serving you some breakfast bangers', and Liz Taylor giggling into her microphone 'These magnificent men in their flying machines are now going to put us down with one of their three-bump specials at Charters Towers.' As we approached Townsville, the pilot came up with a really soothing announcement. 'Although I can see the runway perfectly and could land us all down there in a couple of jiffs, I'm afraid I've got to keep my eyes closed and pretend we're in the dark. The RAAF (which has a base at Townsville) has to earn its keep somehow, so it's making us fly round in circles and come in blind by radar. Have to trust them, I suppose.'

After a flight like that, everyone on the ground seemed reassuringly normal. Townsville is the biggest Australian city north of Capricorn and the largest all-white tropical city in the world. It has a population of 70,000 which is expected to rise to 90,000 by 1975. It stands 984 miles north of Brisbane, 500 miles east of Mt Isa and is the main port and refining centre for Mt Isa Mines. Townsville is one of the world's friendliest and most informal cities and likes to be called the capital of Australia's Booming North.

All these facts were vouchsafed to me by eager informants within five minutes of arrival. But as the day wore on, my most vivid impressions of Townsville were not those of its present importance, but rather the gaping opportunities of its immediate future potential. Merv Norman, Chairman of the Townsville

Development Bureau, took me on a revealing tour of his city: 'Things are just wide open here,' he said. 'Tourists spent 8½ million dollars in the town last year, yet no one's seriously trying to win their custom with really good hotels and services. 130,000 head of cattle come into the meat-works, but when the new feeding techniques get going, there'll be half a million. 4,000 soldiers and their families will be coming here over the next couple of years or so when the Laverack Barracks are built and there aren't any places for them to go in the evening. The University College is soon going to be a university proper and that'll double the number of students to around a thousand. 800 houses are going up a year and all the builders are overworked. It's possible to buy here just about the world's cheapest silver, lead and copper straight out of the refinery, but there's not one single manufacturer taking advantage of it. I reckon Townsville must be just about the easiest place in Australia to make a fortune.'

Townsville's business community isn't quite as sleepy as these comments suggest, for later in the day I met a good number of men who were already piling up considerable fortunes. One retailer said he had stocked swimming flippers for the first time that year and to his amazement had sold over 1,000 pairs. A small builder claimed his annual profits were now running at over $100,000 having been a tenth of this sum two years before. An insurance agent said he'd made $10,000 on the side by renting his boat to tourists who wanted to go out and see the Great Barrier Reef. Kevin O'Shea, 37-year-old son of a railway conductor, had within six years from nothing built up a million-dollar a year electrical business employing 80 people. 'Times are good here,' said the local Labor Member of Parliament, Tom Aikens, 'but not everyone cares about money when a boilermaker can earn 50 quid a week, which is all he needs and more. If you ask why some of the opportunities here are being missed, you get your answer from the local saying "It's Townsville", which really means that in this town life sets its own pace, and it's not worth hurrying faster.'

They try to hurry a little bit faster 580 miles down the coast on the Fitzroy River at Rockhampton (population 49,000), the un-official capital of Central Queensland. It used to be the State's second largest city until Townsville overtook it, but there are some Rockhamptonites who reckon that the order will change again—in their town's favour. One of these enthusiasts is Frank Rudd, Chairman of the Rockhampton and District Regional Research and

Promotion Bureau. This sonorously titled organization was started by Rockhampton's Mayor Pilbeam in 1962, after the 1961 census proved that the town's population was sliding backwards. 'Up to that time, Rockhampton was a stagnant place living in the bygone era of Queen Victoria,' says Judd. 'Now we know we're right at the point of take-off. There are one-third of Queensland's sheep and two million beef cattle in the Fitzroy basin, and they're going to double during the next ten years because 13 million acres of brigalow scrub are steadily being torn up and seeded by new farmers under the Queensland Government's special Brigalow Scheme. There's a $4 million new meat-works just opened here in addition to the existing Lakes Creek meat-works and already between them they're slaughtering 1,000 tons of beef a week. But there's much more to Rockhampton than cattle and meat-works. There are big new coal deposits and a promising nickel strike in the area, in addition to the old Mt Morgan mine which produces a steady 100,000 ounces of gold and 8,000 tons of copper. Tourism is doubling every four years, and that means a lot of extra money about too. I've got a few old caves on my own property which are quite interesting, so I put up a sign saying "Come and see my limestone caves" on the main road and last year I took in 20,000 tourists at 5s. a head just like that. Also we've got a brand new $15 million Institute of Technology in the town which will attract several hundred students, a new storage system of fresh water which will hold 16 million gallons of the Fitzroy each day, and a new cement works. The population's rising steadily again, now the word's got around that Rock-hampton's woken up.'

Standing just five miles from the edge of the Tropic of Capricorn, Rockhampton is a stately, dignified-looking town with broad streets, coconut palms and mango trees. A lot of the buildings have a decaying nineteenth-century look to their exteriors, but their activities within can tell a different story. I stayed at the Criterion Hotel (a real gem of architectural Victoriana) where I saw notices giving directions to an evening function organized by the Australian Institute of Management (Rockhampton Branch). Curious to know what such a body could consist of in a quiet country town, I went along, and was amazed to find some 70 neatly suited executives getting a high-powered lecture from the Professor of Psychology at the University of Queensland called 'Problems of communication and human relations in industrial management'. The standard of discussion and questioning was

L.O.F.—4

extremely high, and I remarked afterwards to one of the executives that I didn't think one would easily find a gathering of this calibre in many British country towns with populations of less than 50,000. 'In the old gold rush days there used to be a saying in this area, "As Rich as Mt Morgan",' my companion replied. 'I suppose most of us are here tonight because we want to learn how to become "As Rich as Mt Morgan" in Rockhampton again. We're a pretty materialistic lot really, but that's what's making Australia tick these days.'

An hour and a half's drive south from Rockhampton along the 'Crystal Highway' (so named because of the number of shattered windscreens that lie on the edge of the road after being hit by flying stones) lies the booming port of Gladstone (population 14,000), which is ticking away so fast that its prosperity has become an explosion. Seven years ago Gladstone was an easy-going quiet port with a population of 7,000. Its shipping facilities could just about cope with the coal produced from one small mine 100 miles inland, and with the agricultural produce exported from the surrounding countryside. The inhabitants were worried about the future in 1962 because the town's meat-works had just closed down and there was a population drift away to the South.

No one is worried about Gladstone today, for it has become a magnet for big developments on account of its superb natural harbour. In this harbour, the wharves are now handling ten million tons of coal, two million tons of bauxite, one million tons of alumina and a million and a half tons of general cargo, particularly grain, caustic soda, pyrites and meat. The population has doubled, the turnovers of most businesses have trebled and real-estate prices have quadrupled. The local paper, the *Gladstone Observer*, used to be a backyard family-run journal with 8 pages and a circulation of 2,000. Now it's a 24-page paper with a 5,000 circulation, and is crammed with lucrative advertising. Mrs Mackay, the proprietress, who used to set and print the entire paper herself, has built a new *Gladstone Observer* building and tripled her staff. She says of the changes: 'We've now got past the stage of excitement here in Gladstone and are entering the stage of panic. No business is geared to cope with what's here. We just can't visualize the future, because it keeps on snowballing.'

One man who has consistently predicted the snowballing future of Gladstone in such visionary terms that he is really the true and onlie begetter of the present boom, is Alderman W. R. Golding, M.B.E., Chairman of the Harbour Board and Mayor of the town. Alderman Golding is locally known as 'Mr Gladstone'. His father was mayor 75 years ago, and he himself has been on the town council for over 40 years. In a life dedicated to community service, he personally planted almost all Gladstone's trees and built most of Gladstone's houses, while as Chairman of the Harbour Board he has been the instigator of the remarkable developments in the port. Driving me round his fiefdom, Alderman Golding out-mayored all the other mayors and development board chairmen encountered on my Australian visits when it came to talking enthusiastically about his town's future.

'We've already moved in five years from being the sixth port in Queensland to the first, because we now comfortably beat Brisbane in tonnage handled. Soon we'll be the Newcastle of Queensland. We'll have a steelworks, several factories, a manganese plant and already the alumina extraction plant here is the largest in the world. There've been four new motels built here in four years, a new water supply system costing $4\frac{1}{2}$ million dollars, and a vast expansion in houses, offices and schools. Nothing can stop us from becoming one of the greatest cities in Australia.'

What started Gladstone on the road to greatness was Golding's encouragement of the Queensland Alumina Company to set up its $160 million alumina extraction plant in the harbour. Over 2 million tons of raw bauxite are shipped straight from the world's largest deposits at Weipa on Cape York down the 1,000-mile coastal trek to Gladstone, are unloaded at a rate of over 1,000 tons an hour, and after a long and complex process are shipped out again as alumina (2 tons of bauxite make one ton of alumina), mainly to Japan. The gargantuan Bayer process plant which spreads its network of crushers, coolers, flash tanks, extractors, carbon electrodes and mile-long conveyor belts over a 1,200-acre site is 75 per cent financed by American and Canadian capital. French investors have a 20 per cent stake in the company and Australians 5 per cent. To exercise this North American control, there are about one hundred US citizens living in Gladstone, and their popularity with the local residents could hardly be higher. As Alderman Golding puts it, 'The American executives have mixed very well. They are a fine type of people and they couldn't have done more for this town if they'd tried. To give some examples, they subsidize the salaries of the doctors at the

Gladstone Hospital, so that say the top doctor there receives an $8,000 regular salary and a $4,000 subsidy from the Americans which means we can get the top medical men in Australia here. Also, the Americans have generously supported many community projects such as the new library, the kindergarten, the musical society and the theatre; they've given invaluable professional advice on the new water scheme, the sewerage scheme and the new railway, while their wives have nursed with the hospital auxiliary, run the subnormal children's committee and have generally played a big part in the social life. In fact, the Americans are so much part of the community here, we don't call them Americans any more. To us, they're now "The New Gladstonians." '

The chief New Gladstonian is Queensland Alumina's Works Manager, 47-year-old Mr John Holeman, an employee of the US Kaiser Corporation, originally a native of Baton Rouge, Louisiana. As the man in charge of the company's 2,700 work force in Gladstone (including 35 top US executives) Holeman is the main influence behind the halcyon relations between Americans and Australians in Central Queensland, and he fully reciprocates Alderman Golding's feelings of warm kinship.

'Australian co-operation here has been better than any local co-operation the Kaiser Corporation has experienced elsewhere in the world. Mind you, this has not happened by accident. I have made great efforts to ensure that Queensland Alumina does not become a sort of Great White Father to Gladstone like Mt Isa Mines is to Mt Isa. To avoid turning Gladstone into a company town, our people have worked hard to blend in with the local citizenry. This has gone so well that many of us now take a deep pride in the development of Gladstone as a community.'

There is much more in these sentiments than mere PR talk from Mayor and Chief Executive. For the combination of American capital and know-how, coupled with Australian enthusiasm, willingness and friendliness, has created in Gladstone a spirit that has brought excellent commercial results and genuine emotional ties. There have been a few hurt feelings among Australian workers whose ideas favouring 'she'll be right', sloppiness and the occasional day's 'bludging' (taking it easy) have been shattered by sharp admonishments from American executives, who are apparently apt to address an errant labourer by the colonial term 'Boy!' Yet on the whole, the Australian-American relationship in Gladstone is a showpiece one, which augurs well for the growing co-operation between peoples of the two countries.

Gladstone, Rockhampton and Townsville are, in their own ways, showpiece cities too, for they share an almost maniacal faith in their futures. Sceptics occasionally claim that the Great Australian awakening is confined to a few holes in the ground in the north-west. This is no longer true, even if the original boom fever did come out of those holes, and a visit to the growing cities of North and Central Queensland is as good a way as any of confirming that the environment of excitement is a nationwide reality.

BRISBANE

Brisbane is different. Its pace of life is torpid, tranquil and tropical. Its prevailing philosophy is 'Not to worry, mate.' Its symbols are shorts, singlets and swallows of ice-cold beer.

750,000 Queenslanders live in Brisbane, and as they all tell you, a Queenslander is something different from an Australian. Queenslanders take life S-L-O-W-L-Y. They're exceptionally hospitable and friendly, they're not crazy for money like those galahs down south in Sinny, and there's not so much of this big-mouth development talk even though they've got just as many minerals as out west. What a Queenslander really cares about is the outdoor life, and 'm'beaut little block of dirt'. Outdoor life comes first, for whether it's surfing at the Gold Coast, cricket at The Gabba, barbecuing on Mt Glorious, fishing at Deception Bay or the trotting races at Rocklea, the Brisbane-based Queenslander throws himself into it with a passion that is remarkable even by Australian standards. As for the block of dirt, Queenslanders don't do any damnfool things with their money like speculating in shares, or leaving it in the bank (savings per head are lower than in any other state). Instead, they buy up quarter-acre plots of undeveloped land, and dream of building their own brick and weatherboard bungalows on their own little real-estate holding. Often they get together with the owners of the next-door blocks and plan the building of a jointly-owned supermarket, or maybe they form a syndicate with half a dozen neighbours, sell their blocks in one lot, and then together buy another larger site somewhere else. Most of this block dreaming and trading is done with maps of virgin bush territory that might conceivably be developed in 15 years' time if the city expands in that direction, so it's all a matter of castles (or, to be precise, bungalows) in the air. This is really the same phenomenon as the frenetic share trading in mining issues which goes on round the martini belt in Sydney's eastern suburbs or Melbourne's Toorak, with 'm'beaut little block of dirt' taking the place of 'a great little nickel search company'. The only difference is that it takes much longer to buy and sell land, but the longer gestation period suits the Queensland character.

Brisbane reflects this character with its quaint provincial style. The centre-piece is the river, which snakes its broad stream round an S bend, splashing with an armada of sail boats at week-ends, although on weekdays it is as languorous as the people living on its banks. Because of the heat, many homes in the city are built on stilts to allow cool air to circulate underneath the wooden verandahs. Although it has been proved that it is far cheaper to buy a modern air-conditioned apartment than one of these timbered architectural antiquities which look as though they might have been transplanted from a Somerset Maugham story set in colonial Sarawak, nevertheless Queenslanders show a marked aversion for anything smaller than a three-bedroomed home. As a result, Brisbane sprawls over an area of 474 square miles, and rare indeed is the building higher than two storeys.

There are certain disadvantages to living in Brisbane. One is the air pollution, which is serious enough to make Brisbane a notorious centre for chronic respiratory diseases. Another medical worry is the high incidence of skin cancer cases in the city hospitals, which is thought to be due to Queenslanders' reluctance to wear shirts except on formal occasions. In character, the somnolence and lack of response to new ideas is more in keeping with the British provincial way of life than the Australian, while Brisbane's dedicated puritanism is unequalled anywhere outside the Bible Belt of America's mid-West. One eminent Brisbane figure who clashed with the local puritans was the former Dean of St John's Cathedral, the Reverend William Baddeley. Dean Baddeley (brother of the celebrated theatrical sisters Hermione and Angela Baddeley) became the target of considerable vilification from the wowser minority after he was photographed in non-clerical dress at a race-course, happily admitting to a reporter that he had backed six winners. The story blew up into a major national controversy, with enraged low-church clerics huffing and puffing from their pulpits with demands for Baddeley's immediate resignation. Although the row rumbled on for an astonished period of time, thanks to much heated correspondence in the newspapers, 'The Racing Dean', as he became universally known, ignored his critics with splendid

Anglican aloofness, pausing only to remark that 'the constant negative attitude of these wowsers can only result in a diminished version of Christianity.' Baddeley thereafter became the most successful clergyman ever seen in Queensland, drawing exceptionally large congregations (some of whom persisted in asking him for racing tips!), adding a new wing to the Cathedral, compèring a weekly TV show, and involving himself in several cultural projects, among them the founding of the Queensland Ballet Company of which he was the first President. Now back in his native Britain as Vicar of St James, Piccadilly, Baddeley says of his years in Brisbane: 'I loved every moment of my time in that city, and particularly I loved its sheer unabashed provinciality. There was this wonderful atmosphere in which everyone knew everyone else, and in which friendship was given so readily.'

Other observers, less ebullient than the Racing Dean, have had harsher words to say about Brisbane's 'unabashed provinciality'. 'Just a branch manager town, a city of also-rans,' was Donald Horne's acid summary in *The Lucky Country*, and it is this feeling of second-rateness, combined with Brisbane's air of smugness, its ludicrous enforcement of censorship regulations, and its complacency about the status quo that tends to madden outsiders who have not been born and bred in Queensland.

But Brisbane is Australia's third city, and although it is stirring itself rather sluggishly to the alarm bells of progress, merely opening half an eyelid while other towns are bouncing out of bed, nevertheless there are places where the adventurous spirit of the New Australia is fighting to break out of this tropical backwater. At the Queensland Department of Mines, the geologists bubble over with excitement when they talk of the state's colossal resources of untapped wealth. Although no geological survey of Queensland has yet been made by the State authorities, vast deposits of coal, phosphate, bauxite and rutile have been found by luck or by accident in the last five years and much more is confidently expected. Equally optimistic in their expectations are the senior men in the Department of Industrial Development, who talk proudly of the engineering achievement of local firms like Thiess Brothers, and eloquently extol the dramatic expansion in coal exports for Japanese industry and agricultural production on the nearby Darling Downs, which has caused the port of Brisbane to double its turnover in four years. At the Wool Exchange, a talk with Sir William Gunn and his team of bright young pastoral experts convinces one that the upstate livestock industry is on the verge of a superboom, thanks to American capital, while down on the waterfront, Brisbane's leading architect, Dean Prangley, produces blueprints that make the city's futuristic skyline look like downtown Los Angeles. Yet the enthusiasm of these visionaries does not seem to fire the imagination of Brisbane. Queenslanders are very set in their ways, the sort of people who would drink with their mates on Saturday night and wash their cars on Sunday morning even if World War III had been declared that week-end. As a result, they are not likely to get excited by the news of an economic, mineral or agricultural miracle on their doorstep. Provided there's a paw-paw on every breakfast table and a few tubes of beer in the ice-box every evening, Brisbane is going to keep on relaxing.

Just about the only time the city's blood pressure rose with any degree of excitement was when President Johnson made a stopover during his 1966 Pacific visit. The Queensland crowds dropped their wonted indifference to interesting events, and thronged the city's narrow streets in thousands to cheer their leading ally in the Vietnam war. During the pandemonium that inevitably surrounded L.B.J. as he 'pressed the flesh' among the hysterical mob congregated outside Lennons Hotel, an illuminating incident occurred when a US Secret Service agent was seen to push a local woman backwards in the scuffling. A Brisbane policeman remonstrated with the Secret Service man, saying, 'Hey, we don't treat women like that in Queensland.' A few moments later, the same US agent was seen again pushing away the same woman, this time rather more ferociously. This was too much for the Brisbane constable, who threw a punch at the G-man and knocked him out cold. Although furious protests were made by the President's security chiefs, the entire incident was hushed up, and no disciplinary action was taken against the chivalrous local cop. Not for nothing is Brisbane a city where 'everyone knows everyone'.

Visits from US Presidents apart, nothing seems likely to quicken the pulse of Brisbane. The rocket-thrusts of Queensland's development projects are being felt far more spectacularly in Townsville, Rockhampton and Gladstone, and they excite more interest in Sydney and Melbourne. Brisbane merely presides, offers a meeting place for the financiers and men of action, and then goes back to sleep again. After the frenetic pace of touring the rest of Australia, Brisbane is a good place to siesta in before travelling on to Sydney to live it up.

4

MIGRANTS

Australia is a nation of immigrants. The country's 13 million population includes 2·7 million who were born overseas, and another 1·2 million Australian-born children of immigrant parents. This means that one in four of the total population either was an immigrant, or had at least one immigrant parent.

Migrants—as they are always inaccurately known in the characteristic brevity of the Australian vernacular—are now arriving at the rate of over 180,000 a year, a figure which accounts for 48 per cent of the annual population growth. Inevitably, these new settlers are making an enormous impact on every aspect of cultural, social, political and material life in Australia, and their importance is likely to become even greater in the next few years, because the continent's need for more people has spurred the Federal Government into making plans for admitting 8 million new migrants before the end of the century at annual intakes of up to 300,000. Australian immigration has thus become much more than a national policy; it is now a major international crusade. The political slogan of the 1930s, 'Populate or perish', which has been disregarded as Australian women are the world's highest collective users of The Pill, now appears to have been replaced by officialdom's amended slogan, 'Attract migrants, or perish.'

They don't actually use this phrase in the Department of Immigration, but it is implied in almost every action its civil servants take. Employing over 1,800 people and spending $50 million a year (it costs roughly $650 a head to import each migrant worker) the Department sends its recruiting agents winging across Europe, giving lectures, showing films, advertising in the press and on television, opening enquiry centres, answering questions, publishing twelve million pamphlets annually in eighteen languages (one of which is American!) and arranging subsidized passages for approximately two-thirds of those who take the bait.

This crusading spirit has been built up since the war by a

determined continuity of policy, supported by all the political parties. The last five Ministers of Immigration, Mr Arthur Calwell (Labor), Mr Alec Downer, Mr Hubert Opperman, Mr Billy Snedden and the present incumbent, 32-year-old Mr Phillip Lynch, have all had to be salesmen rather than statesmen, for the nature of the portfolio demands a zeal for rising graphs, globe-circling promotion tours, go-go advertising methods and an emphasis on business efficiency for attracting and delivering the customers.

Perhaps the most successful of these Ministers was Mr Billy Snedden. In the $3\frac{1}{2}$ years he presided over the Department (1966–69), the migrant intake rose by 30 per cent, immigration agreements were signed with several new source countries and the first trickle of regular Asian arrivals began.

Snedden is one of the most interesting figures in Australian politics and a possible future Prime Minister (he finished fourth in the 1968 leadership race following the death of Harold Holt, although, at 41, he was the youngest candidate by thirteen years). The sixth and youngest child of a British stonemason who emigrated to Australia early in the century, Snedden decided at the age of 8 (the year his father died) that he wanted to be a politician. After a brief moment of war service in 1945 ('The Germans heard I'd joined up—so that ended it'), he determined to travel overseas, and to further this ambition he went to work for the organization he later presided over. He served as an immigration officer in Italy and Britain, then returned to Melbourne to practise law and was elected to the House of Representatives in 1955. He became Attorney General in 1963 and Minister for Immigration, 'the most exciting challenge in politics', in 1966 until his promotion to Minister of Labour and National Service in late 1969. Working in somewhat uneasy harness with 54-year-old Sir Peter Heydon, the sensitive and loquacious scholar who has been the Department's chief civil servant since 1961, Snedden bulldozed immigration policy into the forefront of Australia's national consciousness. For during the later 1950s and increasingly in the 1960s the atmosphere created by immigration changed from that of a cosy all-British club into a spicy Europeanized melting-pot, which is now beginning to be garnished by unusual new elements such as Americans, Turks, Asians and South Americans.

This heady mixture has inevitably aroused a certain amount of controversy. The debate about White Australia, the reaction to well-heeled adventurers from rich America, the influence of the

New Australians and the grumbles of the British have all made headlines over the years and are discussed later in this chapter. But immigration debates have taken a new and unexpectedly subversive turn ever since an influential section of intellectuals recently began arguing that Australia already has enough people and would be better off curtailing the immigration programme. Professor Fred Hoyle of Cambridge University spoke in 1969 of Australia's folly of trying to achieve national greatness through forced population growth. 'There is a grave danger,' he said, 'in Australia striving to become a great and powerful nation like the United States . . . it is too horrible to contemplate.' Hoyle's thesis, which was supported by the editorial columns of *The Australian* and in some other significant quarters, claimed that Australia had reached a stage where it could and should be concentrating on the quality of life and society rather than striving for power through size. Arguing that the work force should expand its skills, not its numbers, Hoyle pointed out that the nation's social facilities such as housing, transport, sewerage, welfare and planning were already becoming inadequate and would not substantially improve as long as a false population growth was imposed on Australia as a matter of national policy.

This interesting theory has won little popular acclaim, largely on the grounds that Australians are conditioned to automatic rejection of such views because it is deeply ingrained into the national philosophy that the wide open spaces must be filled by building up the (white) population at the fastest possible rate. When Hoyle's opinions were first broadcast, I was drinking with a group of educated Australians who up till that time had appeared politically perfectly sensible. All agreed that the Cambridge professor's thesis was 'Communist propaganda'.

As this is likely to be a fairly common type of reaction among fair dinkum Aussies to any suggestion that expanding migration totals is not necessarily beneficial, it is more or less certain that the policy of '8 million new migrants before the end of the century' is here to stay. True, the Federal Government did announce in July 1970 the setting up of an inquiry on whether or not the migrant intake should be reduced and the funds directed to social improvements instead, but senior immigration officials were at pains to stress in off-the-record briefings that this move was only a sop to vociferous press critics. If correct, then the sole obstacle to Australia's mammoth immigration programme is the attitude of the migrants themselves.

Every year a substantial number of disappointed migrants leave Australia and return either to their countries of origin or to other migrant-accepting countries. The exact size of this number is shrouded in vagueness. The Department of Immigration says 'somewhere between 9 and 16 per cent' (i.e. between 13,000 and 28,000). A 1968 Report tabled in the House of Representatives put the figure at 50,000 (including permanently departing Australian citizens). Most observers say that the number works out at just over 500 a week (25,000 a year). But any way the calculation is made, it is still far too many. The patriotic Aussie view of this phenomenon is to castigate the departers as 'no-hopers' who should never have come at all. This is doubtless justified in some cases, but the total is too large to escape the conclusion that a great many would-be settlers don't settle simply because Australia isn't attractive enough to hold them. Herein lies the possible Achilles heel of the whole future of Australian migration.

The incentives and disincentives to emigrate to Australia are complex and often highly personal. Any examination of them must begin with the people who are Australia's largest, best and worst migrants—The Poms (British).

THE WINGEING POMS

Without the Poms, Australia would be a backward country, for 70 per cent of the population is of British stock (in 1947 this figure was 99.5 per cent) and just under half of the annual intake of migrants still originates from the Mother Country. The latest statistics show that in 1970 79,000 British citizens waved goodbye to the White Cliffs of Dover and set off for 'Down Under'. 73,500 of these were on assisted passages, which make it possible for each individual to make the 12,000-mile trip for $20. Although these totals are records, the annual number of departures has averaged out at over 50,000 for more than two decades, with the result that there are now well over a million and a quarter first-generation British migrants ensconced in their adopted country. Because of the sheer size of the emigration programme from Britain, it is fair to say that the recruitment and results from this massive cross-section of settlers holds the key to the success of Australia's present and future immigration programme.

The nerve-centre of Australian immigration recruitment in Britain is Canberra House, a mini-skyscraper tucked away in a side street just off London's Strand. Here the Department of Immigration processes 135,000 written and 70,000 telephoned annual enquiries from would-be migrants; organizes the spending of over $800,000 on Press and TV advertising; and employs a staff of 390 spread across seven regional offices. The man who presides over this evangelical empire is George Kiddle, a 49-year-old Melbournian who has been the Commonwealth Government's Chief Migration Officer in Britain since 1965.

I asked Kiddle why 1970 had been a record year for departing British migrants, and his answer was a revealing one.

'It's a combination of many reasons. When we ask people why they're going to Australia, the most common answer is "For the sake of the children". There seems to be a growing sense of frustration in the UK, particularly a widespread discontent with the economic conditions—or rather the way they're presented here. Mind you, it's like committing blasphemy in a cathedral when we try and point out to an Englishman that the UK taxation isn't all that high by international standards, because presentation has just made him believe that Britain's the most highly taxed country in the world. But the feeling that things are generally too tough here has just got many people down, and they leave because they want to get a better deal for their children.

'Another big reason is the climate. People hit us for singing the praises of sunshine and surf and beaches in our advertising, but for crying out loud, that's what Australia is renowned for. Our departure totals are certainly up this year because the summer here has not been a good one.

'There are a lot of other reasons too. Our regional centres are now upgraded in comfort and efficiency to the equivalent standards of airline offices. Australian companies and the State Government offices have become much more active in their recruiting and advertising. The news of our mineral boom has made quite an impact. Many UK residents are finding the overcrowding and congestion in their own country just too much. But what it basically boils down to is that people migrate to Australia for better opportunities, and they often think of these in terms of further chances for their own children more than for themselves.'

It's an interesting experience to go along and hear about these opportunities at one of the evening film shows and talk sessions for potential migrants regularly organized by the Department of Immigration in London. Although the room (a favourite venue is the Festival Hall) is usually packed to overflowing, the atmosphere is not one of mass excitement or even intense curiosity at the prospect of restarting life in a new country, rather a muted taken-for-granted feeling that a marginally better deal exists for Englishmen at the other end of the world. The film commentaries and the official speakers do not attempt to thrill their audience with tales of propitious openings for new arrivals and case histories of antipodean Dick Whittingtons. The approach is more one of reassurance and 'you'll soon feel right at home'.

If punches are pulled on these occasions (as is often subsequently alleged by returning migrants), it is not the fault of the immigration officials, who on the whole are perfectly straightforward in their replies to questions. It is much more a case of the listeners hearing what they want to hear and misinterpreting the land of promise for a land of promises.

For if the Festival Hall sessions I have attended are accurate guides to form, it appears that the average British migrant fits Lord Devlin's famous description of the average British juryman as 'middle-aged, middle-class and middle-minded'. Certainly they look and sound like it as they sit asking tediously technical questions about whether or not duty is payable on the family saloon, as they demand assurances about the transferability of life insurance policies, and as they nobly reiterate that they are taking this step 'for the sake of the children'. Surveys show that it is rarely a blinding flash of light on the road to Damascus that makes a potential migrant fill in an advertisement coupon and send it in to Canberra House. Migration is most frequently evolved through the catalyst of the camel's back, by which is meant a long accumulation of reasons for quitting Britain. These suddenly burst into a decision to emigrate when the Ossa of some quite trivial last straw—such as a winter power cut—is piled on the Pelion of long-harboured resentments. In short, the decision to emigrate from Britain to Australia is made in far too many cases for purely negative reasons.

The fruits of this negative approach are apt to turn predictably sour once the migrants have reached Australia. Accepting the figure of approximately 500 disappointed settlers leaving Australia each week, one also has to accept that probably over 350 of these returnees are British. Because they usually have the advantage over continental migrants of speaking the language, of not being awed by civil servants, and of being used to reasonable living standards, the Poms are far and away the biggest wingers (grumblers) when it comes to expressing discontent at Australia's shortcomings, and often the wingeing develops to the point of booking a passage home.

The alleged Australian shortcomings that appear to cause the most trouble are the high rents for poor accommodation in migrant hostels; the unexpectedly penal rates of taxation for middle income earners; the high cost of land and housing (substantially higher than in Britain in most areas); and above all the fact that the Australian way of life turns out to be more of a struggle and less of a featherbed than many Poms expected. It is reasonable to sympathize with some of these grievances, notably high taxation and the Nissen-hut-and-institutional-food approach of some migrant hostels—of which former Immigration Minister Snedden says: 'I admit that the quality of some of the hostels used to be low, and the rents are fairly high because we are already subsidizing people in hostels to the extent of $5 per person per week. But we are upgrading living standards, embarking on a $24 million rebuilding programme, and in addition we are building several hundred new flats in key cities for migrants. It all adds up to a very substantial all-round improvement in the welcome we are going to give to new arrivals.'

The winges with which it is difficult to have much sympathy are those which fulminate against the inherent competitiveness of Australian life. In the economic jungle of Down Under, the races are won by the strong, and that means the muscular labourers prepared to put up with tough conditions for high wages, the Greek and Italian migrants who work 16-hour days running their businesses with cheap family labour, and the energetic hustling businessmen. Freeloaders, and those used to being cushioned by British Welfare State benefits such as family allowances and free prescriptions, find the pace of their new life about as comfortable as an icy showerbath. Many, of course, are stimulated by these first shocks and adjust to becoming bonza Aussies. Those who make good fastest tend to be the 37 per cent of the total intake who come out under the Personal Sponsorship scheme, which simply means that they arrive and are met by relatives, friends, or merely pen-pals whose correspondence and personal attention has given the migrants some idea of what to expect. Taken as a whole, the contribution of successful British migrants to Australia has been an outstanding one, and there are over a million happy settlers to prove it, but the returnees remain as the immigration programme's most vulnerable weakness.

My own view is that there is nothing wrong with the quality and quantity of British migrants that wouldn't be cured by a new approach in advertising and promotional techniques. If the Australian Government was to hire one of the more creative big advertising agencies and tell it to run a campaign based on the excitement, novelty and Midas-like opportunities of the island continent, then one would soon see a more enterprising type of Pom sending in his enquiry coupon to Canberra House. The present emphasis on sun, security and suburbia does very well, particularly, one suspects, among discontented second-raters, but it completely fails to interest the hundreds of thousands of younger UK citizens who are mildly frustrated by life in their own country yet cling to the widespread fallacy that Australia is somehow a boring backwater. Australia deserves a better image than the one created by the play-it-safe propaganda of its immigration advertising.

But as any fledgling account executive knows, all the most brilliant image-building techniques of Madison Avenue will ultimately fail unless the end product is up to scratch. As I hope the rest of this book makes clear, the quality of life in Australia is today very much better than 'up to scratch'. Yet surprisingly enough there are still certain barriers and pockets of inconvenience which must be swept away before Australia can offer a good deal to the type of migrants who are needed most.

IMPORTING EXCELLENCE

'What Australia lacks is excellence, or call it high-class professionalism. There are far too many third-rate people around with a "She'll be right, sport" attitude and nothing much else.' The speaker was a 35-year-old Welshman, Gareth Powell, who emigrated to Australia in 1967 with a total capital of $43 ('I could have brought much more but the Income Tax people in England wouldn't give me clearance') and now heads a zany but apparently flourishing Sydney publishing empire. Powell is not everyone's idea of an excellent migrant, since his main contribution to Australian letters has been the publication of a chain of girlie magazines whose contents have brought him into fierce conflict with the Australian censors. Nevertheless he has a point. Australia is certainly in need of more migrants with special skills, professional qualifications, entrepreneurial initiative, executive experience and capital. Where are they going to come from?

The greatest obstacle to wooing exceptional migrants to Australia is the increasing prosperity of Western Europe. Germany was one of the best sources of skilled and professional migrants until her economic boom began around 1961. Then within two years the annual total of German migrants arriving in Australia had fallen from 12,000 to 3,000. From time to time the same thing has happened, in rather less dramatic terms, to other European immigrant-source countries.

The rule that migrant totals decline when times are good can also work the other way round. London's Canberra House is an interesting barometer of Britain's economic prosperity in this respect, for every time the Chancellor of the Exchequer announces another freeze, squeeze or taxation rise, the Department of Immigration receives an inevitable flood of increased enquiries about migration opportunities. However, given the not unreasonable assumption that the sick men of Europe will slowly improve their economic health, it is likely that potential migrants of exceptional ability will in future find adequate opportunities in their own countries. Is there anything Australia can do to reverse this probable trend?

There are two rather surprising deterrents against highly qualified Europeans trying their luck in Australia. The first is Australia's taxation system which, although reasonably generous to the indigent and affluent, nevertheless puts an oppressive burden on the middle-income earners. A 1969 article in *The Bulletin* (approximately the Australian equivalent of *Newsweek*) showed that Englishmen who earn between £2,000 and £9,000 a year would be better off in taxation terms if they stayed in their own tax-ridden country. Migration is apparently profitable only for those earning the princely sum of £10,000 ($20,000) a year. The new Liberal Government is anxious to change this aspect of the tax structure according to its election promises, but reform is unlikely to come before the early 1970s—if then. Until it comes, many able potential migrants from Britain and other less taxed European countries will not be attracted by the economic future Australia is offering them.

Another deterrent to the exceptional migrant is the reluctance of Australian professional bodies to accept the qualifications of overseas professional bodies. Only British and some American degrees are recognized. Continental migrants who are accepted throughout Europe as fully qualified doctors, scientists, engineers, vets and dentists have to take special courses and sit special examinations *after* they arrive in Australia. They cannot obtain their Australian qualifications before they leave their own countries, and the consequent uncertainty about getting re-qualified on the other side of the world undoubtedly stops some professional men and women from leaving Europe.

The Department of Immigration fights a running battle against the insularity and xenophobia of certain Australian professional bodies, but with limited success. 'Some of these organizations have been guilty of extreme selfishness,' says former Immigration Minister Snedden. 'Public opinion must force them into change if we are to attract enough qualified people to Australia.' Snedden quoted to me one recent example of what he called 'sheer bloody-mindedness' by a professional body. The Australian pharmacists (who qualify after three years of examinations) have long recognized the credentials of British pharmacists (who are also required to pass three years of examinations). But in 1968 the British Pharmaceutical Association raised its standards by increasing the qualification period to four years. This, of course, should mean that pharmacists arriving as British migrants in Australia would be even better qualified and therefore, one might have thought, all the more acceptable as pharmacists. Not so. The Australian pharmacists, in a fit of pique, announced that they would refuse to recognize British pharmacists who came out as migrants until their association returned to a 3-year qualifying period equal to Australia's. By some tough arguing, Snedden managed to prevent this particular piece of jealous lunacy, but the incident is illustrative of the mentality of certain Australian professional bodies towards migrants.

Despite the hurdles of unexpectedly high taxation and getting overseas qualifications accepted, Australia is nevertheless attracting a steady trickle of exceptional overseas talent. On a recent two-day visit to Perth, I met at random several migrants who appeared to be making a remarkable contribution to their adopted country. They are worth a brief mention because the fact that such people are now settling in Australia is the best evidence of the exceptional scope for opportunities available to men who have already been successful in their own countries.

Among the most interesting members of the Perth migrant community that I met were: Paul Ritter, a Czechoslovakian-born town planning expert from Nottingham, who after a turbulent spell as Perth's City Planner is now a city councillor, freelance architectural consultant, inventor and author; John Brunner, former assistant manager of the London *Observer*, now Chief Economic Adviser to Broken Hill Proprietary Ltd and a successful mining investment expert; George Barker, a Yorkshire builder who sold his £200,000 turnover construction business in Britain and came to Perth to pioneer a revolutionary new building process using plastic bricks; John Berman, a Polish migrant, now director of the Perth Arts Festival and a senior lecturer at the University of Western Australia; Bill Thompson, an East Anglian farmer who had swapped his British farm for a massively larger and more profitable sheep station; and George Sava, a well-known White Russian plastic surgeon and best-selling author (*The Healing Knife*) who had just opened consulting rooms in Perth. With the exception of Sava, who eventually returned to the United States after finding that he was paid a maximum of $75 in Perth for operations which earned him $1,500 in Los Angeles, all the above migrants have done outstandingly well in their new homeland, most of them after only a very short time.

Australia needs many more migrants of the calibre of these individuals I came across in Perth, for the country offers glittering prizes to overseas arrivals with talent, and best of all with some capital behind them to get started. At present, the number of such arrivals is minute, although there are signs (such as the growing interest of Americans described later in this chapter) that certain categories of exceptional migrants may be on the increase. In London, Australia House has set up a special unit headed by an adviser on professions specifically to cater for the highly qualified migrant. This unit handled 200 enquiries per month in 1967, and 1,000 enquiries per month in 1970. a statistic which reflects the growing interest in Australian migration from the professional sections of the UK population. Last year, just under 800 professional people left Britain to live in Australia (a 300 per cent increase on the previous year), and of these the largest groups were engineers (mechanical, electrical, civil and chemical), management executives, doctors, accountants, lawyers, computer programmers, architects, biologists and geologists.

But despite the encouragingly rising curves of the Department of Immigration's graphs charting arrival totals of professionally qualified migrants, the fact remains that they are rarities in relation to the total intake. Whether or not this situation changes depends largely on the patterns of future American migration, and also on the future relaxations, if any, on the intake of migrants from Asia—which by a strange irony of the present 'White

Australia' policy is currently Australia's best market for migrants of excellence.

THE NEW AUSTRALIANS

During the last twenty years one million migrants from continental Europe have arrived in Australia. Their main countries of origin (in order of totals) were Italy, Greece, Germany, Holland, Yugoslavia, Poland, Malta, Russia, Hungary, Austria, Latvia, Czechoslovakia, Lithuania, Spain, France, Finland, Estonia, Norway, Switzerland and Sweden. 'New Australians' was the label tagged on this heterogeneous mixture, and they have certainly lived up to it by introducing so much novelty and innovation into Australian society that they are now acknowledged as the most dominant influence in changing the traditional fair dinkum Aussie way of life.

The Immigration Minister for 1966–69, Mr Billy Snedden, says that the New Australians were greeted by their adopted countrymen 'first with resistance, then with acquiescence, and now with enthusiasm'. The enthusiasm probably stems from the gastronomic revolution which the New Australians have created, for one quick way to an Australian's heart is through his stomach.

Contrary to the popular international myth about there being three Australian dishes—steak, egg and chips; chips, steak and egg; and egg, chips and steak—it is now easy to eat in any big Australian city almost as Lucullian a repast as can be enjoyed in the *haute cuisine* restaurants of world capitals. The credit for this goes to a small nucleus of wine-growers, market gardeners, delicatessen-owners and restaurateurs, most of whom are first or second generation migrants from continental Europe. My own favourite and fairly typical New Australian restaurant proprietor is Nico Frangi, patron of the celebrated Buonasera at Sydney's Kings Cross ('Sydney has at least 200 high-class restaurants,' said a noted London gourmand and food columnist in a recent moment of hyperbole in Mascot Airport's departure lounge). Frangi, who is half Spanish, half Italian and born in Cairo and says of himself, 'I am like Australian Turkish Delight which in Sydney is made by Greeks,' claims to be the only person in Australia ever to get a liquor licence at the first attempt—even before the restaurant opened. He achieved this distinction by making a personal appeal in court to the Judge. 'Sir, I am opening on

Christmas Eve. How could you possibly let me open without a liquor licence.'

Frangi arrived penniless in Australia, saved up his wages from building fences on sheep stations and with them bought the dilapidated Kings Cross fruit shop which is now Buonasera. He potters around his 48-seat goldmine in bow tie and monocle, exuding proprietorial charm until the small hours of the morning. Young couples are often greeted with, 'Ah, you look so beautiful, you must sit at the special table for lovers', and single men without female companions are told, 'You shall sit near the window at the table which gives the most delightful view of the pretty girls' legs.' All are served with exquisite food and wine at very reasonable prices. The only way to get bad service, or rather no service at all, is to ask for a beer. 'But all my patrons are connoisseurs. You cannot drink beer here. I insist you have a glass of wine,' says Frangi. A remark like that would have got a restaurant owner's nose punched in the Australia of a few years ago.

New Australians have conquered many other worlds beside the gastronomic one. Italians dominate the prosperous tobacco and sugar-cane growing industries in Northern Queensland; Greek shearing teams have a reputation for outstripping the performance of their Australian competitors (a 34-year-old migrant from Messene, Demetrios Stathopoulos, who had never seen a sheep when he arrived in 1956, holds the Australian record for the most lambs shorn in a working day—370 in 7 hours 48 minutes); Central Europeans tend to proliferate in the tough new mining centres in the north and west (the General Manager of the giant Western Mining Corporation is an Estonian war refugee); and in the more intellectual spheres such as the arts, entertainments, universities and architecture, continental migrants are almost invariably playing a prominent part. The entrepreneurial spirit seems to be more prevalent among New Australians than other migrant groups. According to the 1961 census, 17 per cent of Greeks and Italians were employers or self-employers compared to 11 per cent of British migrants.

These achievements have earned the respect and sometimes even the affection of the indigenous population. Now that the nation's booming economic prosperity has obliterated the memory of the days when Australian workers' jobs were threatened by immigrant labour, migrants are no longer a focal point of resentment, and pejorative labels like Wop, Dago, Gippo, Pedro, Eytie, Hun, Wog and Reffo are gradually dropping out of saloon-bar vocabulary. There is, however, one cloud on the New Australian horizon and that is the growth of closely packed urban ethnic communities which some observers are already referring to as ghettoes.

In Sydney I was once driven by a taxi driver who ostentatiously clipped a clothes-peg on his nose as he drove through the admittedly fragrant area of the city which he called 'Little Malta'. In Brisbane I was told of street fights between the densely populated Greek and Italian enclaves, although when I asked the honorary Greek Consul for Queensland about these tensions, he replied that the only time they had come to his notice was on an occasion when he had received a 3 a.m. telephone call which ran: 'Hello Greek Consul. Me Italian woman. Next door Greek baby cry all night. You stop.'

In Melbourne, some experts were expressing anxiety about a 1969 survey which showed that a third of the schoolchildren in 42 inner suburban schools were New Australian migrants. Most of these children spoke English so badly that they could not be adequately taught, yet only two of the schools had the manpower to assign special teachers to give these pupils extra coaching with their English. Said one social worker, 'This means our schools are soon going to be turning out generations of school-leavers whose faulty command of our language will inevitably condemn them to being second-class citizens, equipped only to do third-class jobs. We could be creating here for succeeding generations almost as bad a problem as Britain now has with her coloured immigrants and America has with her Negroes.'

This is probably an unnecessarily Cassandra-like view of the situation, but there is a disturbingly casual tendency among Australian officialdom to pooh-pooh all the problems and danger signals of these ethnic communities, and instead to extol virtues such as their low crime rate (20 per cent less than among native-born Australians), their industry (New Australian workers have a good reputation for willingness to take on long overtime hours), their regular churchgoing habits and their cultural contribution to Australian society. But for all the compliments, assimilation and integration of these newcomers is all too often more honoured in the breach than the observance. Approximately two-thirds of marriageable New Australians pick their spouses from within their own ethnic groups rather than uniting with Australian-born partners, and even the teenage generations of both camps tend to keep themselves separate. One morning I sat in on a sixth-form class at Sydney Church of England Grammar School. For my benefit, the Headmaster, Mr B. H. Travers, asked his pupils to vote on a number of faintly provocative questions such as whether Australia should become a republic (70 per cent against it) and he ended by asking, 'Would you like your sister to marry a Greek or Italian migrant?' With one dissentient, the entire class voted against such a matrimonial mixture. When posing a similar question in one or two other schools elsewhere in Australia, the result was much the same, although by a less overwhelming majority. It would be wrong to draw any dramatic conclusions from such amateur Gallup poll results among teenage school-children, but the indications do not bode well for those who hope to see the 'New' dropped, at least in spirit, from the 'New Australian' label.

If the Immigration Planning Council's forecasts prove accurate, by the early 1970s there should be 100,000 new migrants from continental Europe arriving each year in Australia. These arrivals will no doubt continue to contribute to the sophistication, cosmopolitan culture and general economic progress of Australian society, and no doubt they will follow their fellow migrants' example of reaping the many material benefits which derive from living in a booming economy.

But, as I discovered from random conversations with New Australians, a certain amount of resentment is developing in their own communities, particularly on the issue of the quality of physical surroundings. When a Cypriot taxi driver who lives in an unsewered and dilapidated semi in Sydney's Paddington starts grumbling about the exotic splendours of the homes in Sydney's eastern suburbs, his complaint has an uncanny ring of repetition to a reporter's ears. It is the same 'I want a piece of their action' message first heard in Watts in the early 1960s, and tragically echoed in many American cities ever since. It would be foolishly melodramatic to suggest that Australian cities are on the verge of rioting or street disturbances—they are nowhere near it. But certain ethnic ghettoes are developing, discontent is beginning to smoulder, and there are some indications—such as the language block on educational opportunities in Melbourne schools— which suggest that the problems could be getting worse. The authorities should be specially vigilant to ensure that tomorrow's New Australians do not become Australia's New Troubleshooters.

AMERICAN MIGRATION

Americans are showing an increasing interest in emigrating to Australia. Last year the Australian Embassy in Washington and its consulates-general in New York and San Francisco between them received over 200,000 enquiries from Americans investigating the possibility of going to live in Australia. These enquiries resulted in over 3,000 US citizens arriving in Australia as settlers. At the beginning of the sixties the figure was less than 1,000. Australian Immigration officials are confident that this rising trend will continue and that the United States is one of Australia's greatest potential sources for new migrants in the future.

The trend is particularly encouraging in one sense because this substantial total of 200,000 enquiries has been achieved without any advertising by the Australian government. The reason why the Department of Immigration does not launch a publicity campaign to drum up migrants in the United States (the only good migrant-source country in which this is not done) is partly due to a reluctance on the part of the US State Department to sanction emigration advertising in a land famous for immigrant opportunity, and partly due to Australian fears that hordes of American Negroes might swamp Australia with applications to settle. Mr Billy Snedden did not himself share his compatriots' apprehensions about a massive Negro interest in moving to Australia, but had to shelve his proposals for advertising for migrants in the United States because of strong opposition from within the Australian cabinet and also from within the hierarchy of his own Immigration Department. Says Snedden: 'The best Negroes won't be interested in coming to Australia because in the present climate of opinion in their own country they are being pushed forward at the fastest possible speed into jobs with very high salaries and very good opportunities. The worst Negroes won't have the initiative and the drive to emigrate, nor the funds to pay the fare to Australia. Perhaps there might be a few Negroes who prove exceptions to that rule and apply to become migrants. They will be welcome in Australia provided they answer to the description we require which is this: for a person whom we describe as a non-European, he or she has to possess skills of positive value to Australia.'

Snedden's argument that the 'best Negroes' will find superior economic opportunities in the United States than in Australia applies equally to white Americans, and is the reason why the encouragingly high total of 200,000 American enquiries about emigration turns into the disappointingly low total of 3,000 actual American arrivals in Australia. Although there is no appreciable difference between the cost of living in Australia and in the United States, there is a yawning gulf between the salary scales (much higher in the US) and a slightly less wide gap between the taxation rates (more penal in Australia, particularly on incomes below $20,000). Thus any American who decides to make the leap across the Pacific must have some special reasons beyond the usual desire for economic self-improvement.

One such special reason appears to be the call of a new frontier. Australian immigration officials[1] (whose number in the US has doubled during the last six months) say that the opportunities for adventure in more or less virgin territory seem to be a major factor in attracting potential American migrants. This will surprise no one who has studied American history long enough to realize that the romantic excitement of the nineteenth-century frontier spirit still looms large in contemporary US society. It is constantly referred to in the rhetoric of politicians (President Kennedy's inaugural address is the outstanding example), in the purple prose of the ad-men and in the language of the TV film, but rare indeed are the chances to indulge in pioneering adventures on the over-developed US continent. Even those who follow the traditional frontier advice, 'Go West, young man', are apt to end up in the disappointing smog and urban sprawl of the Southern Californian megalopolis. Perhaps that's why by far the largest percentage of US enquiries about life in Australia—30 per cent—originates from Californians who apparently want to go even further West.

Other researches on American motives for becoming Australia-bound migrants suggest that anxieties about the future of US society are partly responsible for the rising departure totals. As Billy Snedden put it: 'The material factors are on the whole slightly less good in Australia than in the United States, and therefore it is other factors which pull American migrants here. Although we get very annoyed whenever some stupid redneck arrives, saying he's come here to get away from niggers, the researches of my department do show that many American migrants have come because of a sense of strain, and an unstated

[1] To avoid upsetting the US State Department, these officials are euphemistically described as 'Australian consular officers dealing with immigration'.

apprehension about the future of their own country, particularly over the issues of law and order and the Negro rebellion.'

Since President Nixon's America seems, at least temporarily, to be cooling down the passions which unleashed so much violence and destruction in the summers of 1967–68, the quieter domestic atmosphere may result in a slight falling off of American emigration to Australia. This would be a severe blow to Australia's hopes for increased migrant totals, for if the Department of Immigration's target of 200,000 migrants a year by the early 1970s is to be achieved, then the United States will have to be contributing at least a tenth of that figure, particularly because English-speaking migrants are needed for half of the total intake and Britain's present migrant figure of 73,000 is thought by some to be nearing its zenith. But while some observers are sceptical about the possibilities of a dramatic increase in American migration to Australia in the next few years, other visionaries argue that given an advertising campaign, a continuing boom in the Australian economy, and a deterioration in America's domestic problems such as the quality of the urban environment and law and order, then in these by no means unlikely circumstances the number of US citizens prepared to seek a newer world on the other side of the Pacific might reach remarkable totals in the region of 100,000 annually.

Should this happen, the effect on the Australia of tomorrow will be revolutionary. The most outstanding feature of American migrants to date is that over half of them bring somewhere between $10,000 and $50,000 of capital into Australia with them. They tend to use this capital on direct investment projects such as farms and small businesses, and in both their social and economic activities they tend to aim for higher standards than the lackadaisical 'She's right' Australian philosophy so cheerfully tolerates. In short, the rising graph of American migrant totals (steadily increasing by around 30 per cent a year) could improve the quality of life in Australia in a faster and more far-reaching way than any other migrant group has yet been able to do.

WHITE AUSTRALIA

'We have to be very cautious about our intake of Asian emigrants. Scratch the surface of Australia and you find discrimination.' With these candid words Billy Snedden sums up the attitudes that have created 'White Australia'. The label is today much less justified them formerly, for since March 1966 there has been a considerable relaxation on the prohibition against Asians wishing to settle in Australia. Although non-European migrants are still discriminated against by selection methods and numbers, nevertheless Australia now admits approximately 3,000 carefully screened Asian immigrants a year. It's not much out of an annual total of 180,000 migrants, but given the background of past and present Australian attitudes to Asian immigration, the 1966 policy change represents a significant step in the right direction.

Before 1966 the ban on non-white immigrants wishing to enter Australia was administered only slightly more humanely than the ban on East Germans wishing to cross the Berlin Wall. Taking as its creed the celebrated nationalist slogan 'Free, White and Great', the Australian Government systematically excluded all non-Europeans except for a tiny handful of 'distinguished and outstanding' applicants (such as Dean Dixon, the Negro conductor of the Sydney Symphony Orchestra). At the discretion of the Minister of Immigration, certain non-whites married or closely related to Australian citizens were sometimes allowed to remain in the country rather than break up families, though even in this category there were some harsh exceptions. One of these was the Gamboa case, when the then Minister of Immigration, Mr Arthur Calwell, decided to deport a US Army Sergeant of Filipino extraction, even though Sergeant Gamboa was married to an Australian girl.

By the mid-sixties, public opinion was clearly ripe for some amendment to the White Australia policy. In a 1965 Gallup Poll only 16 per cent of all Australians wanted to exclude Asians altogether; 7 per cent didn't know; 6 per cent wanted unrestricted Asian immigration, and 71 per cent favoured selective Asian immigration. Among the younger generation, the desire for change was slightly stronger. A 1966 survey published in *The Australian* revealed that 4 out of every 5 young Australians between the ages of 16 and 25 would favour allowing Asian migrants to settle in the country, although of these youthful reformers 47 per cent favoured the admission of only highly skilled and educated Asians.

The politicians took their cue from these manifestations of public opinion, and under the leadership of Prime Minister Harold Holt, who was genuinely and enthusiastically interested in Asia, a relaxation of the immigration restrictions on non-Europeans was announced in the House of Representatives in March 1966. Under the new policy, Asian immigrants were to be admitted to

Australia in numbers 'somewhat greater than previously'. The guiding rule in deciding whether or not to admit an Asian applicant for immigration is, in Mr Snedden's words 'whether he or she possesses skills of positive value to Australia'.

During the first four years of the new policy the Department of Immigration approved 4,800 applications from non-European migrants, mainly from Hongkong, India, Malaysia, Burma, Ceylon and the Philippines. In the same period, 5,000 temporary visitors of non-European origin were granted resident status and a further 4,000 non-European arrivals were relatives of people already in Australia. None of these would have been allowed to enter before 1966.

These new Asian migrants tend to be hand-picked and well qualified. Amongst the 1970–71 intake of approximately 3,000, there was a high proportion of doctors, engineers, university lecturers, dentists, teachers, and technicians. In answer to the obvious criticism that such a policy of 'special skills only' does a disservice to the underdeveloped nations in Asia who are crying out for citizens with professional qualifications, Immigration Department officials reply that Australia is not just attracting Asians from their own countries as one-third of the applications in the non-European category come from Asians living in Western countries. Officials also stress that in some countries, notably Hongkong, there are already more professionaly qualified people than there are jobs available, particularly in such fields as mechanical engineering, architecture and electrical sciences, and therefore no disservice is done by Australia admitting skilled migrants in these trades. In any case, no Asian nation has yet seriously complained that Australia is siphoning off its professional people.

These new Asian migrants are not quite the only non-white element in Australia's twelve and a half million population. Apart from the 140,000-odd Aborigines, there are approximately 20,000 Asians who hold Australian citizenship through birth or registration. These are mainly the historical remnants of the gold-rush days of the nineteenth century when adventurous Chinese could arrive and settle in Australia as they pleased because immigration restrictions had not been invented. There are another 8,000 Asians who have been given varying degrees of temporary resident status for business and trading purposes. Many of these will eventually qualify for citizenship. Finally, at any one time there are 12,000 Asian students at Australian universities, 10,000 of them privately financed, 2,000 given government sponsorship under the Colombo Plan.

The government's policy towards these Asian students is and always has been that they must return to their own countries when their studies are completed (or when they have failed their examinations too many times). The only exceptions to this rule are students whose professional qualifications are not needed in their own countries, and students who marry Australian citizens. During the 1940s when Arthur Calwell was Minister of Immigration, a Chinese student called Johnny Wong wanted to remain in Australia. His case was massively supported by the fans of Darwin Football Club, for whom Wong was in the habit of scoring a large number of goals. So keen were the citizens of Darwin to keep their star footballer that a group of them actually found a sports-loving Australian girl prepared, in the interests of avoiding the deportation order, to become Mrs Wong. Unfortunately, this chivalrous gesture was thwarted by Immigration Department sleuths who discovered that a Chinese Mrs Wong already existed. This detection enabled Mr Arthur Calwell to justify his deportation order with the immortal crack, 'The trouble is, two Wongs don't make a white.'

Although many Asian students would dearly like to remain in Australia, there seems little hope of relaxing the rules which now require them to leave the country soon after graduation. One absurdity of the present system is that the Australian Government cannot force students to go back to their country of origin. They can only be compelled to leave Australia. The result is that each year many Westernized Asian graduates leave their Australian universities and settle in Canada or the United States. Many of them would much rather have stayed where they were, but their pleas are almost invariably turned down by the Immigration authorities. Says Mr Snedden, 'I take the view that the Americans and Canadians are being somewhat avaricious in the way they positively encourage highly qualified Asians to come in. We see ourselves as a part of Asia, and so we believe we have a duty not to hold on to Asian students who could be making a valuable contribution to their own countries.'

When discussing Asian immigration with Australian politicians and senior officials, I was always conscious of their immense caution on the subject. This stems from their apparent concern for forces of innate conservatism in Australian public opinion. Although the Gallup Polls now suggest that the Australian people are rather less conservative about keeping their country 'Free, White and Great', the Australian establishment is taking no chances.

Sometimes this establishment caution extends into outright discrimination, as candid Ministers have occasionally admitted. Early in 1971 Mr Vance Dickie, Immigration Minister for the State of Victoria, said publicly in London that Australia's immigration selection procedures were racist. His comments followed a controversial episode involving a Jamaican-born British citizen, Mr Jan Allan, who was refused an assisted passage to Australia because he was a person of non-European descent. There have been recent complaints that black Papuans, though technically Australian citizens, are not allowed to settle on the Australian mainland. Further criticisms of Australia's policy were made at the 1971 Commonwealth Prime Ministers' Conference in Singapore, and the then Prime Minister Mr John Gorton replied to them by frankly and unapologetically stating that his country did control its admissions on a discriminatory basis. But since Australia now annually admits more non-white immigrants in proportion to its population of 13 million than Britain does in proportion to its population of 55 million, it seems that Australia's acknowledged degree of discrimination is a comparatively moderate one.

The sixty-four thousand migrant question for Australia now is: Does the 1966 policy change represent the first step in a steadily expanding programme of non-European immigration, or is the present meagre trickle of 3,000 highly skilled Asians merely a carefully measured token concession to liberal opinion? Because of the desire of officialdom that immigration should be a non-party issue, immune from political controversy, the chances are that any expansion in Asian immigration will be extremely gradual. A 1968 report by the Immigrant Planning Council on immigrant prospects for Australia in the following five years made no mention of Asians in its 140 pages. Mr Snedden, who talked futuristically of finding 8 million migrants at rates of up to 300,000 a year between 1970 and 2000 if Australia is to reach its predicted population of 28 million by the end of the century says of the non-European element: 'So far as my human eye can see, the Asians will not be making a significant contribution to achieving those totals, although we will probably be making a slight increase in the annual intake.'

This then is the official attitude of the Australian establishment. If there are going to be any important changes in the present rate of Asian immigration, they look as though they will have to emanate from Asia itself.

5

AUSTRALIA AND ASIA

Australia and Asia appear to be on the brink of starting a mutual love affair. Whether this turns out to be a superficial flirtation for reasons of political convenience, or a shameless exploitation by the latter of the former's physical resources, or a genuine friendship that could ripen into an international equivalent of matrimony, are all premature questions. What is interesting, in the light of previous xenophobia about 'The Near North', is that a relationship between the two continents should be getting off the ground at all.

Australians showed no serious interest in Asia until the mid-1950s, except to mutter darkly about 'The Yellow Peril'. The man who started to change such attitudes was Richard Gardiner Casey, Australia's Minister of External Affairs from 1951–60 (later Governor-General 1966–69). He was a tireless enthusiast for good relations between Australia and Asian countries, making numerous official visits to Asian capitals during his period of office and in 1954 publishing an influential book *Friends and Neighbours,* urging closer links with the Near North. As long as Sir Robert ('I'm British to my bootstraps') Menzies was Prime Minister, new diplomatic links with Asia always took second place to his old personal links with the British Royal Family, but a very different attitude came from Menzies' eventual successor, Harold Holt.

Spurred perhaps by a need to have a different political style from that of his predecessor, Harold Holt made fresh overtures to Asian countries from the day his premiership began in January 1966, and his first official overseas visit was not to London or Washington, but to Cambodia, Laos, Malaysia, Singapore and Vietnam. Holt had a delightful personal manner in his leader-to-leader style of international diplomacy, and his blend of bonhomie and naïvety went down extremely well among Asian statesmen accustomed to being treated with arrogance and condescension by other eminent Westerners. In a few months of mutual exchange visits, together with some increased aid grants, a few tariff relaxations and a modest amendment to the White Australia policy, Harold Holt did more good for Australia's image in Asia than had been done in the previous 65 years of the century, an achievement which became fully recognized at the time of his tragic death through drowning in December 1967.

Harold Holt's funeral underlined this fact, for the leaders of the 1,500 strong congregation at St Paul's Cathedral, Melbourne, on December 22nd, 1967, made up the greatest galaxy of international political talent ever seen on Australian soil. President Johnson flew from Washington in Air Force One; the British delegation consisted of The Prince of Wales, Prime Minister Harold Wilson and Opposition Leader Edward Heath. But what would undoubtedly have pleased the mourned Australian leader most was that eighteen heads of state or national leaders had made the journey from Asia to pay their homage, among them Prime Minister Lee Kuan Yew of Singapore, President Park of Korea, President Marcos of the Philippines, Tun Abdul Razak of Malaysia, Field-Marshal Thanom Kiitichorn of Thailand and President Thieu of South Vietnam. Since President Johnson took advantage of the period before and after the service to have top-level talks with his allies in the Vietnam war and with other statesmen, it could be said that this was Australia's first and finest hour as an accepted member of the Asian community.

But Asian countries did not just confine their manifestations of regret about Harold Holt's death to sending eminent representatives to Melbourne Cathedral. Despite the differences of language and religion, several Asian nations honoured the Australian Prime Minister with special memorial services on their own ground. Perhaps the most impressive of these was held in Luang Prabang, the royal and religious capital of Laos. At the gold-roofed royal pagoda of Wat Mai in the presence of the King, Queen and full cabinet council, the Bonze (Patriarch) of the Laotian Church and a choir of saffron-robed Buddhist priests chanted prayers, lamentations and carried out incense-burning rituals for Holt's soul in a baroque ceremony which lasted for $2\frac{1}{2}$ hours. 'It was an unprecedented tribute,' said one senior US diplomat who attended. 'The leaders of Laos were genuinely moved by the Holt tragedy and they mourned him like one of their own—far more than they mourned the late President Kennedy. It made us all appreciate that Australia really did have a special relationship with some of the Asian countries.'

A special relationship is certainly what Canberra's Department of External Affairs would like to have with Asia, and there are signs that this policy is succeeding. Because of Australia's relative smallness in relation to the world powers, and because Australia has no imperialist history (except that of being a colony itself), the complexes and suspicions which complicate Asian countries' relations with Washington, London or Paris do not threaten their relations with Canberra. Some Asian diplomats even argue that the down-to-earthness of the Australian national character makes a positive appeal in the inscrutable Orient. The High Comissioner for Singapore in Canberra, Mr Stanley Stewart, has publicly declared that Australians fit without self-consciousness into the Asian scene because they tend not to find any task menial. 'Whereas British and American executives in Asia are apt to supervise work without actually participating themselves, in an Australian-supervised job you are likely to find the Australian down in the ditch with his shirt off and as dirt-stained as the Asians with whom he is working.' High Commissioner Stewart went on to argue)hat because of this different approach, Singapore tradesmen who were merely polite to American and British customers were prepared to crack jokes and extend social invitations to Australians, and herein lay the basis for Australia's special relationship with Asia.

Although there is something in this thesis, a far stronger basis for the new *entente cordiale* across the Coral Sea is mutual self-interest. The government of Singapore, for example, last year started investing heavily in Australian equities to build up its slender reserves, and the Finance Minister, Dr Goh Keng Swee, is on record as saying that his country's holdings in companies like Broken Hill Proprietary, CSR and Western Mining 'could rise to perhaps five times, possibly ten times, what they are at present'. Hong Kong's exports to Australia, now running at $36 million annually, are up 90 per cent since 1966, and trade figures with some of the smaller Asian countries are showing equally dramatic percentage increases. But trade is not the only element in the relationship, for Australia's natural desire to live peacefully on the periphery of an increasingly uncertain Asian mainland has caused the Commonwealth Government to make substantial increases in its aid programme (particularly to Indonesia), and to promise to retain a token military presence in Malaysia and Singapore after Britain's final withdrawal from the area in 1971. These developments have stirred Australian interest in the Near

North. Most newspapers have at least one full-time correspondent based in the region, while *The Bulletin*, Australia's prestigious newsweekly magazine, presciently started a new section in July 1969 entitled 'The Neighbourhood' whose reporters and editor concentrate exclusively on stories from South-East Asia. Thus there is a growing curiosity and appreciation about Asia in Australia today, and this interest inevitably focuses on two countries in particular—Japan and Vietnam.

AUSTRALIA AND JAPAN

'Australia spent the first half of the century as a farm for the British. Now it looks as though we may spend the second half as a quarry for the Japanese.' These words of Australia's Opposition Leader, Gough Whitlam, sum up the national dilemma about the booming new relationship with Japan. To date, most of the whispers of doubt about the rocketing trade figures between the two countries have been drowned by the ringing of the cash registers, yet for all the wealth being generated by their links with the Land of the Rising Sun, some thoughtful Australians are expressing serious fears about the future of the Pacific's newest and strangest alliance.

Ten years ago the Japanese were still widely hated among those considerable sections of Australian opinion for whom wartime feuds die hard. Trade between the two countries was confined to wool sales and the idea of serious political or diplomatic co-operation on international issues seemed laughable in the Menzies era. Even as late as 1967, there were frenzied national protests when the Japanese Consul in Perth was invited to lay a wreath on the local war memorial. But today, such prejudices are fast receding, for Japan is Australia's biggest customer, buying over $700 million worth of goods a year. 25 per cent of Australia's total exports are going to Japan, and 12 per cent of Japan's exports come to Australia. All these figures are increasing by an annual rate of over 10 per cent.

Looked at from Japan's point of view, this relationship is a happy and prosperous one. The giant complex of industrial factories along Honshu Island's 200-mile long Tokaido corridor is ravenous for raw materials, all of which have to be imported. With bulk shipping costs fallen by half over the last fifteen years, Australia is a relatively short and inexpensive haul for Japan's supercargo ships, to such an extent that it is actually cheaper to move iron ore from Western Australia to Tokyo than it is to ship it to Broken Hill Proprietary's blast furnaces in New South Wales. As a result, Japan is now taking 88 per cent of Australia's iron-ore exports and there is plenty of room for expansion, for the Japanese iron and steel industry expects to have increased its output by one-third by 1972 and by then to be needing 170 million tons of imported iron ore each year. But despite the colossal Pilbara resources which could eventually enable its mines to supply twice this amount annually, Australia is unlikely ever to contribute much more than about a third of Japan's total requirements for reasons which were explained to me in Tokyo by Mr Shigeo Ngano, the President of the giant Fuji Iron and Steel Company.

'We Japanese like doing business with Australians. They are efficient, they keep to their delivery dates, and of course Australia is a very stable country politically. But in the Japanese iron and steel industry we have a definite policy of not buying all our raw materials from one source. At present, we buy large quantities of ore from America and Canada, where prices are higher than in Australia, and in future we will buy from India and Brazil as well as from Australia. Although it would be more efficient and more cheap perhaps to buy everything from the Hamersley company, this would be too much of a risk, because one strike, or a breakdown of the railway or harbours could mean that our mills would have to shut down. For this reason, we will not take more than about a third of our raw materials from any one country, whatever the cost. So you see, Japan is more important to Australia than Australia is to Japan.'

Despite such characteristic self-satisfaction from a Japanese tycoon, and despite Gough Whitlam's *cri de coeur*, the message about Australia's growing economic dependence on her northern neighbour seems to be lost on most government and commercial leaders.

In addition to iron ore, Japan is the biggest buyer of Australian wool (with the textile mills of Osaka taking up 35 per cent of the total export clip), and is also the largest purchaser of Australian sugar, coal, copper, hides, nickel and manganese. Certain other Australian exports to Japan, particularly beef and wheat, are increasing at a prodigious annual rate. Although capital investment from Tokyo's finance houses has been low until recently, it is now starting to loom large in key mining projects. As for Japanese imports, these are inevitably concentrated on motor cars and consumer goods. Starting from scratch three years ago, Japanese car manufacturers have already captured 15 per cent of the Australian market in motor vehicles, and this share of the total is expected to double by the mid-1970s when firms like Toyota, Nissan and Honda have expanded their export production output, particularly in the field of higher-powered cars and jeeps. Japanese industrialists admit that Australia figures prominently in their plans for increased exports during the next decade. When I visited the headquarters of the giant Matsushita Electrical Industries near Tokyo, a senior vice-president told me: 'We regard the Australian market as a naturally advantageous one for us, because it is so underdeveloped. Less than 20 per cent of Australia's imports are finished consumer goods, and although it is a country rich in primary produce, there is very little secondary manufacturing, particularly in the sophisticated technical equipment we specialize in. Our future prospects there are almost limitless.

The Japanese leaders have done their homework well, for as the above comments indicate, Australia's secondary industry is weak and vulnerable, and could be bought under the table to-morrow by any of Japan's big trading companies. Secure in the knowledge that their country's standard of living will, at present rates of economic expansion, comfortably overtake Australia's within the next 15 years, the average Japanese attitude to their Anglo-Saxon neighbours is one of mild condescension. While foreign-office officials in Tokyo talk deprecatingly of 'Little Australia', businessmen remark that labour disputes in Sydney and Melbourne factories show that 'Eikokubyo' (literally: 'The English Sickness'—meaning strikes, absenteeism and laziness) is obviously soon going to spread to the British Empire's most virile outpost. Japan, they infer, will shortly have to carry the white man's economic burden throughout the Pacific.

Such sentiments are no doubt very galling to Australian listeners, but the facts are that Japan is now an immensely rich and arrogant trading nation, with every intention of increasing its wealth at its neighbour's expense. Those who pontificate about Australia's future being fossilized by the residual influence of British traditions, or vulgarized by the cultural impact of America, are overlooking the third and more important force, for a much more likely obstacle to the Australianization of Australia is economic colonization by Japan. This will occur because Australians do not realize that it is going on now, and are not bothering to try and understand their Japanese economic invaders.

To be fair, an influential section of Australian opinion is suddenly doing its best to bridge the understanding gap. Many schools and all universities now teach Japanese, and at the University of Western Australia there is a newly-instituted Faculty of Japanese Studies. Mining companies have sponsored scholarships for post-graduate work in Japan, a flourishing Japan-Australian association has started up in Sydney, and *The Bulletin* now publishes a special section, 'The Week in Japan', which is often longer and better journalism than its long-standing 'The Week in America' feature. Even Australia's politicians, who have in the past led the nation on foreign policy matters from a political stance scarcely distinguishable from that of the Retired Servicemen's League, are now making some interesting noises about Japan. Charles Court, Western Australia's dynamic Minister of Industrial Development, persuaded his state government to set up a special Western Australia office in Tokyo, which is on a small scale no less effective than the Australian Embassy, and Australia's Commonwealth politicians too are making some enterprising moves. At the United Nations in the summer of 1969 I heard a speech by Australia's then Minister of External Affairs, Mr Gordon Freeth, in which he publicly urged the Japanese Government to play a more forceful role in Asia. This was the first time an Australian Government spokesman had ever admitted in a policy speech that Japan had any major role at all in Asia, let alone calling for Japan to exercise its power actively. The address so surprised Japan's Foreign Minister, Kiichi Aichi, that he paid effusive private compliments to the Australian delegation, and twenty-four hours later proposed that the United Nations should give serious consideration to admitting Japan as a permanent member of the Security Council.

But compared to trade, the political and cultural links between Japan and Australia are of very small importance. Already the gnomes of Tokyo are paying the Australian piper. How long—on some looming problem like increasing the rate of Japanese immigration to Australia—before they start calling the tune?

VIETNAM

When Air Marshal Nguyen Cao Ky, as Prime Minister of South Vietnam, made an official visit to Australia in 1967, he brought with him in his entourage a mysterious woman who locked herself in her bedroom on arrival at Government House, Canberra, and remained there throughout the entire trip in a state of obvious sulk. This performance vexed the Governor-General, Lord Casey, and positively infuriated Lady Casey who herself had to carry trays up to the recluse because of the over-strained staff problems at Government House. Only when Ky was back in Vietnam were Australia's secret service chiefs able to discover and disclose to the Caseys what had been going on. The mystery woman was, in fact, the wife of one of Premier Ky's chief rivals in the South Vietnamese political power struggle. She had been taken to Canberra as a hostage, to guarantee that there would be no anti-Ky coup while he was out of the country.

This incident is illustrative of much of Australia's involvement in the Vietnam conflict, for throughout the adventure it is fair to say that Australia's leaders have spent a good deal of time way out of their depth. Sir Robert Menzies was Prime Minister when Australia was first asked by President Johnson to become a war ally, and he agreed without serious hesitation. 'Big Ming' had never been a reluctant partner in previous military enterprises with Australia's 'great and powerful friends' as he liked to call Britain and America, and at Washington's request he swiftly up-graded the 1964 force of thirty Australian instructors training Vietnamese soldiers in jungle warfare into a 1966 force of 4,500 combat troops (later increased to 8,000). The next Prime Minister, Harold Holt, was even more of an enthusiast for the Vietnam war than his predecessor had been. Fêted and flattered by President Johnson on his visits to the US in the early days of his premiership, Harold Holt proclaimed on the record that Australia would 'go all the way with L.B.J.' He repeated the remark in London as he urged the British Government to despatch troops to Saigon, and successfully fought an election on the same slogan.

As a result of this uncritical adulation of Johnson's war policies, the Australian-American alliance touched new heights of friendship. In October 1966 L.B.J. became the first US President to set foot on Australian soil, and amidst scenes of mounting hysteria he roared in Melbourne to the cheering crowds, 'Hurray for Australia! The Aussies are my brothers. A is for America, A is for Australia. Long live A A!' The tour continued on this lyrical note, so apart from a few anti-war demonstrations and a row with the Governor of Victoria over precedence, the visit was judged a whirlwind success, ending with the Presidential comment, 'If I ever get kicked out of America, I'm coming to Australia.' In private conversations, Holt said of the President, 'He's the biggest fish I ever speared,' while L.B.J. said of Holt, 'I like to come out and look my Prime Ministers over.'[1] Both remarks apparently pleased their recipients. Because of this ecstatic welcome in Australia, and also because of the unqualified support which Australia continued giving to the Johnson administration's line in Vietnam, Harold Holt became L.B.J.'s closest friend among international leaders, and one of the administration's most valuable assets in soothing the war anxieties of American public opinion.

The death of Harold Holt thus came as both a personal and political blow to Lyndon Johnson. It also came at a particularly bad moment in the war, for by December 1967 the White House knew from enemy troop movements that the Vietcong were about to launch the major military thrust which became known as 'The Tet Offensive'.

Thus when President Johnson came to Australia for the Prime Minister's funeral he used the occasion to brief the cabinet on the coming Vietcong onslaught and personally requested that more Australian troops should be committed to Vietnam without delay. According to Theodore H. White in *The Making of the President 1968*: 'On December 21st in the Cabinet room of the Australian Government in Canberra he [the President] personally briefed the Australian Cabinet on the dark days ahead; the kamikaze attacks we might expect in the coming offensive; the American troops being flown out; the promised new division from Korea; the need for greater Australian exertion in the common cause.' At this historic meeting were Acting Prime Minister John McEwen, the Federal Treasurer William McMahon, the Minister for External Affairs Mr Paul Hasluck, the Minister for Defence Mr Allen Fairhall and the leader of the Government in the Senate Senator John Gorton. At that moment, all were contenders for taking over the leadership of Australia, and perhaps because of the oncoming power struggle, they unanimously turned down the President's request for more troops. The Australian-American honeymoon was over.

But the end of the honeymoon has by no means meant the end of the marriage. Although the incoming Prime Minister, John Gorton, enjoyed nothing like as idyllic a relationship with the White House as did his predecessors, nevertheless Australia has by and large remained the United States' staunchest ally in Vietnam. When I had an off-the-record talk with Prime Minister Gorton

[1] Quoted by Hugh Sidey, *A Very Personal Presidency*, André Deutsch and Atheneum.

on December 24th, 1968, he answered my questions on the war
with a lecture on the folly of appeasement-type sentiments which
he said he learned the dangers of during his undergraduate days
at Oxford in the late 1930s. Since that interview, despite rapid
US back-pedalling by the Nixon administration, the Gorton
government has made no significant alteration in Australia's
military and political commitment to Vietnam, and indeed made
a positive virtue of this policy at the 1969 General Election. (The
Australian Government has since that interview, with some degree
of public reluctance on the part of the Prime Minister, withdrawn
one battalion—1,000 men approximately—from Vietnam.) In
short, talking to politicians and public officials in Canberra about
Vietnam, one is left with the impression that Australia's leaders
have not thought deeply about the origins of the war, and that they
have neither worried overmuch about its course, nor concerned
themselves with the wider implications of their military involvement on Australia's future role in Asia. What has motivated and
influenced Australian policy all along has been the desire to please
the United States. Troops have been sent to Vietnam as payment
of an insurance premium, for Australia's first objective is to
guarantee that the American fire-brigade will turn out if ever
Communist forces threaten antipodean soil. That any future US
government would be bound to help defend Australia against
Asian aggression whether Australia had supported the Vietnam
war or not is a thought which does not seem to have been seriously
considered in Canberra. 'Support America, right or wrong' appears
to have been Australia's motto for the Vietnam conflict, and even
if this philosophy had produced the right policy, it is an unworthy
posture for any sovereign state to be quite so slavishly and un-
thinkingly tied to Uncle Sam's apron-strings.

   But the apparent dearth of Australian thinking and political
planning over Vietnam should not detract from the military
excellence with which Australian troops have carried out their impossible duties in the war. Early in 1967, when doing a stint as a
Saigon-based war correspondent, I went down to the Australian
Tactical Area of Responsibility in Phuoc Tuy province, travelling
by an RAAF Caribou flown most of the way at tree-top height to
avoid sniper fire. Landing at the base camp of Nui Dat, I found
an atmosphere very different from that of the many US headquarters I had visited. In the first place, the security checks were
strict and highly efficient. Most American base camps had South
Vietnamese visitors dropping in, peasant girls serving food at the

General's table, and local villagers hanging around watching the coming and going of aircraft and equipment. The Diggers (as Australian troops are always known) took no such chances with their Vietnamese allies. No villagers were allowed anywhere near the base camp, and on the rare occasions when exceptions to this rule were made, even as eminent a visitor as the local mayor was blindfolded on the perimeter of the area and brought into the interviewing tent before being allowed to see where he was. One might have thought that such tough tactics would have aroused considerable local resentment, but all available evidence suggested that in the 'winning the hearts and minds' campaign, the Diggers were doing a good job. Around Hoa Long, the Australian Army's civil action group had, at that time, transformed what twelve months earlier had been a troublesome and atrocity-racked Vietcong provincial capital into a showpiece of tranquillity. The methods of the officer in charge, Major John Donoghue of Melbourne (who was the target of three serious assassination attempts during his tour of duty) were particularly interesting, and contrasted sharply with the lavish generosity and military ostentation of American pacification programmes in other areas. While US soldiers working in civil aid groups were apt to lash out with munificent donations to 'the natives' of everything from candy to cement, Donoghue's men seemed positively mean by comparison, and went out of their way to avoid giving the impression that the Australian base camp up the road was an all-providing big brother. Apart from the troops actually assigned to the civil action programme, no soldiers were allowed within the pacification area. If Australian jeeps had to pass through pacified villages, they were required to keep below the speed limit of 15 miles per hour in order not to frighten the women and children, and so strictly was this rule enforced that speeders automatically received 28 days confined to barracks. Any brothels that opened up in the province were smartly closed down by the puritanical Digger officers, another sharp contrast with the policy of some US units whose answer to this inevitable problem was to post the local brothel's address on the camp notice board and to open an expensively-equipped VD clinic adjacent to the offending establishment. Above all, the Diggers set out to conduct their civil action operations in as discreet a style as possible, showing the villagers how to do things for themselves, rather than showering them with gifts and doing things for them. These sensible attitudes certainly seemed to be paying off, for Hoa Long was the only place where I heard

Vietnamese villagers greeting officers by name and where I saw children offering sweets to soldiers rather than the other way round.

Unfortunately, Phoc Tuy proved, in the long run, to be an unpacifiable area because Vietcong and North Vietnamese Army troops were in the region in such large numbers. Recent estimates claim that only 42 per cent of the population of Phoc Tuy are loyal to President Thieu's government, and although this degree of support has doubled from what it was two years before, nevertheless it still leaves the province as one of the most treacherous in South Vietnam. Good though the Diggers' pacification efforts have been, their limited manpower resources have enabled them to do only a partially adequate job.

The same can be said of the Australian Task Force's military activities in Phoc Tuy. On the face of it, the Diggers are just about the best combat troops on the allied side. Their discipline is strict enough to eliminate flaws which exist in some US units such as talking on patrol, lighting up cigarettes and playing transistor radios in the jungle. Their morale is high, the relationship between officers and men is a good one based on mutual respect (as one Major put it, 'Australians are easy to lead, bloody hard to order'), and Digger gallantry in battle has lived up to the Gallipoli legend. But for all these virtues, Australian troops have failed in their assignment in Vietnam for the Phoc Tuy province is still, in 1970, a Communist stronghold, containing around 1,500 active Vietcong guerillas, often supported by 2,000 North Vietnamese Army forces coming in from Bien Hoa province. The Diggers have 8,000 men on their base, 5,000 of whom are regular combat troops. They have to train South Vietnamese units, take on emergency duties outside their own tactical area of responsibility, run the pacification campaign and fight the enemy. The manpower for all these duties just is not there. When the Australians built a seven-mile fortified fence around Dat Do to cut off Vietcong supply lines, they patrolled it so inadequately because of troop shortages that the Vietcong not only broke through the fence repeatedly, but added injury to insult by digging up 7,000 mines from the fence and re-planting them in Australian patrol areas, thereby killing 15 Diggers and seriously injuring 134.

This sort of failure has been repeated in miniature many times in Phoc Tuy province, where the Digger efforts may be compared to those of the celebrated Mrs Partington, who spent her life trying to keep the Atlantic Ocean from her doorstep with her mop.

Australian military activity has been too small to be really effective. Although some 330 young men have been killed in action, there is little to show for it. Defence spokesmen in Canberra like to point out that the Australian Task Force's 'kill ratio' (that macabre statistic indicating the number of allied soldiers killed in relation to enemy losses) stands at 1 to 10, whereas the US average in that part of Vietnam is 1 to 5. But what's the use of this if Phoc Tuy province remains firmly under Communist control? One can praise the Diggers for their military skill, for the toughness of their conscripts trained at Queensland's School of Jungle Warfare, for their pacification efforts, and even for their humanity (there have been at least two instances where Australian troops were killed by snipers hidden because officers refused to burn down hamlets or throw grenades at suspected houses). But the end result has been negligible. Drinking in the Nui Dat officers' mess, under a portrait of the Queen, one Australian officer said to me, 'We've bitten off more than we can chew.' It is a fitting epitaph for Australia's entire Vietnam involvement.

AUSTRALIA—POLICEMAN OF ASIA?

Thinking Australians spend a lot of time arguing about their country's future military role in Asia. The debate gets considerably more media coverage than that given to Australia's present martial activities in Vietnam (where amazingly not one national newspaper or TV station thinks it worthwhile keeping a full-time staff correspondent) and was a major issue at the 1969 election. From all the heat that is generated on the subject, an outside observer might be forgiven for assuming that the Australian commitment to Malaysia-Singapore which causes all the fuss must be at least as large as say, Britain's diminutive forces in the Persian Gulf (9,000 men), but in fact Australia has a mere 1,200 troops in Asia outside Vietnam. Most of these are infantrymen based at Selangor in northern Singapore, and they are supported by two RAAF squadrons of Mirage fighters hangared at Butterworth Airfield in Malaysia. All are at least 2,000 miles from Australia's northern frontiers. What are they doing up there?

Originally, Australia sent troops to Malaysia-Singapore as an extra arm to the substantial British commitment (40,000 men) in the region. Then, following the 1968 devaluation crisis in Britain, the Wilson government decided, as an economy measure, to withdraw all British forces East of Suez by December 31st, 1971. The announcement of this move, coming after several firm promises to the contrary made by Prime Minister Harold Wilson and Defence Minister Denis Healey to the Australian High Commissioner in London, Sir Alec Downer, inevitably caused alarm and confusion in Canberra. The chaos was increased by several wild off-the-cuff remarks about Australian defence policy by Prime Minister John Gorton, who at various moments indicated enthusiasm for withdrawal, for stepping up the commitment, for establishing a forward air defence system centred on the RAAF's as yet non-existent F111 squadrons, and for starting an experimental force of 'Israeli-type commandos'. With so much shooting from the lip going on, the Australian cabinet settled for the comparative peace of a major defence review, which took some eighteen months to complete. The final judgment on this review can best be summarized by quoting the relevant policy statements of the political party leaders at the last election. Mr Gorton said, 'We have decided that even though Britain withdraws from our north, we shall keep ground, sea and air forces there as a visible expression of our continuing interest in helping to preserve that region against possible external attack.' The Opposition leader, Mr Gough Whitlam, said, 'We will withdraw all forces from the area, because the garrisoning of token military forces there is so restricted physically and politically that it renders our presence useless and meaningless.'

From this altercation, it is evident that Australians are somewhat divided about their military role in the Near North. Since Mr Gorton's party narrowly won the election, 1,200 Diggers are now in Malaysia-Singapore to stay, but they are under some peculiar restrictions, of which the strangest was the former Prime Minister's own dictum at the 1969 five-power Asian Defence Conference that the troops can be used for defending 'Malaya' (which does not exist) but not for 'East Malaysia' (which does not exist either). Mr Gorton's verbal arabesques should not, by this time, necessarily be taken with the seriousness normally awarded to statements by a head of government. It is expected that the new Prime Minister, Mr William McMahon, who took office in March 1971, will soon clarify Australia's military role in the region.

At present there are several possible threats to the security of Malaysia-Singapore, which include Chin Peng's communist guerillas in North Malaysia, Filipino attempts on Sabah, and a second dose of 'confrontation' by Indonesia. More serious than any of these are the communal problems between the Chinese and

Malay races within Malaysia, which have already exploded into full-scale rioting on one or two occasions and are likely to do so again in the face of increasing militancy from the young Chinese, who no longer accept the compact granting Malay political supremacy which their fathers entered into 15 years ago. Prime Minister Gorton has made it clear that Australian troops will not be involved in maintaining internal law and order in Malaysia-Singapore, but the big difficulty lies in deciding when rioting is merely an administrative internal problem of law and order or when such disturbances have been stirred up and promoted by outside subversive forces, such as Peking's Red Guards. Since the Malaysian government invariably believes that evil external influences are working against it, and since the sensitive communal problems of Malaysia are likely to get worse before they get better, Canberra could well have some tricky decisions ahead of it in determining when to commit Australian troops for the purpose of maintaining stability in the region. The lesson of Vietnam shows how easy it is for an Anglo-Saxon military power to get bogged down in the quicksands of Asia in the name of suppressing external aggression and subversion, and critics of the Liberal government's policy like to point out that in 1960 the US commitment to Vietnam was only a few hundred men. Of course, the racial tensions in Malaysia may sort themselves out with the minimum of trouble, but they could be fanned by Communist activities into a fire next time that will give Australia as proportionately bad a burning as America has had in Vietnam.

Alert officials in Canberra are well aware of this potential disaster, and like to stress that the Australian policeman will probably be stationed on the Malaysia–Singapore beat for a temporary period only. For example, Lee Kuan Yew's new defence plan (costing over 20 per cent of the entire budget) will give Singapore a regular and reserve army of 30 battalions or 45,000 men by 1979. They will be backed up in the air by squadrons of Hawkers, Hunters, Provosts and Alouette helicopters (commanded by the recently retired Commander-in-Chief of Britain's Far East Air Force, Air-Marshal Sir Rochford Hughes) and supported at sea by a flotilla of eight naval patrol ships. When this force is fully trained, Australia's present unit of 1,200 men may seem superfluous.

Most of Australia's political leaders would certainly be pleased to see their country's policing activities on the Asian mainland phased out during the next few years as and when the capitalist countries of the region can do the job for themselves. To this end,

Australia takes in officers from Indonesia, Singapore, Malaysia and Thailand for special training programmes; exchanges visits with Taiwanese warships: keeps an RAAF training unit in Thailand; and has donated 10 Sabre jet fighters to the Malaysian Air Force. Future possibilities that have been seriously canvassed include the setting up by Australia of a recognizable services training unit in Asia, and the creation of a joint air defence system based on Malaysia–Singapore. Such schemes in the long run are far more likely to win friends and influence people for Australia in Asia than a long-term physical presence of Diggers in explosive Asian areas 2,000 miles from home.

INDONESIA AND WEST IRIAN

Indonesia is Australia's nearest Asian neighbour and the one that worries her most. The first time I visited Canberra, an official in the Ministry of External Affairs told me in sepulchral whispers of a secret document just captured by intelligence agents in Djakarta, which revealed the existence of an Indonesian plan to invade Australia. The details included even the Indonesian place-names for new settlements and townships in the North, but fortunately omitted any mention of how the four-ship Sukarno navy was going to transport the tens of thousands of invaders across the Indian Ocean. 'I think we can regard these plans as academic for the moment,' said my informant, 'but it makes bloody hairy thinking about for the future.'

At that time (1965) even the most absurd rumours about Indonesia's future intentions had to be treated with care, for the 100 million-strong nation a mere 300 sea miles from Australia's northern coast was in a state of turmoil. The vicious aggression against Malaysia known as 'confrontation' was at its height, the flamboyant President Sukarno was spewing forth daily diatribes of maniacal hate against the West in his radio broadcasts, and hysterical mobs burned down the British Embassy, no doubt *pour encourager les autres*. But since the overthrow of Sukarno, a more peaceful tone has entered into Indonesian foreign policy. Australia now enjoys good relations with the Suharto government, giving Indonesia the largest slice of her foreign aid programme ($13 million), and offering educational and training opportunities in Australia for Indonesian students, professional men and army officers. Nevertheless, despite the present harmony between the two nations, Australians are still somewhat nervous of their volatile neighbour. The nervousness is likely to increase in the coming years because of the impending problems surrounding the state of West Irian.

West Irian (a new province of the Indonesian Republic) shares a frontier along the 141st meridian with Papua–New Guinea (Papua is fully Australian, New Guinea is an Australian-administered UN Trust Territory), and all of them are situated on an island landmass 80 miles north of Queensland's Cape York. Papua–New Guinea is in reality, if not in name, an Australian colony, and a very backward one at that. Its population of 2¼ million indigenous tribesmen and 35,000 Australians is unimaginatively guided by Canberra, and as a result the Territory's House of Assembly is small and unrepresentative, the schools are rudimentary and often teach only pidgin English, and the employment opportunities are poor. Inevitably, in this anti-colonialist age, there is a vocal West Papuan Freedom Movement, demanding independence. An independent state of West Papua is not a practical proposition, for the 'Mastas' (as the native pidgin dialect terms Australians) will not stomach the thought of a power vacuum on their borders, which might all too easily be filled by some Castro-like troublemaker. On the other hand, if Australia keeps firm control of Papua–New Guinea, this is almost sure to strain relations with Suharto, for the inhabitants of these territories are militantly anti-Indonesian.

At the moment, the problems of co-existence between West Irian and Papua–New Guinea are of minor importance. But it is easy to draft a scenario of independence riots on the island, emotional passion generated in Canberra and Djakarta on the issue, and an impulsive Indonesian leader in the Sukarno mould. In such circumstances, the Indonesia–Australia confrontation could make the earlier version with Malaysia look like a vicarage tea party by comparison.

AUSTRALIA'S ASIAN FUTURE

From the preceding studies of Australia's links with individual nations in her Near North, it seems that her future role as a South-East Asian power is hedged with far more long-term problems and difficulties than are at first apparent. Reverting to the analogy of Australia and Asia's present relations being akin to those of two people on the brink of a love affair, it would be fair to say that the Australian side of the courtship is now starting to have serious doubts about certain aspects of the romance. Nevertheless, commitment is already far too deep and overall mutual attractions far too great for there to be any possibility of the relationship being broken off. The worst one can say about Australia's intentions towards Asia for the 1970s is that they may be becoming slightly less serious and intense than they were in the later 1960s.

In one sense this shift in emphasis should be welcomed for its realism. When former Prime Minister Harold Holt swept through Asia's capitals declaring exuberantly, 'Australia is part of Asia', he was making the same sort of idealistic oratorical flourish as President Kennedy's famous cry from the Berlin Wall in 1961, 'Ich bin ein Berliner.' A more down-to-earth view of the situation came from Prime Minister Gorton when he said, in an April 1969 speech to the Imperials Services Club of Sydney, 'It is a popular proposition that we in Australia are part of Asia. That is woolly thinking. We hold a sparsely settled continent in the name of Western culture on the periphery of Asia.'

Contrasting the sparse settlement of Australia, the least densely populated country in the world (12 million people to 3 million square miles) with the overcrowding and high birthrate of Asia—which already holds 53 per cent of the world's population and is expected to increase by 400 million people before the end of the century, one can understand why Australians fear an eventual take-over bid for their rich and empty continent. This take-over bid is not, of course, inevitable. Any Asian power might be put off from annexation plans by the realization that one-third of Australia is uninhabitable desert; by the colossal logistic difficulties of mounting an invasion across several hundred miles of ocean; and by Australia's (allied presumably to America's) military defences. But far and away the best prevention of an Asian take-over is by Australia demonstrating her good faith and good works towards Asia so effectively over so long a period that she becomes accepted as a useful and beneficial member of the Asian community, and cannot possibly be regarded as a selfish, isolated, or hostile enemy.

This is presumably the objective of Australia's present Asian policies. As far as trade goes, the patterns seem to be following the right lines. Australia is already using her natural resources to assist Asia's industrial revolution, and developing her agricultural potential to combat present and future Asian hunger. Even the McCarthyite anti-communist consciences of pastoralists in Australia's Country Party have been assuaged by $100 million of annual wheat sales to Peking, and it now seems to be accepted that Australia's destiny as a trading nation is inextricably linked with Asian customers of all political persuasions.

Yet in two other spheres of policy, aid and immigration, many experts argue that Australia's activities are giving or soon will give considerable cause for offence in Asia. Criticism of Australia's foreign aid programme has been pithily expressed by Donald Horne in *The Lucky Country*: 'Australia has not the resources to play Lady Bountiful to all Asia but it has been unexpectedly mean in what it does do. Australians congratulate themselves on their 'aid' to Asia. But as a proportion of gross national product the aid is only 0·35 per cent, a remarkably insignificant percentage for a nation that is so concerned in the future of the Asian sub-continents. *Per capita* national income in Australia is sixteen times that of Asia. Despite its internal democracy, Australia plays an aristocratic role in the society of Asia—rich, self-centred, frivolous blind.'

As for immigration policy, there is as yet no evidence of a massive demand from Asian countries for sending settlers to Australia, since migrant applications from the entire sub-continent appear to be running at the feeble rate of 3,000 per year. Thus Australia's immigration policies are a matter of international public relations more than anything else, but in these terms critics argue that the restrictions do considerable damage to Australia's image in Asia. Here they are probably right, for although no one now disputes the right of a host country to impose strict controls on immigration quotas, a nation with an open-door policy like Australia's is exposed to unanswerable allegations of discrimination if, out of a total annual intake of 180,000 arrivals, less than 3,000 are from Asia. If Australia wants to avoid incurring the hostilities of fierce emotional attacks on her immigration policies from Afro-Asian leaders (some of whom have already voiced their indignation on the subject) then the Department of Immigration must increase its percentage intake from non-European sources. This, of course, is a decision for Australia's top politicians, because stressing the importance of getting along with Asia is not much of a vote-getter, while advocating the virtues of living alongside Asians could be quite a vote-loser. Nevertheless, those leaders who think of the next generation, as opposed to the next election, will be well advised to support a modest increase in Asian immigration, for apart from possible future economic jealousies, the present immigrant restrictions are the most likely cause of friction and bitterness between Australia and Asia in the years ahead.

But although it is easy to criticize certain imperfections in Australia's relationship with Asia, the most important aspect of it has been the amazing upsurge of Australian enthusiasm for diplomatic, political, commercial and cultural contacts with Asia during the last five years. 'Fortress Australia' thinking is dead or dying fast. Although the Holt concept of Australia as an integral part of Asia has not found favour, it is now widely accepted that Australia must play some other substantial role in its own region. This role has been felicitously described by the Foreign Editor of *The Australian*, Robert Duffield, as 'that of the outrigger on the Asian canoe—an essential stabilizing influence but not part of the main craft.' Even this task is an expensive and delicate one, but Australia's new willingness to take it on is the most convincing evidence of her growing weight and maturity as an international power.

6

AMERICANIZING THE WIDE OPEN SPACES

Flying across the Atlantic ocean one sees many more signs of human existence on the surface of the water than one sees on the surface of the earth when flying across the Australian outback. This is just a roundabout way of saying that Australia's wide open spaces are cavernous in their emptiness, and that the outback (a generic term meaning the back of beyond) looks and feels like a desolate graveyard.

On first inspection, a Lazarus-type miracle would seem necessary before wealth and prosperity could be resurrected from this grave-yard. In Australia's northern and central regions, thousands of square miles are totally uninhabited, and thousands more are populated at the meagre rate of less than one human being to every ten square miles. Life for those who inhabit this wilderness is tough and rugged. Driving down the most famous of all outback roads, 'The Track' from Darwin (the only bitumen route going southwards through the Northern Territory), one passes through some of the bleakest and most primitive countryside in the world. The soil looks parched and barren, with hardly a blade of grass to be seen; much of the ground is covered with quartz chippings, rocks, cattle skulls, scrub and spinifex; for three-quarters of the year the temperature remains constantly at 90° F or over and the rainfall averages less than one-twentieth of an inch of rain per month; while for the remaining quarter the rain gods take revenge by pouring water down from the skies in quantities of up to five inches per day.

This land is so hostile it almost literally eats people. Drivers who suffer breakdowns are well advised to obey the Number One rule of outback motoring, 'Stick to your vehicle', for those who wander away from their cars in search of help are sometimes not discovered until several days later—and then only as sun-scorched corpses. Houses tend to be little better than rudely built shanties,

liable to collapse in the face of cyclones and floods during the
rainy season, and to become incandescent ovens during the dry.
The blazing heat sends many outback residents into madness,
more into alcoholism. Those who resist these temptations (and
they are not easily avoidable in a region with so much isolation and
rural poverty) have to battle for survival against poisonous snakes,
crop blights, crocodiles, plagues, tempests, droughts, dingos and
devastation by insects. 'A poor dried-up land, afflicted only by
fever and flies', was how the nineteenth-century Australian
explorer, Matthew Flinders, summed up the outback, and except
in the eyes of a few visionaries, there was nothing happening in
the area, until very recently, to make it worth anyone's while to
challenge that description.

The heart of the outback is the Northern Territory, which,
excluding the town of Darwin, has a population of only 36,000
(12,000 of whom are aboriginals) in its 520,000 square miles—a
ratio of 13 square miles per person. The region has all the hall-
marks of frontier hardship—including a dash of Wild West
lawlessness. Half-way down the Track I shared a roadside beer
with Police Constable Harold Darwin of the Northern Territory
Police. A migrant from Preston, England, his beat now covers
22,000 square miles, and his lot is not entirely a happy one:
'It can be rough in these parts. I get called out to a good many
fights, and occasionally they've been knife or gun fights. Abos
with the grog in them make a lot of trouble, and the same goes
for drivers. The Territory doesn't have any speed limits and the
pubs stay open 24 hours a day. As a result, there's a steady stream
of bloody terrible crashes, and the death toll on the roads is the
highest in Australia. Another of my big worries is the number of
fugitives from the south who come up here to try and hide away
from the law. They can be nasty when they're cornered. Not long
ago I had to arrest a bloke and we had the one hell of a punch-up.
After a bit, I got him on the ground and sat on his head as I
tied him up. Darn me if the bugger didn't take a bloody great
bite out of my arse. I'm scarred for life there now.'

If the posterior of a policeman is one symbol of life in the wide
open spaces, another must certainly be the interior of a pub.
624 pints of beer per head are consumed in the Northern Territory
each year, and as that statistic includes all the women and children
in the 'per head' part of the calculation, some people must be
positively drowning in the excesses of liquid pleasure. 'And why
not?' said my neighbour at the bar of the Adelaide River Hotel.

'A newcomer don't get accepted as a Territorian until he's proved he can drink. That's the way it should be. There's nothing much else to live for up here except grog.'

The Adelaide River Hotel is about 70 miles south of Darwin, and despite its imposing name, it is scarcely superior to an enlarged corrugated-iron hen-coop. However, its ice-box works well and its beer flows freely. On my visit, well over half the customers were Aboriginals, who amused themselves by throwing darts first at a dart-board and then at each other until the inevitable brawl got them forcibly ejected. The self-appointed bouncers, who evidently enjoyed their regular exercise of 'boong-clobbering', came back into the pub and pointed out to me a large crocodile skull and a pair of giant buffalo horns hanging on the walls. Amidst gales of laughter, they recounted how an American had come into the bar and said to his companion, 'Gee, I just bet those darn great horns came off that darn great skull.' The same informants also told the story of a young Englishman who entered the bar and asked for a beer. The bartender obligingly thumped the usual bottle down on the counter and ripped the cap off with his teeth, whereupon the refined young Englishman asked, 'Could I have a glass, please?' At this unique request, the barman leant over his customer and said menacingly, 'And what part of fairyland do you come from, mate?'

Territorians are proud of such rough edges, and take pleasure in teasing visitors from 'Down South' about the privations they will have to endure because of the local shortage of nightclubs and pink champagne. A year or two ago this type of mocking was apt to take on a slightly bitter note, but now the jokes remain very good-humoured. The reason for this change, and also the reason why so many observers from the Eastern Cities are making the 2,000 mile trek north, is that the outback suddenly looks like becoming an immensely valuable and profitable tract of agricultural real estate. Unbelievable though it seems even to the 1970 visitor as his eyes survey the apparently barren wastes of simmering scrubland, the Lazarus-type miracle is about to happen in the outback, and the graveyard is soon expected to prove itself to be paved with gold.

The Midases who are effecting this transformation are mainly Americans, or Australians with a strong American orientation. Their stories are as remarkable as those of their fellow pioneers in the mineral world, and their rewards could ultimately be almost as substantial, for at best their achievements will improve agricultural production in certain parts of the outback by anything from four hundred to four thousand per cent. Such startling predictions are highly credible in the light of the area's past agricultural history, for previous pastoral developers of Australia's north and centre seem to have been inept managers with the Midas touch in reverse. Because of the difficult climatic conditions, large-scale attempts at planting cash crops have had a long and miserable record of failure, and because of the dearth of scientific breeding, fencing and seeding techniques, livestock has fared little better. Although cattle are supposed to be the economic mainstay of the outback, 100 acres of open range scrub are usually needed to support one beast and even then the animal in question is likely to be a mangy cow with a tick-infested hide flapping like soggy sailcloth across the protruding spars of its rib cage. There's no agricultural Eldorado to be found as long as the end results are like these.

But despite all the failures and disappointments, experts have been arguing for at least a decade that the agricultural potential of the outback could be revolutionized into immense profitability if only someone with capital would implement certain forms of pasture improvement. Government research scientists authoritatively claim that there are 280 million acres in Australia north of the 30th parallel which are suitable for improvement. By certain professional methods such as clearing the scrub, planting special pasture grasses, spreading nitrogen-producing fertilizers, erecting fences and introducing new breeding strains, it is officially estimated that beef production can be increased at least tenfold even in the most barren areas. Of the 280 million acres designated as suitable for these kinds of improvements, only 7 million acres have so far been developed. The early results on these pioneer properties are encouraging enough to show that the potential production increase stemming from these new techniques is staggering in its magnitude. Indeed, there now seems little reason to doubt that the wide open spaces of Australia are on the threshold of what people living in them like to call 'The Great Awakening', and that the agricultural gold rush will be second only to the great mineral boom.

WILD GOOSE CHASE

One of the first Americans to appreciate the agricultural potential of the outback was a legendary entrepreneur from Los Angeles, irreverently known in Australia as 'Wild Goose Chase'.

An investment banker now in his fifties, Allen T. Chase first came to Australia in 1937, and has since made more than seventy visits to the continent in the course of which he has directly channelled more than twenty-five million dollars of American money into buying up properties and cattle stations. Taking note of his example and initiative, many more US investors have been indirectly encouraged to put tens if not hundreds of millions of dollars into similar schemes, thereby making Allen Chase perhaps the most important single influence on the Americanization of Australia's wide open spaces.

Chase's first steps were not easy ones. The sobriquet 'Wild Goose' derives from a disastrous agricultural failure which occurred in 1953 when he and a consortium of American financiers sank $4 million into a rice-growing project on the Northern Territory property named Humpty Doo. After expensive dams, irrigation channels and paddy fields had been created, production costs were found to be far too high and the project was abandoned. A contributory factor to the débâcle were swarms of wild magpie geese which dug up sedge bulbs in the paddy fields, thereby damaging some of the rice plants. Chase rather unfairly laid the entire blame on the geese, and his nickname dates from this episode.

But Chase's faith in Australia's food-producing potential remained undimmed, and working from an office in Los Angeles' prestigious Kirkeby Centre, he brought a steady stream of big-money US investors to Australia throughout the fifties and sixties. I first met him early in 1967 in the Ord River township of Kununurra, when he was taking a small party of wealthy Californians around attractive property situations in the north-west. A sleek dark man, bearing remarkable facial resemblance to the late Humphrey Bogart, Allen Chase was taking the evening sun in Kununurra wearing a startlingly formal costume for that casual environment, consisting of sharkskin flared trousers and a frilly white silk shirt with sleeves rolled down to elegantly cuff-linked wrists. With a polished, highly courteous manner of speaking, and a tendency to make theatrical waves with his hand, he seemed more like a soigné metropolitan conjuror than a pioneer frontiersman whose exertions have changed the face of large parts of Australia. I asked Chase how and why he had got started on these trans-Pacific investment missions:

'What was the great stroke of genius that brought me to Australia? The answer is that I just liked to ride on boats, got myself a trip to Australia way back in 1937 and became so interested in the country that from then on Australia became my hobby. I believe that Australia is the future bread-basket of Asia, and that the potential for well-improved properties here is just fantastic. When I first sank money into Esperance, the land cost me 50 cents an acre, and a lot of my friends said "God, that crazy man Chase, going mad about that desert". Now, of course, the land round Esperance is worth at least 30 dollars an acre. I and my associates still have 750,000 acres down there which are getting more valuable every day.'

Allen Chase has had interests in several Australian properties at various times in the last ten years, but he is most proud of his Australian political achievements, by which he means his successful efforts in persuading the Government to change their rules to allow United States citizens to own land in the Northern Territory.

'Harold Holt was my great friend. We first met in Mexico in 1949 through his knowing a girl friend of mine. Our friendship became very strong, and he came and stayed at my home in Bel Air. I used to say to him, "The set-up in the Territory is all wrong. You need American capital to develop it, but no American is going to be interested unless he can get freehold title to his land. Harold, you must change that," I told him.'

Harold did change it soon after he became Prime Minister, and American capital has been flowing into the Northern Territory ever since. Allen Chase himself has done well out of the change as an expert adviser and partner to various landowning syndicates, but since 1969 his interests have been concentrated in a 1,001 square-mile property at Fitzroy Crossing, Western Australia. When I talked to him in October 1969 at his sumptuous apartment in the Riverina Country Club, Los Angeles, Chase expressed the belief that he had found a new agricultural breakthrough for a part of the Western Australian coastline which will make for sensational future profits: 'I've got 10,000 head of cattle on Fitzroy, so it's doing well by any standards, but the fantastic part about it is that the property has an 80-mile frontage on the Indian Ocean. I own a new company, Australian Ocean Products, which has exclusive rights to fish on this 80-mile beach. Well, do you know that this bit of coast has 26-feet tides, and a four-mile shelf to it. Every time the tide comes in it brings with it 15 lbs. of fish per acre. With the right equipment I can just take off all these fish on 80 miles of beach and four miles of shelf and sell them to Japan. I've had Japanese engineers and research scientists investigating this project, and their most conservative estimates show that I can catch 1 million lbs. of fish per day at costs of less than one hundredth of a cent per lb. Did you ever hear such a story? I'll be making myself a fortune down there all right.'

Allen Chase deserves his fortune, for although he is not universally beloved in Australia the former UCLA and London School of Economics graduate had the vision to see the island continent's agricultural potential long before any other outsider:

'I always saw that there'd be a hungry world, and that Australia had the resources to solve the hungry world's problems. This is possible now that US money is pouring in. I reckon there'll be a steadily increasing number of Americans coming out to buy land in Australia, because opportunities for mass agricultural production in the US are now minimal. I guess I must have really started something.'

ESPERANCE

The biggest project started by this adventurous Angeleno was Esperance, a district where the initials B.C. mean Before Chase. Until his antipodean peregrinations took him by chance in 1954 to this beautiful coastal corner of Western Australia, some 370 miles south-east of Perth, Esperance was a totally barren sand-plain. The countryside supported no domestic animals at all, and the township was a struggling service port for the old Kalgoorlie gold-fields, exuding an atmosphere of run-down hopelessness that belied the district's name.

Thanks to Chase's early interest, Esperance is now to Australian agriculture what the Pilbara is to Australian mining. After discovering from Australian research scientists that by sprinkling zinc, copper and molybdenum trace elements on the soil certain kinds of sheep-fattening clovers and grasses would flourish, Chase formed a company to develop $1\frac{1}{2}$ million acres of the area. He suffered an early financial setback because his group tried to accelerate the two-year build-up period needed to fertilize the sand-plain, but his efforts were more successfully followed through by a different syndicate of US investors calling themselves the Esperance Land Development Company. Under their and Chase's auspices wealthy Americans such as TV personality Art Linkletter, David Rockefeller of the Chase Manhattan Bank, financier Benno C. Schmidt, Henry Luce III of Time Inc, film stars Anne Baxter and Robert Cummings and many others have invested over $15 million in Esperance. Most of them are now enjoying at least a 20 per cent return on their capital from farms concentrating on sheep, beef cattle and cereal crops.

The star American property at Esperance is 'Linkletter's Place', as the lofty lettering on its wooden Arc-de-Triomphe-style gateposts call it. A visitor sweeps up its mile-long drive lined with specially planted tuart trees and immaculately painted fencing, feeling as though he might be visiting a showpiece farm on the Sussex downs or in the lush pastures of Wisconsin rather than an outback sheep station in what until recently was a Western Australian desert. At length the homestead is reached, where Linkletter's 36-year-old Australian manager, John Hagon, offers guests tea on a silver tray and reels off statistics that indicate he could well have afforded to offer champagne in gold chalices.

'This property consists of 22,000 acres, which originally cost less than 50 cents an acre, and is probably now worth about $45 an acre. Mr Linkletter has spent well over a million in improving production here, and the return on his investment is over 20 per cent. In addition to fencing and pasture improvement, we're particularly pleased with our computers which we use for checking breeding and feeding techniques, and for improving efficiency. With an enterprise costing system we have reduced what used to be twenty minutes of man-time per head of sheep a year down to twelve minutes per head. At the moment we have about 35,000 sheep and 500 Aberdeen Angus cattle on the property, but we should double this within the next year or two.'

The proud proprietor of this concern, Art Linkletter, is the main catalyst behind American participation in Esperance. He has a genuine passion for all things Australian; he makes the 6,000-mile trip to his property anything up to six times a year; and spends many hours in his native California publicly lecturing on and privately enthusing over the agricultural prospects in Australia for US investors. The publicity given in the US to his activities on the other side of the Pacific has undoubtedly stimulated many Americans into participating in similar projects, and Linkletter has gone so far as to call himself 'Australia's Number One unofficial ambassador to the United States'. He evidently takes his diplomatic duties seriously, for he amazed White House and State Department officials soon after President Nixon's inauguration by unilaterally declining the (unoffered) post of American Ambassador to Canberra!

Although Linkletter and his fellow Americans set the pace in Esperance, they have avoided accusations of establishing a US colony by taking care to share some of their good fortune with Australian farmers. The Esperance Land Development Company has an arrangement with the Western Australian Government by which it disposes of half of the 100,000 acres it develops annually to local buyers. Under this scheme, it has so far sold off over 120 two-thousand-acre blocks of land to Australian owners, at prices in the region of $8 an acre. For this sum, the purchaser gets land which has been developed one-third of the way towards productivity. He probably needs to spend at least another $30,000 before a profitable farm exists, although there are good local examples of owners who got leases direct from the State Government and have made good starting only with $1,000 and a second-hand tractor.

Although one might have expected to find considerable latent anti-Americanism in a district where US outsiders have made big profits by using Australian ideas to make money on Australian land and selling it off to Australians, in fact there is nothing but praise for the spirit that made Chase, Linkletter and others put Esperance on the map. One man who has seen it all happening from a relatively detached viewpoint is an Esperance-based priest, the Venerable Dennis Bryant, holder of the euphonious ecclesiastical title 'Archdeacon of the Gold-fields'.

Bryant, a former RAF pilot and curate in the London suburb parish of Wimbledon, emigrated fifteen years ago after successfully answering an advertisement in the *Church Times*: 'Pioneer Priest wanted for Esperance'. He started the hard way. 'When I began, life here was pretty bleak. Toilets were always just holes in the garden, we were so isolated that we couldn't pick up any radio station, and a fresh-water supply didn't exist. People drifted in and out of the town, but it had no community feeling. Then after all this American money came in it was like being thrown into the days of Buffalo Bill and the Wild West, there was so much excitement. The people who have come here are the best people I have ever met in my life. They are incredibly generous. If I pop into a homestead to say hello, before I know what's happened my car's been filled up with petrol and a sheep carcass has been shoved in the boot. But most important of all, the new farmers created a community spirit and ended the feeling that the vastness of this countryside is somehow frightening. No one here slacks at all now. Because of the example set by the Americans, everyone

realizes that we are building something in Esperance, and that it's
something really big.'

Now that minerals have been found in the surrounding region,
Esperance is likely to get even more prosperous as a port and
commercial centre. Quarter-acre blocks of building land in the
town centre, which used to be auctioned off in Before-Chase days
for as little as $5 each, now fetch around $3,000. The population
has trebled to 6,000, the port is full of towering cranes and bulk
wheat silos, and the atmosphere is one of cheerful rural prosperity.
Esperance, in short, is an agricultural miracle that worked thanks
to American risk capital. There are millions more acres awaiting
similar treatment.

BIG GUNN OF GOONDIWINDI

Hearing the stories of the financial killings made by American
investors in Australian agriculture, an observer soon poses the
inevitable question, 'Why don't the Aussies themselves seize a
bigger piece of the action?' The quick answer, and it applies
equally to the world of minerals, is that Australia is chronically
short of Australian capital. Although there are plenty of middle-
rich Australian investors doing very nicely with their 2,000-acre
properties in New South Wales, Victoria or even Esperance, rare
indeed are the home-grown plutocrats who have large sums of
ready cash available for Texan-dimensioned developments. When
it comes to projects on the scale of the million-acre plus cattle
stations in Australia's North, the most lucrative economies of size
are unfortunately available exclusively to the very rich—and that
usually means exclusively to Americans.

In these circumstances, there is a predictable school of thought
which argues that if Australia's wide open spaces can only be
developed by American dollars, then it is better that they should
not be developed at all. In a country where national pride is the
established religion, particularly among the more conservative
inhabitants of rural areas, this argument might well have taken
root with prohibitive consequences. That it has not done so
is due to the persuasive enthusiasm of certain pro-American
Australian leaders, whose vision is broad enough to see the benefits
to the whole community of a transformed and profitable outback,
even under overseas ownership.

One such leader who has perhaps done more than any other
individual Australian to encourage the Americanization of the

Wide Open Spaces is a celebrated figure known to the headline writers as 'Big Gunn of Goondiwindi'. Standing 6 foot 3 inches in his socks, and weighing 20 stone, this craggy giant with the jowls of a prizefighter has immense prestige throughout the continent's agricultural industry, partly because of the excellence of his own 30,000-acre property near Goondiwindi and partly on account of his successful chairmanship of Australia's Wool Board. In this capacity, Sir William Gunn (he was knighted for his services to agriculture in 1961) travels over 150,000 air miles each year promoting international wool sales (which earn $800 million annually for Australian exports—twice the value of mineral exports) and presides over the destinies of the nation's 100,000 wool growers and their 140 million sheep. He fulfils this important role on a part-time basis, being paid a nominal salary of only $5,000 plus expenses, for his main interest and business activity is pioneering the development of the north.

Big Gunn's pioneer headquarters are a suite of modest offices above the Wool Exchange in Brisbane. From here Sir William, his 29-year-old son Bill, and a team of a dozen energetic young executives (average age 28) whom he calls 'the boys', administer a 15-million-acre pastoral empire whose frontiers are as much as 1,200 miles away and whose commercial ambitions know few limits. Gunn's company, The Gunn Rural Management Pty Ltd, owns about 1½ million acres of this empire and manages the rest for a handful of American owners, who hail mainly from Texas and Florida. Gunn offers these owners a pastoral management service which, he claims, can transform poor land supporting one low-grade head of cattle on every 40 acres into good land supporting one high-grade beast for every 3 acres—an improvement of 1,300 per cent.

To carry out such a transformation, Gunn buys for his client, or syndicate of clients, a property in the tropical zone of Australia of not less than 100,000 acres in size and preferably up to a million acres. The land, which might perhaps be situated in the Northern Territory or in the Cape York district of northern Queensland, is priced according to the estimated number of cattle already on it, and this will usually work out at an average cost of 50 cents per acre. Once the deal has gone through, Gunn's first step is to fence in the existing cattle (who have hitherto ranged free in a totally wild state); to give them tick and parasite control by pushing them through dipping vats; and to improve the breeding strain by shooting the scrub bulls and introducing new ones. The second step comes shortly before the rainy season, when the property is sprayed from the air with a mixture of Townsville lucerne grass seeds blended with super-phosphate fertilizer. This dramatically improves the quality of the feeding, which can be upgraded still further if the third step is taken, namely the planting of crops like soya beans and grain sorghum. The entire cost of the improvement operation is approximately $10 per acre and takes three years to implement. At the end of that period, the client has an investment which should bring him a regular return of between 10 and 30 per cent on his capital, together with a property and a herd of cattle worth many times what was paid for and spent on them. Big Gunn, who was the first Australian to encourage extensive numbers of Americans to invest in northern cattle stations, believes that the widespread use of these techniques, which he stresses are not at all new but merely an application of existing agricultural knowledge, will revolutionize the north, provided investors keep coming forward.

'We've bought ourselves a gold-mine here,' he says, 'but it's a gold-mine which wouldn't exist if it weren't for these Americans. The blokes who keep on grumbling about the dangers of foreign capital are putting their heads in the sand. For a start, anyone who puts their money into the land here can't take it out again without first contributing an enormous amount of money to the development of this country. Another point is that the management of these companies is entirely Australian, and the managers usually get a good share of the profits. The most obvious point of all is that Australia just can't afford to do these kind of improvements without outside capital. The biggest venture in the north right now is Tipperary. I worked damn hard for 12 or 18 months trying to get the development of Tipperary Station financed in this country, but Australian investors just weren't interested in backing such a proposition. American investors are much more prepared to run certain risks for high rewards. Good on them if they do all right in the end.'

TIPPERARY

It's a long way to Tipperary, Australia, from Midland, Texas—9,200 miles to be precise—but the journey looks like being a profitable one for attorney William Neely, the Northern-Territory-based Executive Chairman of the largest and most revolutionary agricultural experiment in the world.

Tipperary was—and most of it still is—an untamed 3,600-square-mile jungle wilderness standing 90 miles south of Darwin. Its only assets appear to be its size; its location in a country acclaimed for its political stability; and its situation on the banks of the mighty Daly river. But these were enough to persuade some 850 Americans in 1967 to sink $6.5 million of equity capital and borrowed funds of up to $18 million into a venture that could radically change the food supply patterns for a hungry Asia.

Tipperary (the name comes from the red Tippera clay of the district) owes its existence to a simple idea. After carefully checking that there was a world demand for grain sorghum, the Tipperary Land Corporation's managers decided on a massive planting of this crop in such quantities that all imaginable economies of scale could be made by devices such as 32-row ploughs, bulk transporters, giant clearing tractors, multi-row seeding machines and other king-sized impedimenta of modern farming. In addition to selling this crop to Asia, cattle improvements of the type promoted by The Gunn Rural Management Company would be used across the station, and the revitalized herds would be able to feed on the stalks of the grain sorghum. Thus the shareholders (the company is quoted on the New York stock exchange) would get a cash benefit from the grain, and a further cash benefit from the cattle fattened on the by-product of the grain.

This plan suffered a major reverse during the first year of operations. The grain sorghum planting was destroyed by a late fall of heavy rain—a freak occurrence which had only happened once before in 90 years of record-keeping—and most of the first year's harvest was literally washed out. There were subsequent rows and management upheavals, which ended in Sir William Gunn's team losing the contract and William Neely moving from Texas to take up residence in Darwin, but the enterprise was continued along much the same lines for a second year, and with much happier results. Some 17,000 acres of cleared scrub-land in 1969 yielded good-quality grain sorghum at a rate of 3,000 lb to the acre, and the bulk of the crop was sold to the Mitsui Group of Tokyo at a contract price of $90,000 for 18,000 tons—$50 a ton. Also, approximately 6,000 open-range cows and calves were satisfactorily fenced in and fattened on ensilage from the sorghum stalks, and although many problems still remain, the outlook for Tipperary is now one of brisk optimism.

To a visitor, the most amazing aspects of Tipperary are its magnitude, and its forthcoming innovations. 'Come and see a bit of clearing,' they said to me when I was in the area in the spring of 1967. I went to Tipperary expecting to see some raking and burning of brushwood, and instead witnessed a destructive operation the Pentagon would have been proud of. Explosives were used to blow up tenacious tree stumps, light aircraft circled the area giving orders by radio, pairs of gargantuan D9 caterpillar tractors, towing a quarter-mile of 12-foot iron chain links between them rumbled like tanks through the bush clawing down all forms of vegetation while petrol fires were started behind them to obliterate the brushwood. There was even a sniper on hand to slaughter escaping rabbits, dingos and kangaroos.

At the end of it all, 42,000 acres of jungle had been transformed into colossal 'paddocks', a word which normally means a field about the size of a sports pitch, but which on Tipperary means rolling vistas of cleared enclosures, each averaging six miles by nine miles. These have been fenced, and have now successfully yielded their first sorghum harvest, although the present results are scarcely even a curtain-raiser for what may be coming.

William Neely believes that in the Northern Territory climate, where frosts are unknown and the rainfall is accurately predictable, it will be possible to get two and three crops a year out of the land, as is done in the Philippines, where farmers with a similar climate get four crops a year. By this double and triple cropping of different varieties of grain, by experimenting with fertilizers and by using even larger farm equipment of 64-row size, Tipperary expects to make massive shipments of produce—perhaps up to half a million tons a year—to Japan, Taiwan, and other Asian countries where agricultural land is limited. By irrigating special drinking places, drilling artesian water bores, and using new supplementary feeding techniques, a tenfold increase in beef cattle production is predicted. Eventually, Neely hopes to clear all of Tipperary's 2·3 million acres and to sell two million of them off to Australian farmers in 5,000 and 10,000 acre lots. All this adds up to quite a dream for a one-time wasteland, which is still 90 per cent covered by virgin bush, but if it comes true the experiment could well, by its example, as William Neely claims, 'provide a practical means of overcoming world hunger.'

Since writing the above account of Tipperary, news of fresh disasters on the property have become public knowledge. Last year's harvest was again a disappointing one; the quality of the sorghum crop was so low that Japanese companies refused to pay an economic price for it; the experiments with 64-row agricultural ploughs proved unsuccessful; and William Neely returned to practise law in his native Texas. However, Neely's vision lives on under new management, for these particular American investors are nothing if not stickers. Tipperary has now embarked on a slightly less revolutionary but no less optimistic phase of agricultural development, and local observers are rather more sanguine about the chances of success. As one expert put it: 'We've spent a lot of time learning from our mistakes. Now it's the moment for the big breakthrough.'

KING RANCH

An earlier American enterprise which has made the big breakthrough and is already providing 'a practical means of overcoming world hunger' is King Ranch Australia. This phenomenally successful offshoot of King Ranch Texas was brought into existence in 1952, following a 10,000 mile tour of Australian cattle stations by Robert J. Kleberg Junior, the parent company's president. Kleberg came to Australia as a result of a visit paid to him in Texas the previous year by a young Melbourne law graduate, Sir Rupert Clarke. Clarke, who had inherited his country's only baronetcy and largest pastoral empire, urged Kleberg to set up a major joint cattle-raising venture in Australia using the hardy Santa Gertrudis breed which King Ranch had pioneered. Clarke believed that if these animals were introduced to the Australian continent, they would revolutionize the cattle industry, because they were much more resistant to drought, ticks and other vicissitudes of the Australian outback than any conventional breed.

As a result of Clarke's faith and Kleberg's tour, KRA was registered as an Australian company in March 1952, and three months later 75 Santa Gertrudis bulls and 200 herd cattle, all direct descendants of the famous 'Monkey' who founded the breed, were shipped from Texas to Brisbane. In the beginning, KRA had one 7,500 acre property at Warwick, Queensland. Today, the company owns seven properties totalling over $1\frac{1}{2}$ million acres, of which the most spectacular are Tully River (51,000 acres in North Queensland) and Brunette Downs (4,750 square miles in the Northern Territory). On all these KRA properties there are now an estimated 170,000 head of cattle, and the Santa Gertrudis breed has been introduced into herds all over Australia with highly beneficial results.

L.O.F.—6

A good way to appreciate the scope of KRA's achievements is to travel 1,149 miles north of Brisbane to the Tully River Station, which the company acquired in 1963 when it was nothing more than a hopeless tropical wilderness. It is the sort of place about which Bob Dylan might have written his famous surrealistic pop ballad 'A hard rain's gonna fall', because the nearby town of Tully is the wettest spot in Australia, averaging 168 inches of rainfall in an ordinary year, and 310 inches a year when St Swithin is on his best form. As a result of these torrential downpours (six times heavier than anything recorded in rain-soaked Britain), the Tully River flora and fauna can be decidedly surrealistic, producing such freaks as the world's biggest bananas (weighing 1 lb. each with bunches over 150 lbs.), colossal specimens of poison peach, lantana and stinging tree, and horrendous-looking crocodiles and snakes. Of the station's 51,000 acres, when KRA moved in 12,000 were tropical rainforest, 12,000 were swamps and the remainder was eucalyptus forest. The Queensland Government, who owned this land, had long been anxious to see it developed and had offered it to four or five Australian organizations, all of whom had turned it down. The reason for their rejection was that nobody had ever before cleared large tracts of rainforest in this heavy rainfall area for conversion to pastoral land, so nobody knew whether the weeds would re-grow too fast or whether the soil was too barren to accept pasture grasses. The King Ranch experts did not know either, but they decided to take the gamble, and with $500,000 of equipment they embarked on a gigantic five-year clearing operation, which was described by Mr J. S. Wilson, company secretary of KRA: 'The rain-forest areas were crashed down by two 40-ton bulldozers working in tandem style and dragging between them a water-filled, nine-ton steel ball on an axle. The rubbish left lying on the ground was left to dry and was then burned. After the area had received heavy rainfall, tropical grasses and legumes were aerial-sown directly on to the ash. The open forest country, which is at a lower altitude than the rain forest area, was cleared in a similar manner. The rubbish on this country was pushed into "windrows" for burning by bulldozers fitted with specially designed blade rakes. Then the area was ploughed and sown, together with several hundredweight of fertilizers. The swampy areas were drained and sown to para and pangola grasses which are more suitable for low-lying areas. All this development was accompanied by the construction of fences, roads, stock water facilities, cattle yards, machinery sheds and modern well-equipped accommodation and houses for employees.'

After five years of this activity, the Tully River Station is today a showpiece property, and is put on the route of every VIP touring Queensland. Its lush paddocks are used for fattening cattle rather than for breeding, and weight gains of 400 lbs. per beast are regularly recorded. 'When mangy animals are moved to Tully from drought-stricken KRA properties elsewhere in the state, they get their heads down and eat like they're in heaven', said one jackaroo. As for the results, they have exceeded all expectations. What was a tropical wilderness in 1963 is now carrying 25,000 head of cattle—one beast to two acres—and turning them off to the meat-works at the rate of 12,000 a year. As Sir Rupert Clarke says, 'It's one big wonderful success story.'

But King Ranch men do not rest long upon their laurels. Their latest venture is the gargantuan 4,750-square-mile property of Brunette Downs, which from the air looks more like the Sahara than a cattle ranch. Only 14 inches of rain a year fall on Brunette, and in one 300-square-mile belt of desert, the average rainfall gets down to 2 inches. This makes life tough for the beasts, and in a year like 1958 when the drought was extreme, 25,000 head of cattle perished from thirst. Disasters like this almost unnerved the King Ranch experts. On one reconnaissance visit, Kleberg's Texan lawyer, Leroy Denman, sent back a letter saying, 'My impression is that the country out here is too big to forgive any serious mistakes, or for any mistake to be a little one.' In fact, very few mistakes seem to have been made, for since it acquired the property KRA has alleviated the drought problem by spending over $2 million in drilling 80 new water bores (there were only 39 before) which are regularly checked by the King Ranch aircraft. This logs 800 flying hours a year, landing on Brunette's 70 airstrips, ever-vigilant in ensuring that the 60,000 animals get adequately watered.

It is on the hot earth of Brunette Downs that the Santa Gertrudis come into their own, for they can stand the heat, resist the ticks, breed well and mature one or two years faster than shorthorns. Consequently, KRA are now breeding out the shorthorns on Brunette and are concentrating on improving the Santa Gertrudis bloodline towards purebred herds.

But there has been an impact made on humans as well as on livestock by King Ranch's activity on Australian agriculture, for the traditional stockman on a big Northern property used to lead a life almost as rugged as that of his beasts. He dwelt (and on many properties still does dwell) in a corrugated-iron shack with no facilities; he slept rough, went out mustering for days living off the land, and when he returned was badly underpaid. King Ranch began to change all that. On Brunette Downs, mobile canteens bring out cold drinks and ice-cream to the cattlemen; their company homes are filled with washing machines, coffee percolators and toasters, not to mention hot and cold running water, and the wages are often healthily above the minimum award levels.

King Ranch Australia, then, has been an all-round force for good, for both the human and the agricultural experiments it has pioneered do amount to a beneficial revolution as foreseen by Sir Rupert Clarke and Robert J. Kleberg Junior in 1952.

COTTON

King Cotton has crossed the Pacific and made good. Seven years ago, Australia did not have a cotton-growing industry worth mentioning, and had to import over $20 million worth of medium staple bales each year for the country's textile mills. Today, virtually all domestic requirements are catered for by the newly established cotton fields in Namoi, New South Wales, Kununurra, Western Australia, and Emerald, Queensland, and in addition a booming trade in cotton exports to Japan has recently developed. That this spectacular birth of a new industry should have occurred at all is due in no small measure to American initiative.

The cotton story first began in 1959 with a display of Australian initiative when the New South Wales Department of Agriculture built a research station in the upstate Namoi Valley to investigate the region's cotton-growing potential. In charge of the investigation was a Hungarian horticulturist, Nick Derera, who had escaped from Budapest at the time of the 1956 uprising and settled in Australia. Derera found that cotton could easily be grown in the Namoi Valley, thanks to the availability of a regulated water supply from the newly constructed Keepit Dam. When he revealed his findings, a local paper, the *North Western Courier*, headlined the story and a news item about the discovery was reprinted as far away as the *San Francisco Chronicle*. There it was read by two cotton farmers in Bakersfield, California, Paul Kahl and Frank Hadley. Because they were being frustrated by the high costs and oppressive acreage controls on US cotton growing, Kahl and Hadley did some serious research into the project at the Australian Trade Commissioner's office in San Francisco, made a trip to the Namoi Valley and ended by buying 'Glencoe', a 4,000-acre sheep property north-east of the sluggish country town of Wee Waa. They paid $36 an acre for the land in 1961. Today it is worth $260 an acre.

The first steps of the new American arrivals were not easy ones, and in the process of making them they trod on several local toes. The easy-going residents of Wee Waa got upset by the ruthless Californian drive that led to excesses such as those of one farmer who dug irrigation canals across a road without waiting for the Shire Council's permission; they became irritated by outspoken American criticism of traditional Namoi agricultural methods; and there were even sharp conversational clashes on political grounds because the locals (and it sounds amazing from ultra-conservative rural Australians) found the newcomers' opinions intolerably right-wing. Certainly the Californians, who numbered about 50 families within three years of Kahl's arrival, were staunch Republicans (there was one Democrat, but he voted for Goldwater in 1964), so much so that when US Ambassador Ed Clark made an official visit to Wee Waa, the leading US residents all refused to have their envoy to stay or to entertain him in their homes on the grounds that he was a Democrat and a Johnson nominee. There were even heated religious arguments in the district when some Californians tried to convert Namoi worshippers to their own esoteric brand of Presbyterian fundamentalism. But despite all these little local difficulties, the Americans were respected for their hard work and for the big risks they took to get established. One of the worst drawbacks of the Namoi region was its isolation. Says Paul Kahl, 'Growing the crop was one thing, but once harvested we had to truck the cotton all of 500 miles to the nearest gin in eastern Queensland.' Transportation problems like these made the building of a Namoi processing plant inevitable, so in a courageous gamble the growers formed the Namoi Cotton Co-operative Ltd, building gins and separating equipment with bank loans, and even, with outrageous self-confidence, appointing a manager at a salary of $10,000 a year at a moment when the co-operative's entire funds amounted to $2,000.

But the gamble paid off in a big way. At present, some 60,000 acres are under cotton in the Namoi. Typical average yield per acre is approximately $320 with production costs at $200, leaving an average net return (including a handsome bounty payment from the Government) of $120 per acre. This prosperity has transformed the region, for the shire of Namoi was a run-down mini-Appalachia before the coming of Kahl and his friends: today it is booming with a wealthy population of around 15,000. Thanks to an influx of Australians who have benefited from the American initiatives, enterprise and cultivation techniques, US citizens now comprise only 40 per cent of the total number of growers, but they still dominate the co-operative and set the pace in the towns of Wee Waa and Narrabri. Perhaps because of their success, local feelings towards the Americans are still mixed. The most prominent Australian grower in the Namoi is Ben Dawson, who was Australian Trade Commissioner in San Francisco when the first enquiry on cotton growing came from Paul Kahl. Dawson got into Wee Waa at an early stage, now owns 4,700 acres there, and lives on his land in a magnificent mansion designed by the US architect of Canberra, Walter Burley Griffin. 'Don't be too impressed by the stories you're given about American achievements here,' he told me. 'The fact is that all the best growers are Australians. The Americans don't make a serious effort to blend in with the local community, they just win the power struggles at the co-operative and trample on anyone who disagrees with them. Although they got this thing going, it's the Australians who are now making the Namoi really big.'

American farmers are much more popular, though less successful, at Australia's second biggest cotton growing area, Kununurra, Western Australia. Kununurra is a symbol of faith. Eight years ago it did not exist. It was created because experts believed that by damming the nearby Ord River and creating a complex artificial irrigation scheme, a breakthrough in northern tropical agriculture would be made. The Ord plan made admirable sense on paper, and so a pilot scheme was launched in 1963 with a $16 million diversion dam able to irrigate 30,000 acres of scrubland; 32 farmers and their families moved in, 10 of them Americans, attracted particularly by the lucrative cotton-growing prospects on land which could be bought outright for $2 an acre.

When I visited the Ord early in 1967, everyone in Kununurra was distinctly bullish about their prospects. Typifying the general feeling of optimism was Henry Kelly, a 44-year-old Oklahoman able to tell an overseas-boy-made-good story about himself that made cheerful listening after the Yanks-go-home rumbles in the Bowling Club at Narrabri. Kelly had been a lifelong labourer in cotton, working mainly in Oklahoma, West Texas and Arizona. His last boss, an Arizonan, having decided to take the plunge and emigrate to Kununurra, offered to take Kelly along with him. Kelly accepted and started working on his boss's Ord farm as a hired hand, until some alert Western Australians, aware of the value of a skilled cotton grower, offered Kelly a 50-50 partnership in their own Ord property. He was to do the work, and they would put up the $60,000 necessary for equipment and development costs. Inevitably Kelly joined them, and his expertise raised the 600-acre property's yield to over 2 bales per acre, thereby putting the Oklahoman's share of the profits into the $30,000 a year class. In addition to his commercial success, Kelly was given high marks for making himself 'a fair dinkum Aussie', on account of his sociability—which even extended to playing cricket for the Kununurra team. Kelly himself was lyrical in his eulogies for his new homeland: 'I am absolutely in love with Australia. It is my home now, and I will soon apply for Australian citizenship. I've just become the father of the first Australian-born American in Kununurra, and I'm glad for him too, because this is a wonderful country offering a lot better opportunities. There are no class or money barriers here like we have back in the States. People accept you for what you are.'

Henry Kelly, like all the Ord farmers I met, spoke enthusiastically of the opportunities for big expansion. By expansion, they meant the construction of the promised main dam across the Ord, a $75 million project which will bring the irrigated water and the soft white fleece of the cotton fields to an additional 150,000 acres of Kununurra's parched red land. But instead of the promised dam, residents of the Ord have had to put up with a flood of promises. Because of a variety of problems, among them an Australian version of the boll weevil which costs a fortune in crop-spraying expenses to exterminate, and the late harvest which puts Ord cotton at a marketing disadvantage, there seems to be a case for saying that the cost of enlarging the Ord scheme is prohibitive in return for the cash results. The man who puts this case most vehemently (and is Public Enemy Number One in Kununurra as a result) is an academic agronomist from Sydney University, Dr Bruce Davidson. In his latest book *Australia Wet or Dry?* Dr Davidson has this to say about the Ord: 'Farmers on the Ord River can continue to farm and make a satisfactory return on their capital only if they receive a subsidy of $14,000 a farm each year and are supplied with water free of interest on the capital the State has invested. They would require a subsidy of $30,000 if they were charged interest on the capital invested in the reservoir.

If Australians persist in expanding the area under irrigation they are simply squandering the nation's resources. The present-day Australian is a poorer man than he would have been if the resources used in irrigation had been invested in dry-land farming, and the future Australian will be poorer still if a policy of expanding irrigation at the expense of dry-land farming is continued.'

Yet such prophecies of doom do not go uncontested. Ord farmers have recently been getting higher yields and better quality cotton by using 'Hopicalia' cotton seeds from the USA, and even more significantly, many of them have made profitable diversifications into cash crops such as grain sorghum and cereals.

There are also the social and human arguments in favour of immediate expansion. These are well expressed by the Ord's most passionate advocate, Western Australia's Minister of Industrial Development, Mr Charles Court. In a nutshell, Court's view is that despite the expense, it is in the national interest to have a viable farming community inhabiting the Kimberleys. Australia's population, he claims, must be encouraged to spread away from the coastal cities by offering people a way of life that is permanent and prosperous.

This view seems to have carried the day, for after over three years of vacillation and indecision, the state and federal politicians concerned finally gave the Ord dam the go-ahead, and construction work on the $75 million complex began early in 1970. When all this is finished and working, a man-made miracle will have transformed the scorched terrain of the Kimberleys into what a poetic phrase of the psalmist describes as 'valleys that stand so thick with corn that they shall laugh and sing'.

TAMING THE WILD WEST

It seems symbolic of the present massive invasion of American capital into northern agriculture that a Texan investor should be willing to build a dam on the Ord only a few miles from the spot where the Australian Government was so reluctant to take a similar risk. The investor is Mr W. R. Goddard, a millionaire cattle king with extensive ranching interests in the western states of America. Under an agreement signed with the Government of Western Australia in 1969, Goddard agreed to build two dams at a cost of over $6 million approximately 30 miles south-west of the present Ord River farm areas. By controlling the flood water from two Ord tributaries, Arthur Creek and Dunham River,

Goddard will irrigate an area of 44,000 acres on his own 986,000-acre Dunham River Station.

It is amazing to Australians that any individual investor should be prepared to sink so much private capital into a scheme of this magnitude, for apart from letting Goddard buy the land at a 'pioneer price' of $1 per acre, the Government of Western Australia is not subsidizing the dams at all. Ultimately, about half of the irrigated area will be sold off to Australian farmers in 1,000-acre blocks, which should recoup the original investment, thereby leaving Goddard with a substantial tract of irrigated land for highly profitable grain crops and intensive feeding of his own beef cattle. But whatever the eventual profitability, Goddard's willingness to undertake such a substantial high-risk investment is typical of the big American capitalists who are now moving into Australia's north in increasing numbers.

This take-over of Australia's big properties by US millionaires is inevitably something of an emotive issue. Newspaper headlines have referred to the 'American land grab' and 'the great Aussie sell-out', while one sardonic commentator suggested that the Stars and Stripes should be hoisted over the Northern Territory as the region's new national flag. Such a gesture would not be entirely inappropriate, for the *Wall Street Journal* recently estimated that Americans now own between 60 and 70 per cent of the 43,000 square miles of the Territory's best pastoral land. There are many nations in the world with much smaller geographical areas than this.

Yet despite the local emotions, the Australian Government is doing everything in its power to encourage American buyers. Ben Dillingham II, a beefy Hawaiian American in command of the antipodean empire of the giant Dillingham Corporation, has publicly stated that his company would not have purchased their 750,000 acres of Northern Territory land without the incentives offered by the Federal Government. The Dillingham Corporation paid approximately 10 cents an acre for a 50-year lease on their Mountain Valley station (total cash payment $460,000) with an option to acquire freehold title to 100,000 acres after 20 years, and a guarantee that the lease would be renewed provided the company made adequate pastoral improvements during their period of tenure.

During their first two years as owners, Dillinghams spent $2½ million in developing the property, destroying the wild scrub cattle, drilling new bore holes and importing a high-quality herd of 10,000 East Coast Brahmins. This was where the Australian Government's encouragement proved invaluable, for the Department of Trade undertakes to pay the entire transportation costs of every head of cattle imported into the Northern Territory across another State boundary. Since the movement of cattle herds, even on the modern beef roads, can take several weeks during which time the beasts have to be fed and watered, the Government's willingness to foot the bill for all this expense is a most munificent incentive. Dillinghams have certainly profited from the deal, for due to the new cattle, the land that cost 10 cents an acre four years ago is today reckoned to be worth $2 an acre—and rising in capital value by 50 per cent per annum. These sort of rewards have attracted a host of US buyers (the US Embassy in Canberra now records more than 3,000 Americans with land in Australia) such as Mr Nelson Bunker Hunt, the son and heir of the Dallas oil billionaire, H. L. Hunt, who at present owns 2,500 square miles of Australia's north and boasts of becoming the biggest landowner on the continent. Other private US investors who have recently bought large Australian stations include steel king Edgar Kaiser, oilman Robert M. Librock, grocery magnates the Duda Brothers from Florida and Indianan electronics tycoon Douglas Howenstine. As yet, very few Australians have invested in large-scale agricultural projects (two notable exceptions are Sir William Gunn and L. J. Hooker, Australia's leading real-estate dealer, who owns the million-acre Victoria River Downs property). This is largely due to Australia's shortage of capital, but partly also to Australia's shortage of imagination. Although the facts about the big northern and western land developments, the beef road schemes and the irrigation dams are all published in the national newspapers, it seems that their excitement has not yet caught the fancy of the public. It is still far easier to spellbind an Australian dinner party, or round up a syndicate of enthusiastic investors, with gossip about suspected minerals underground, than it is to raise curiosity or cash with solid facts about abundant harvests and healthy cattle above ground.

It would be intriguing to know why American investors have, on the whole, neglected the Australian mineral market (there is minimal US buying of even the most glamorous mining shares) and plumped so heavily for direct investment in agriculture. Some observers put it down to the interest equalization tax imposed on US share purchases in Australia, others claim that the American cattlemen are the only people experienced enough in

large-scale pasture improvements to appreciate the profit potential
of the north, and are particularly attracted by the generous
incentives and tax concessions for agricultural development in
Australia. But my own view is that the Americanization of the
wide open spaces is only partly motivated by economics, and that
the romantic notion of conquering a harsh and untamed land
bearing remarkable similarities to the nineteenth-century American
Wild West has been an important factor in bringing so many US
investors across the Pacific. This concept of a romantic motivation
for investment and settlement in Australia's outback was lucidly
expressed to me in Kununurra by the Reverend David Nurse, a
parish priest extraordinary from the Australian Inland Mission.
His cure of souls covers a geographical area of over 100,000 square
miles of wilderness, running from the Northern Territory boun-
dary through to the west coast, a celestial empire which he can
cover only by piloting his personal aircraft for more than 60,000
miles a year. Nurse says of his parishioners: 'They are all engaged
in a romantic struggle, although the last impression you get from
the people here is that they are romantic types. Nevertheless, like
me, they are entranced by the sheer poetry of the north-west and
captivated by their titanic battle against this rugged countryside.
As soon as a man comes up here and starts to dig the Ord valley
he is right back in the book of Genesis—"go forth and subdue."
Because of this fight for subjugation, it is no use talking to these
people about units of cost expenditure, or profit projections, or
other slide-rule calculations. They'll argue about them, but in
their hearts they know that they could make more money by selling
up and putting everything into stocks and shares. The reason they
don't is that they're spellbound by the romance, by the poetry,
even by the religion of this pioneering life. There's no feeling of
loneliness up here like you often find in a big city. The degree of
interdependence is immense. Ask the question here "Am I my
brother's keeper?" and the answer is invariably "Yes." This is a
life which gives men back their souls, and it is this that captivates
us all, from American billionaires to struggling labourers.'

But whatever their motivation, it now seems certain that the
big American land-buyers are in Australia to stay. Feelings of
xenophobia against their presence are rare and getting rarer.

On a local level, there is increasing acceptance of the fact that
Americans are bringing new work, better conditions and increased
prosperity to a wasteland, and that their long-term participation
in the nation's agriculture is likely to be akin to that of the Scottish

landowners whose money and know-how developed the agriculture of nineteenth-century Texas without affecting American
sovereignty.

On the national scene, Canberra politicians speak hopefully of
these influential new property owners being able to lobby US
Senators and Congressmen into improving the beef import quota
to the United States from Australia, and there is even more
sanguine talk of the American agricultural presence boosting
Washington's concern for Australia's long-term military security.

'The best thing that can happen to Australia,' said one Liberal
Cabinet Minister, 'is for a million Americans to settle here with
their capital and buy land.' If this remains the prevailing view,
the Americanization of the wide open spaces should prove one of
the most beneficial and exciting aspects of the New Australia.

7

RECREATION UNLIMITED

SURFERS PARADISE AND THE BEACH GENERATION

Surfers Paradise is a place where no mother should let her son go out after dark, for the capital of Queensland's Gold Coast (a 50-mile strip of surfing beaches just south of Brisbane) is also the capital of Young Australia's most uninhibited hedonism. Each year some three million visitors descend on the Gold Coast at a rate of 150,000 a week in the peak summer period. Most of these visitors are in the 16 to 27 age group, and about two-thirds of them are girls. They come to Surfers after a year of living at home in suburbia, hammering at typewriters in soulless offices, and dreaming of the holidays for which they are saving up. In their reveries they yearn for idyllic vacations packed with sun, surf and sex, and on the Gold Coast such dreams are easily made to come true.

Thanks to the numerical ratio of approximately two girls to every man, any self-respecting male can effortlessly transform himself into a Casanova or Don Juan on the Gold Coast, and many do. A high percentage of romances appear to begin in the lounge of Coolangatta Airport. Here one can observe, just before aircraft departures, large numbers of touchingly passionate farewell embraces. Yet no sooner have the frequently tearful feminine halves of these parting couples embarked into the aeroplane than their faithless escorts remove the lipstick smudges from their faces with a backhand wipe and then wait around to pick up the best selections from the next arriving airload of beauties.

The Gold Coast is well geared to cater for the pick-up industry. There are about 3,000 establishments offering accommodation, ranging from the middle-aged respectability of the Chevron Hilton (about $15 a night), through Miami-style high-rise apartment blocks with California names like 'Surfside 6' and 'Santa Barbara' ($80 a week), racy neon-lit motels with slightly suggestive titles such as 'The Ova-Nite' or 'The Snugglers-Inn' (about $7 a night), down to inexpensive teenage hostels with names like 'Sunset Strip' or 'Fun House' (about $3 a day for full board and lodging). The hostels cater for the teenage market, and are organized by 'House Captains', usually in their mid-twenties who, in return for a free holiday for themselves, arrange picnics, surfing parties, and excursions for the hostel inmates. House Captains are theoretically supposed to maintain discipline within their hostels, but the theory exists exclusively in the minds of suburban mums, whose daughters have escaped to the land of immoral promise only by making promises about morals. When a girl arrives at a hostel (many Gold Coast visitors don't bother about bookings), by way of introduction she is often made to sing a song, recite poetry or tell a story to the assembled company of fellow boarders. She is then either snapped up immediately by some hostel Romeo, or more likely she gets together with one or two other lonely hearts and roams the popular Gold Coast meeting places in search of prey. The most popular arenas for these manhunts at Surfers are the Beer Garden (excellent beer, but as it is concreted all over the only flowers are human ones) and the Skyline Bar, where anything up to 1,500 young Australians paying 60 cents a time congregate nightly for an evening of rock n'rum. The music, which on my Saturday night visit was provided a group called The Rhodesians, only one of whom had ever set foot in Africa, is invariably performed at an ear-splitting decibel count. The most popular drink is rum and lime, which is poured down thirsty throats in such liberal quantities that lonely hearts soon lost their inhibitions to the point of following the felicitous suggestion of The Rhodesians' vocalist 'Everyone who isn't fixed up, make a UDA—Unilateral Declaration of Availability!' These declarations, proclaimed with all the subtlety of a herd of buffaloes charging across sheets of corrugated iron, came in three stages. Early in the evening, the girls' technique seemed to consist of edging up to selected men at the bar and saying, 'Shout me a drink, gorgeous!' Later on, the approach had changed to waving at males drinking peacefully at their tables and screaming, 'We think you're beaut!' By the end of the evening, those who had still not found a partner were resorting to shrieking, 'How about a naughty, then!' Since the phrase 'Having a naughty' is a strine colloquialism for love-making, it can be seen that the girls of Surfers do not shirk from methods of direct attack, but then they need to use extremist tactics to catch Australian men, who usually do not think of going to bed until their intake of alcohol has made it difficult for them to stand up. Ignored until the last possible moment, then insulted, possibly injured, and often inadequately served, the life of an Australian Miss Everage on holiday at Surfers is not exactly a romantic bed of roses. Girls of any other nationality would reject suitors who approached them with such charming introductions as 'Hello Horseface!', 'Hi dimmo!' (dimwit), and 'G'morning yer dopey old slough!', but the hedonists of the Gold Coast are apparently so grateful to have escaped from the cloying puritanism of suburbia that they take these humiliations in their stride, and regard them as acceptable preludes to the eventual goal of 'having a naught'.

Life at Surfers Paradise is remarkably similar to life around the surf beaches of Southern California, where the manhunting activities of strip chicks, groupies, score girls and teeny boppers are no less predatory than those of their Australian sisters. Two big differences are that West Coast girls don't bother to put up a hypocritical charade of virtue when they return home, while West Coast men are decidedly more courteous to, and covetous of the fair sex than are their equivalents in Queensland. Unfortunately, the golden age of chivalry is not merely dead in Australia, it has never been alive. Australian young men are natural misogynists, they face women in groups as if they were afraid to face them alone, and armour-plated with booze and boorishness they greet even their steady girlfriends more contemptuously than Indian chiefs dismiss their squaws. Individuals who deviate from the norm and show a little charm and tenderness towards girls have to endure ribald aspersions being cast on their masculinity by their former drinking companions. Absurdly, it is somehow thought 'unmale' for men to pay attention to women, and that's why at free-living Surfers so many girls make the running themselves.

The Gold Coast is a good place for a reporter to study the behavioural trends of Young Australia, for Surfers Paradise is the headquarters of the Beach Generation. This label was first pinned on the unsuspecting hordes of under-30s who go down to the sea in swimsuits by Australia's leading pop sociologist, Craig McGregor, who wrote of them in his book *Profile of Australia*— 'Affluent, city-bred, education, mainly middle-class, and the product of a changing and restless society—that is the background to this new generation . . . they are going to be very different from their parents, and they are going to cause profound changes in Australian society. They are sharp, up-to-date, ambitious, image-conscious, materialist—and more than anything else they are aware: aware of ideas, fashions, cults, overseas trends, music, business techniques, in a way very few groups of Australians have been before. This awareness is their greatest characteristic and it will probably be their most valuable contribution to adult society.'

It may be a case of overseas visitor myopia, but I don't entirely share Craig McGregor's lyrical enthusiasm for the Beach Generation. Its members are certainly different from their parents, but they strike me as being considerably less likely to change society than their contemporaries in colleges and universities in Britain or the United States. In a country which is bulging with easy targets for young dissenters—such as censorship, wowserism, political illiberalism, Vietnam, and restricted immigration—it is amazing that so few ripples of disagreement with the status quo have broken on the surface of young Australia. As for awareness, the fashions, cults and trends of Australian youth rarely originate domestically, but are derived from London, Paris, or New York about nine months after the pace-makers in these cities have dropped them completely. Finding an excessive quantity of intellectual dullness and lack of originality amongst this particular milieu in Australia, I am inclined to take the view that the beach is not making a generation more aware, but stopping it from being more interesting. For too many surf lovers, beach leisure is not so much a relaxation, more a way of life, and at its most extreme, this way of life becomes the cult of the Surfie.

Surfies are the hippies of the ocean. Like their landlocked cousins of Haight-Ashbury, they have dropped out of society, are tuned in (but to the customs and language of the surfboard subculture) and get turned on (not by pot, but by riding the great rollers of the south-eastern Pacific). They tend to live in communes on or near the more remote surf beaches, wear their hair to shoulder length in sun-bleached salt-caked tassels, pad about the streets in bare feet and super-casual garb, and deliberately set out to make themselves an identifiable minority tribe in young Australia. One of the tribe's most singular characteristics is its argot. I once heard a surfie describe his afternoon's activity in terms which went something like this: 'Well, I was out there riding the Dee Why swell when along comes a beaut set of tubes, so I front up and get m'plank hard on the green shoulder. Then away we shoot and before you can say Ned Kelly I'm sliding the curl, and then I'm riding the nose, hanging five, then hanging ten, and just when I'm real stoked along comes a bloody egg who clobbers my tab and it's a real dead loss wipeout, hit by a dumper so bad that I chundered real terrible, and had to hit the sack until one of the femlins woke me.' The essence of this story is that the surfie got his board on a big wave, rode with it so well that he was able to edge to the front of his board getting ten toes over the top end. Then he was hit by a novice in the rear, crashed, vomited, fell asleep and was woken up by one of the groupie-type girls who hang around surfboard riders.

Within the surfing community, exotic nicknames are used such as 'Supertank', 'Virgboard', 'Splasher', 'The Tiger', 'Sharkie', 'Biggles' and 'Greenie'. The proud bearers of these sobriquets talk about their sport in romantic fantasy language that is very reminiscent of hippies eulogizing Acapulco gold. 'Man, surfin's a mind-blowing thing. Very kinetic, superheats the ego and sends a charge right through yer, from yer scalp to yer toe callouses. Can't get no satisfaction anywhere else except on top of the tubes, but when I'm there—wowie-zowie!—it's ecstasy—pure ecstasy, baby!'

True surfies are full-time enthusiasts, having no visible means of support except occasional casual labour jobs, often in surfboard factories. Despising 'hibernators' (riders who put their boards away after the summer), they don their psychedelic painted wet-suits and move north to the Queensland beaches in order to surf throughout the winter when the waves are at their best. If conditions are good, you can watch them as early as seven in the morning, paddling their malibus out to the point where the rollers are breaking. Sometimes they stay in the water from dawn until dusk, happily missing breakfast and lunch if the tubes (good size waves concave on the outside) look good. If the surf is disappointing on a particular beach, devotees of the sport think nothing of driving three or four hundred miles along the coast in search of more permanent waves. Because of these distances, and the isolation of the beaches which makes nude surfing a perfectly acceptable activity in some areas, true Australian surfies are really more nomadic gypsies than urban hippies. They sleep by the surf, live in the surf and are psychologically and emotionally hooked on the surf. Yet for all their mental vacuity and commercial indolence, the members of this tribe are happily tolerated and even glamourized by the rest of society. There are too many plastic surfies around—talking the language, weekending on the beaches, painting astrological signs on their boards, and sometimes bleaching their hair with Ajax—for anyone to get uptight with those who have gone the whole hog and dropped out completely. Also, most middle-aged Australians have at one time or another been slightly hooked on surf, at least to the extent of frittering away an afternoon at Bondi or Surfers or Sorrento when they should have been at work. It's just part of the national way of life that when the surf's up, a disproportionate number of office and factory workers 'take a sickie' (sick leave).

Members of the Beach Generation then are not so very different from their forebears in attitudes to leisure—they just want more of it. Perhaps this is all to the national good. Australians are cheerful, happy and relaxed people and the contribution of beach life to this atmosphere of contentment cannot be underestimated. Moreover, surf is symbolic of the present national mood. Just as a surf-rider knows that once he has caught a wave, barring accidents, he will be carried inexorably in towards the shore on an exciting ride, so an Australian knows today that his country has now caught a wave of mineral, pastoral and commercial development that will, barring accidents, carry the nation on an exciting ride into the front rank of international wealth and power. Perhaps the Beach Generation's new spirit embodies this knowledge. Certainly the previous Australian generations had no comparable spirit, for they suffered from fears of economic depression and from an international inferiority complex. But now that young Australians can feel proud of their very superior country because of its riches, they will be building a boring though gold-plated future for themselves if they let the cult of prosperous leisure cocoon them into a mood of self-satisfied, unimaginative unawareness that in my observation now characterizes too many members of the under-30 age group. Sir Winston Churchill's prophecy that 'the only empire of the future will be empires of the mind' contains a warning for Australia, which was labelled in 1964 by the national Boswell, Donald Horne, 'A nation without a mind.' No observer now doubts that Australia has an exciting future commercially, or that it offers its citizens a wonderful quality of life in terms of leisure. What remains to be seen is whether the Beach Generation is interested in making Australia into a future 'Empire of the Mind' as well.

THE SPORTING LIFE

Sport is the religion of Australia, and Saturday is the day of worship. Gallup Polls indicate that two-fifths of the population play some sport regularly and that three-quarters of the population watch it. This national obsession is reflected throughout the mass media, in the public acclaim given to sporting heroes, and above all by the packed grandstands, pavilions and stadia throughout the country on a Saturday afternoon.

Australian fathers indoctrinate their sons into the sporting life at the earliest possible moment. On many beaches one can see toddlers being instructed on how to kick footballs and hold catches before they can even walk properly. For the slightly older age group there are innumerable beach clubs, such as 'The Narrabeen Nippers' (Narabeen is a beach 30 miles from Sydney) which gives lessons to 5–10-year-olds in swimming, running, cricket, life-saving, tug-of-war and any other games that can be played on sand. The Jesuitical fervour of sport teaching to the young is continued at all schools, and many organizations exist for athletic school-leavers to join. A man who personifies these organizations is Judge Adrian Curlewis, who in addition to presiding over a Sydney courtroom is the nation's leading establishment figure-head in sport, being Chairman of the National Fitness Council; Chairman of the Surf Life-Saving Association; Chairman of the Duke of Edinburgh's Award Scheme for Australia; and Chairman of the Outward Bound Course. Approximately 15,000 adolescents collect certificates of proficiency from Curlewis' varied stables each year, and their chairman says of them: 'The youth of this country has fantastic opportunities for sport and on the whole they make good use of them. I believe that one of the best ways of influencing the minds of young people is through their bodies, and that much of the self-confidence which now typifies the young people of this country is due to their tremendous bodily activity in their formative years. I myself lead a bit of a Jekyll and Hyde existence, as I spend five days a week putting young people into gaol, and two days a week trying to keep them out of it. Frankly, there are some worrying trends in Australian society these days. Seventy per cent of the customers who come up before me in court are between 17 and 22 and most of them are a pretty unhealthy lot. The great battle in this country today is against spectatoritis. There is too much encouragement of the expert, and not enough of the amateur, that is why spectatoritis is growing so fast and undermining the moral fibre of Australia.'

One would hardly think that the nation's moral fibre was being undermined from the scene in any Australian city on a Saturday. Everywhere there seems to be frenzied activity by the man in the white flannel shirt. Players have been on the golf courses since dawn, on the cricket pitches since noon, and on their yachts since the night before. The most popular participant sports seem to be tennis (there are 300,000 registered tournament players and an estimated 600,000 unregistered players, figures which mean that at least 1 Australian in 13 plays tennis regularly), bowls (a quarter of a million men and a hundred thousand women play it each week), and from June to October, skiing (despite the expense, which in fashionable resorts like Thredbo runs up to $200 per head per week), for over 300,000 Australians now take an annual winter sports holiday, most of them in the Kosciusko and Falls Creek regions. On top of these, there are the spectator sports such as cricket (a Test match will pack in 75,000), Australian Rules football (which draws the biggest and most frenzied crowds of all —six matches attracting a regular weekly gate of 120,000) and racing (the Melbourne Cup, the Derby of the Southern Hemisphere, gets 90,000 on-course spectators and eight million listeners or viewers). Despite the gloomy comments of Judge Curlewis, no one should be deceived into thinking that the Australian spectator at these events is a passive animal. In fact, he is very often a great deal more active than some of the players, giving his all to his vocal explosions of approval or disapproval, which are always prefaced by the great Australian adjective. 'Bloody well bust 'is nose!' at a big fight, 'Stop using yer bat like a bloody butterfly net,' at Sydney cricket ground, and 'Get yer head down prop'ly and stop sniffing at everyone's bloody arse,' at a Melbourne Australian Rules football match were three memorable cries from barrackers that wafted across to my surprised British ears at various sporting occasions.

Even without barrackers, emotion often runs high among Australian crowds. In 1967 I saw a horse named Tobin Bronze win the Caulfield Cup at Melbourne's Caulfield racecourse. For reasons of past injuries, and because he carried top weight this horse, with a fine record behind it, was considered to be the underdog of the race. When it put on a burst to take the honours at the winning post, the grandstands erupted with melodramatic excitement. Middle-aged matrons threw their flowered hats in the air, granite-faced graziers sobbed with joy, and one dressy young socialite did a circuit of cartwheels around the paddock, while Australia's silver-tongued racing commentator, Ken Howard, put so much passion into his voice that he sounded like a 45 r.p.m. record of Billy Graham describing hellfire speeded up to 78 r.p.m. If Peace had been declared in Vietnam, one would not have seen a tenth of the public excitement that was then being generated by Tobin Bronze's victory.

Australians are justifiably proud of what they like to call their 'sporting heritage', for with a population smaller than that of Greater London, they have in recent years produced many of the world's top sportsmen, including tennis players Lew Hoad, Ken Rosewall, Rod Laver, Roy Emerson, Fred Stolle and Margaret Court; swimmers Dawn Fraser and Jon Konrads; runners Herb Elliott and Ron Clarke; cricketers Richie Benaud, Neil Harvey and Norman O'Neill; golfers Peter Thomson and Kel Nagle; the boxers Lionel Rose and Johnny Famechon. No other nation of comparable size can approach Australia's athletic success, which is attributed to such causes as the country's abundance of high-protein food, the cheap and plentiful sporting facilities (Sydney, for example, has over 30 Olympic-sized swimming pools—most international big cities are lucky if they have one) and above all to the climate and the life-style.

Yet the emphasis is steadily changing in Australian sporting life, away from team and competitive games towards individual sports which allow a degree of self-expression. For explosive growth, nothing can touch surfboard riding, which had an estimated 20,000 devotees in 1959 and now has around half a million regular riders. The sport's stylish champions like Midget Farelly and Nat Young are national heroes as much as any tennis or boxing stars, yet in their way they are anti-heroes, spurning the team spirit of regimented organizations like the Surf Life-Saving Association and chasing the lonely waves. Skiing, spear-fishing, skin-diving, squash, trampolining and car rallying are other individualist sports which are booming with a new popularity, from which it can be assumed that some of the older games are waning in their appeal. There is nothing to despise in this changing trend. All it means is that Australia's younger generation treats sport less as a religion, more as a hedonistic form of individual paganism.

INDOOR SPORTS

If you find an Australian indoors, it's a fair bet that he will have a glass in his hand, as drinking is far and away the most popular national pastime and social activity. A comparison of international brewery and distillery figures indicates that Australians are the world's heaviest beer drinkers, consuming over 210 pints of the stuff per head per year (an 18-pint lead over their nearest rivals, the Belgians). This achievement is partly due to the climate, and partly to the skill of the national breweries in producing such remarkably potent and potable concoctions, for Australian beer comes ice-cold, is deliciously light, and contains 8.5 per cent alcohol compared to the 7·7 per cent alcohol of the headiest British and German ales.

Since Australians are also high in the league table of international wine drinkers (approximately twelfth, consuming almost two gallons per head annually), and are by no means backwards in the consumption of spirits, the statistics confirm what observers have suspected for a long time: Australia is just about the hardest-drinking nation on this planet.

This pre-eminence has had an important effect on the national character, for the immense friendliness and informality of Australians probably stems from it. When interviewing for this book, I found the pace of my researches getting considerably slowed by the compulsory alcoholic intake. Even when calling on government ministers at nine in the morning, the questions would quite probably be interrupted by an invitation to 'have a snort', and by the time I had snorted in other places, 'shouted' the taxi-driver a beer at mid-day (the strine word derives from the days when one had to yell to get the barman's attention), downed a couple of middies over lunch, and maybe sampled a glass or two of the local wine as well, I was making many friends, but not many notes.

Hospitality to visitors should not necessarily be equated with normal practice, but the vast proliferation of pubs and clubs, and the number of private bottles in offices confirms that friendly conviviality plays an intergral part in the average Australian's working day. In bars, beer consumption is something of an act of ritual. It is common to see two men standing side by side in a pub, drinking steadily for an hour or two without apparently communicating at all, save for the mechanical unison of their glass-lifting movements, and their split-second timing which enables them to finish their beers simultaneously. One is told that these men are 'mates', and that they have worked together for several years. 'Mateship' is a sacred Australian relationship, baptized with the sweat of mutual toil, and consecrated nightly by deep immersion in beer. Although mates don't talk much to one another, they think, drink and feel as one, and in times of trouble can be relied on for all forms of mutual help and assistance.

Mateship apart, Australian drinking friendships tend to be only gin-deep. This superficiality becomes most obvious at younger parties, where the boozing is apt to be much more important than the socializing. Such events begin with a telephoned invitation to 'Bring yer own grog', and end when the grog has run out—sometimes not for 24 hours. During the long watches of this kind of party, many of the men will 'chunder' (vomit) in the bathroom several times, always returning to the scene of the action where they resume their drinking and proudly announce their latest chunder score. Between chunders, some far-gone imbiber is likely to perform a 'Hambone' which is a male striptease dance peculiar to the antipodes. Its astonishing popularity (I've seen it done three times at random parties in Sydney's eastern suburbs) is surely the ultimate proof that Australia is a man's country.

Not surprisingly, such parties are disliked by many girls, and in recent years something of a female rebellion has been staged in protest against the manners and courting methods of Australian men. The chief rebel is Miss Sue Rhodes, a Sydney journalist, and author of *Now You'll Think I'm Awful*, a book published in 1967 which takes as its provocative theme, 'Of course, we all learn sooner or later that sex to the Australian man is more a means of relieving himself than of expressing feeling, affection or even hot desire', and has outsold (150,000 copies and still going strong) most other works in Australia except the Bible. With the unerring accuracy of one who has spent years dedicatedly researching her subject, Miss Rhodes picks off the easy targets of young Australia's sexual customs. Her hilarious invective has, it is said, caused a sharp drop in hambone performances, and requests beginning with the phrase 'Come and have a naughty'.

After drink and sex, Australia's most popular indoor activities are television-watching, reading and gambling. Gallup polls claim that the mythical average man spends 30 hours a week in front of a TV set, 10 hours a week with a book and 9 hours a week thinking about, reading about or placing his bets. The televiewing statistic is about a third higher than the average man's equivalents in Britain and the United States, while the figures for books and bets show that Australians are, by a huge margin, both the most literate and the most profligate people in the world.

For 'a nation without a mind', Australia's dedicated reading habits come as an everlasting surprise, and are discussed in detail in the next chapter. As for gambling, Australians will have a flutter on anything at any time, often literally on the two proverbial flies crawling up the pub wall. I was once drinking peacefully in a

Brisbane bar when two workmen came over to me. 'Scuse me, mate, will yer settle a wager for us. How tall are yer exactly?' they asked. On receiving the information that I stood at 6 foot 3½ inches, five dollars changed hands, the bet having been 'That stranger's not a fraction over 6 foot 2.' This kind of zany gambling, which is very evocative of the absurd Regency betting books in London clubs, is an omnipresent feature of the social scene. No other people except Australians would be mesmerized by 'Two up', a punting game which depends entirely on the spin of two coins. It became so popular that the wowser Canberra Parliament of the thirties felt obliged to make it illegal, but it still flourishes in places like Broken Hill and Port Hedland where the constabulary willingly turn a Nelsonian blind eye. There is also much illegal gaming on baccarat and chemin de fer, and a wide variety of fully legal betting on all forms of racing from yachts to horses, not to mention poker machines, sweepstakes and lotteries. It is estimated that Australians spend more than $1,500 million annually on these variegated forms of gambling, which is double what they spend on their defence or social services. The astronomic scale of Australia's betting mania is steadily increasing and is probably connected with the national economic superboom. As John Pringle has written in *Australian Accent*: 'The Australian worker proves his basic indifference to money by gambling it away on the race-course. Why not? He has all he wants and can always get more.'

One interesting trend in Australia's indoor vices (if such they be) is that the younger generation drinks much harder and bets far more recklessly than the middle-aged group. Elsewhere in the Anglo-Saxon world, boozing and betting are thought to be rather old-fashioned kicks, and have definitely been wounded by such new-fangled cults as permissiveness and pot, but in Australia the generation gap merely consists of about four pints of beer. Dad may chunder earlier and prefer to be sick into the pub spittoon rather than the cocktail lounge's aspidistra, but otherwise he and Junior just get along fine. As an undergraduate comedian said at one Sydney University party I went to, 'Our fathers are a pretty degenerate lot. They spend most of their wage packets on beer, and on the horses—and then the rest they just waste!'

THE CALL OF THE WILD

Australians live in cities, but their hearts are often i
It is no coincidence that the national symbols are i
outback images like koala bears, kangaroos, emus, billy-cans and
boomerangs. Those who find this sort of thing a trifle corny are
underestimating the strength of the Australian rural heritage, for
the bush—a vague generic term meaning the wild countryside
beyond the cities—casts a mystic spell over the emotions of
millions of metropolitan suburbanites.

The mysticism is reflected in a wide variety of ways. The bush
and the outback (they are the same, but the outback is theoretically
further away, wilder and more rugged) have long been an inspiration to poets, writers or artists, and their inspirations are now
appealing to the mass of the Australian public. Prints of desolate
rural paintings by Sidney Nolan and Russell Drysdale hang in the
lounges of fifty thousand semis, along with bark paintings, mulga-
wood souvenirs and Aboriginal carvings. Books about Aboriginal
folklore by specialist authors like Douglas Lockwood are best-
sellers. Children are told bush legends such as the tale of bush-
ranger Ned Kelly as bedtime stories. There is a pressure group
lobbying to make 'Waltzing Matilda' the national anthem and a
poem by Dorothea Mackellar, recited by generations of school-
children, has been described as 'a national apostolic creed'. Its
first stanza runs:

> I love a sunburnt country,
> A land of sweeping plains,
> Of ragged mountain ranges,
> Of droughts and flooding rains.
> I love her far horizons,
> I love her jewel sea,
> Her beauty and her terror—
> The wide brown land for me!

To some outsiders, it seems peculiar that anyone should love
a 'wide brown land' as harsh and ugly as Australia's, with its
parched scrub, its pallid, twisted gum trees and its overpowering
atmosphere of haunted gloom.

An early visitor to Australia, D. H. Lawrence, caught this
atmosphere brilliantly in his novel *Kangaroo*, whose central
character, Somers, feels revulsion against the bush. 'He felt it was
watching and waiting. Following with a certainty just behind his

back. It might have reached a long black arm and gripped him. But no, it wanted to wait. It was not tired of watching its victim. An alien people—a victim. It was biding its time with a terrible ageless watchfulness, waiting for a far-off end, watching the myriad intruding white men.'

But Lawrence was writing nearly fifty years ago, and he saw only a small part of the continent in his four-month stay. Although some contemporary visitors are, like Lawrence, positively repelled by the bush, today's Australians have grown to love it because they know they can beat it. They appreciate the historical drama of how their country was carved out of this hostile wilderness, and their appreciation (all the stronger because the fight is still going on) makes them feel an emotional involvement with the land that they and their ancestors have conquered.

Today, this involvement is most often expressed through tourism. Australians are great enthusiasts for seeing their own country. Their idea of a beaut vacation is to pack the kids and the snake-bite kit into the back of a station wagon and set off, towing a caravan into the bush. Since very few roads are bitumenized and since the wide open spaces really are wide open, it is easy to feel cut off from civilization within an hour or two of leaving a big city. A typical family might take two or three weeks driving nomadically towards the continent's desert interior, spending the days clocking up vast mileages and their nights barbecuing jumbucks and waiting till their billys boil. It's difficult at first to understand why such holidays are usually so blissful. The scenery remains so much the same that one could amend an Agnewism and say that once you've seen one gum tree you've seen all of them; the physical discomforts of the sweaty, fly-blown drive are considerable; and the only real points of interest in the interior, such as Alice Springs and Ayers Rock, are over-rated and over-photographed touristana. But to raise such querulous objections is to show a lack of understanding about bush mysticism. Despite having been born twelve thousand miles from the nearest gum tree, I myself have felt the call of Australia's wild on several occasions, and have appreciated something of the sensual primitivism of the outback's spell. One night in Northern Queensland, I remember gazing upwards from my sleeping bag and being moved almost to tears by the indescribable beauty of the night sky. The Southern Cross galaxy was shimmering incandescently across the cobalt firmament as if it was a celestial display of crown jewels. The atmosphere was one of majestic stillness, prevented from being overpowering by the orchestrated buzz of a million coloratura cicadas, the distant deep bass pounding of the surf, and the occasional counter tenor of a wild dingo baying for his prey. No less moving was a dawn at Geehi, a remote staging-post in the wilds of the Snowy Mountains. Roused by the hysterical cackling of the kookaburra bird, who seemed to be sharing jokes with a family of tuneful currawongs, I wandered through dense foliage until coming upon a large clearing in which somewhere between five hundred and a thousand kangaroos and wallabies were bounding joyfully about in the matutinal sunshine. Standing on the edge of the forest, the birds above my head going berserk with vocal excitement, the roos leaping through the thick grasses ablaze with a glory of exotic wild flowers, and the trees looming darkly ahead like serried ranks of impassive sentries, I had a strong feeling of being a gauche intruder at the brilliant court of King Nature, whose realm seemed infinitely preferable to the urban squalor of mankind.

A third spellbinding bush scene was a storm in the heart of the Northern Territory, when I saw thunder, rain and lightning hurtling down from the heavens with a ferocity that made the celebrated tempests of Delphi in Greece seem like a light shower. It was as though the Australian Zeus had flown into a sadistic rage, and was determined to lash the bleak landscape into pulp. The local inhabitants were terrified, for scrub cattle charged blindly round in circles, terrified emus squawked hysterically as they rushed headlong to nowhere in their famous 40 m.p.h. sprint, giant goannas shot themselves into the most substantial rock crevices they could find, and even the somnolent crocodiles were being swept away in the rising muddy torrent of the river in flood. We humans, helpless in our waterlogged Land-Rover, sensed stronger passions and forces in this natural environment than anything we had seen or felt before in the world of machines.

These three personal reminiscences of scenes from the outback may perhaps provide a clue to the depth of emotional nationalism aroused by the countryside. Perhaps D. H. Lawrence caught it best, when in *Kangaroo* he eventually grudgingly acknowledged "the strange, as it were invisible, beauty of Australia which is undeniably there but which seems to lurk just beyond the range of our white vision'. It is this beauty, the primitivism of the land, the untamed wildness of the flora and fauna, the primeval intensity of the light and the dramatic extremes of the elements that combine to captivate human spectators, unleashing in them an urge to return to their ecological origins. One can draw a valid comparison between Australia's inland tourists and the rich Bedouins of Kuwait, whose idea of a really enjoyable weekend is to drive their Cadillacs way out into the barren wastes of the Arabian desert and there to feed on charred slabs of barbecued goat-meat, and afterwards to sleep in discomfort on the sand dunes. It is the back-to-nature syndrome that produces such behaviour patterns, and they come strongest from peoples whose development of their land is most recent.

Australians rank highest among wealthy Western nationalities in displaying a preference for domestic tourism above overseas travel. Partly this is due to the high cost of getting away from the isolated south-west corner of the Pacific, but the tremendous increase in conducted tours of outback properties, air charter holidays around the mining centres, and bus trips to the interior, all show that Australians are genuinely more interested in Australia than in anything else. Some may think this too parochial or introspective an attitude, but it can convincingly be argued that Australians need to know more about their own soul now that they are in the process of gaining the whole world. In this respect, their attempts to trace their spiritual and social roots through the magic of the bush is an understandable and attractive side of Australian hedonism.

A PLAYGROUND FOR THE WORLD?

In 1960 Australia was visited by 50,000 overseas tourists. By 1970 the figure had increased sevenfold to 350,000. Between them they spent approximately $750 million, thereby earning more foreign exchange than Australia's entire exports to Japan.

International tourism is thus big business in the antipodes, and it is likely to get much bigger when the Jumbo jets start increasing the rate of trans-Pacific air travel in the 1970s. At present, the cost of travelling to Australia for a tourist holiday is prohibitive to all but the wealthy, as the London-Sydney return economy air fare is $1,240 (£579) and the New York-Sydney equivalent costs $1,110 (US $1,250). But competition on the trans-Pacific air routes is hotting up, and the combination of charter flight bargains, package tours, and more frequent scheduled services from more carriers all points to a still more rapid growth in tourist traffic.

It is easy to see why northern hemisphere holidaymakers might wish to flock Down Under in droves. The strongest pull is the attraction of 'The Great Outdoors', which in terms of sunshine and surf is at its climatic best when the European and North American winters are at their worst. For many British visitors there will be the additional emotional attraction of migrant relatives, who have hitherto been out of range because of the expense, while a different emotional inducement is thought likely to tempt Americans into sampling Australia's pioneering frontier atmosphere which is so close to that of the United States' Wild West a century ago. A new growth factor is the influx of Japanese tourists, who are showing a sudden propensity for the agreeable recreational facilities of their giant Anglo-Saxon neighbour. If lower costs and bigger aircraft attract visitors from these categories to Australia in the numbers predicted, there should be well over two million overseas tourists arriving annually before 1980.

SENATOR REG WRIGHT

The man who is master-minding the plans to cope with this expected invasion is Senator Reginald Wright, the Federal Government's Minister for Tourism.

Reg Wright is a marvellous tourist attraction himself, for both visually and vocally he is perhaps the most entertaining character in Australian politics. Son of a Tasmanian farmer, Wright started his working life as a barrister, making a legendary reputation by the baroque splendours of his court-room rhetoric. This made him greatly feared as a prosecuting counsel, causing one fellow barrister to say of Wright that he had 'the same capacity as Dickens' celebrated Buzfuz for adding the most sinister overtones to everyday action'.

In a country notorious for the inarticulateness of even its most eminent public figures, Wright's love of oratorical crescendo together with his ability to quote extensively from the great classical authors soon made him a force in political as well as legal circles. But when he won his way to Canberra as the Liberal Senator from Tasmania, some of Wright's political colleagues were uncertain as to whether the new arrival was a force entirely on their side. Their concern was understandable, for during 25 stormy years on the back benches, Wright voted against his own party on well over one hundred occasions, usually justifying his division-lobby perversity with gifted eloquence. Such independence, which would certainly be frowned on by the party whips of Washington or Westminster, caused fury among the much more regimented

Liberal Party caucus bosses of Canberra, and their wrath made Wright something of a political pariah. Sir Robert Menzies, who for 20 years led the Liberals with an arrogance worthy of Louis XIV, regarded the mischievous actions of the turbulent Tasmanian with considerable distaste, particularly because Wright's main quarrels with his party were over his allegations of unconstitutional and autocratic ruling methods on the part of the Prime Minister. The net result of this entirely mutual antagonism was that Wright was kept out of office for a quarter of a century. However, soon after Menzies' retirement, the Tasmanian Senator's undoubted gifts were recognized and at the unusually advanced age of 62 he came into the Ministry—a remarkable transformation from *enfant terrible* to elder statesman without any intervening period for repentance.

Reg Wright today looks every other inch the Grand Old Man of Australian politics. With a rubicund countenance crowned by dancing bushy white eyebrows and a rotund figure encased in heavy tweeds, he seems the perfect sturdy countryman to be promoting Australia's tourism. Sitting in his spacious office on Parliament Hill he will wax lyrical about the loveliness of the hawthorn blossoms, the excitement of the mountain air and the fascination of the bush. If one can bring him down to earth from quoting Virgil to illustrate the bucolic beauty of Australia, Wright will rattle off statistical information about future programmes and projects with impeccable ministerial zeal. Tourism is the 8th biggest export earner in Australia; 50 per cent of all towns have now appointed a Tourist Officer; $55 million was being spent on hotel construction in 1970 compared to $13 million in 1960; Government spending on tourism is increasing by 13 per cent a year; and more than two million tourists are expected annually by 1980.

Yet there is more to Reg Wright than statistics. Catch him late at night after a festive dinner party and he can reveal himself as one of the most fascinating conversationalists in the English-speaking world. With bawdy anecdotes worthy of Rabelais, beery witticisms comparable to those of Brendan Behan and a sense of political mischief-making not unlike that of Lord Beaverbrook's, Wright is one of those rare talkers who can spellbind any company. If Australia really wanted to double its inflow of tourists, one sure way to do it would be to offer each arriving visitor the chance to spend a convivial evening in the entrancing company of the Minister for Tourism.

QANTAS

Whether coming to see Reg Wright, Ayers Rock or any other historical monument in Australia, the chances are high that the arriving visitor will travel on Qantas, the national airline. Unlike most IATA carriers, Qantas has a distinct and original flavour of its own. This is partly due to its age (50 years old in 1970), partly to the unusually long distances it flies, and partly to Australians' own view of their airline's extra-aviational role. As Qantas General Manager, Captain R. J. Ritchie, C.B.E., puts it, 'It's often said that Australia's best image around the world is created by Qantas. We believe this, and we think we're more than just an airline. We're a national emblem.'

There is more in these words than the natural pride of a chief executive, for Qantas really does have a unique position both in the past folklore and present nationalism of Australia. As one senior airline executive put it, 'In terms of traditions and public esteem we're on a par with the Services. Australians think in terms of the Army, Navy, Air Force and Qantas.'

The name Qantas derives from the original title of the company 'Queensland And Northern Territory Aerial Services Ltd.' This outfit was founded in 1920 thanks largely to the energy and dedication of Lieutenant Hudson Fysh, an Army pilot then recently demobbed from the First World War. Fysh was a passionate believer in the future of commercial aviation (then unknown in Australia), and thought the best chances of success for a company lay in starting a mail and passenger service linking the rich pastoral districts of north-west Queensland. With the financial help of local businessmen and graziers, Qantas was founded in the small Queensland town of Winton on August 19th, 1920. Its first aircraft were a 65-m.p.h. 3-seater Avro Dyak biplane, and a 60-m.p.h. 2-seater BE2 biplane, and they operated on a six-town route in Queensland and the Northern Territory. Old-timers in this area will, at the sight of a 707 30,000 feet overhead, still spin hair-raising yarns about the early days of Qantas. Its crashes (twenty in the first ten years), its rows with local councils and government ministers, its extravagant prospectuses, its navigational errors by pilots who couldn't tell one outback air-strip from another, its mechanical disasters solved by bits of string and its numerous financial crises all add up to an air saga worthy of the pen of Antoine de Saint-Exupéry. Thanks to the books of Lieutenant (now Sir) Hudson Fysh—Chairman of Qantas until his retirement in 1966—many Australians are at least partly aware of this saga, and know about the airline's steady development via Tiger Moths, flying boats, converted bombers and Super-Constellations to its present pre-eminence as the tenth largest international jet airline of the world.

Qantas today takes the lion's share of Australia's battle to win visitors and beat isolation. With a government-financed fleet of 30 giant 707s (and 4 Jumbo jets ordered for delivery in 1971), the airline carries over 650,000 passengers a year, each one flying for an average of 4,300 miles. Seasoned travellers are critical of Qantas's refusal to relieve the tedium of long-distance flying by installing the film and music equipment for in-flight entertainment, but thereafter almost all comments are laudatory. In particular, punctuality, efficiency, food and service all get high praise. One interesting deviation from the normal human appearance side of cabin staff is that a surprising number of surf-bleached Qantas stewards look blond and fragile, while many of the stewardesses look dark and muscular, but since both types do their job of cosseting the passengers equally well this subjective visual impression is unimportant.

On the ground, Qantas strives mightily to boost the Australian image, promoting art exhibitions in far-flung capitals, organizing trade fair displays in cities with export potential and pushing out a highly original paraphernalia of PR material and souvenirs (passengers are even invited to take home their serviette hooks as a memento of their flight with Qantas). Much of this originality is due to the airline's go-go publicity chief, John Ulm. Son of a famous Australian pioneer aviator, Ulm is an establishment-looking senior executive inside whom there is a talented creative writer bursting to get out. His 3,000-word piece written early in 1969 on the inaugural flight of the Boeing 747 Jumbo jet contained so many Tom Wolfe-like jewelled phrases, onomatopoeic expletives, and dramatic punctuation marks, that it became acknowledged as a classic of aeronautical journalism. Headlined 'Roll Anthem Drums for this is History!', Ulm's article managed to combine a marvellous send-up of inaugural flight hysteria together with a profound and informative analysis of what the Jumbo will mean to world air travel.

According to Qantas top brass, the coming of the Jumbos will not bring down the expensive fare tariffs to and from Australia, even though the giant birds will certainly bring in more tourists.

Says Qantas General Manager, Captain R. J. Ritchie: 'Our biggest problems are raising the massive capital expenditure for these big new aircraft, keeping our costs stable and meeting the ever-increasing competition of other airlines. At the moment, things are tough. The Jumbos have increased seat capacity on US airlines by 140 per cent, and as a result of this everyone else in the business, including Qantas, feels the draught and maybe goes broke. Last year the seat factor across the Pacific routes was 44 per cent. That's far too low a load since the break-even point is 54 per cent. But these new arrangements of bigger aircraft and increased competition will bring the seat-occupancy figure down to 29 per cent. That is a really bad exploitation of the IATA Bermuda Agreement, and what it means is that it is impossible for us to bring fares down in the foreseeable future. However, we're not gloomy about the long-term prospects from Qantas's point of view. We're sure that tourism will grow massively across the Pacific in the next few years— far more than from any other area. To this end, we're putting a great emphasis on building more first-class hotel rooms and on producing a better and more frequent service. In the long run, Australia's tourism will bring an immensely profitable boom both to the economy and to Qantas.'

REG ANSETT

One airline tycoon who is well prepared to cope with this boom within Australia is 61-year-old Sir Reginal dAnsett, the founder, Chairman and Managing Director of Ansett Transport Industries, a holding company which controls some 70 subsidiaries, including an 85-aircraft airline, a fleet of over 300 buses and a chain of 16 hotels.

Ansett has done more than any other individual in Australia to overcome what one historian has described as the continent's 'tyranny of distance', for his buses are now the Australian equivalent of United States companies like Greyhound and Trailways, providing cheap travel throughout the country; his jet-line is the nation's best and biggest (the government-owned Trans-Australia Airlines is a pale and less profitable shadow), while his hotels have transformed previously inaccessible wildernesses such as Hayman Island, the Interior, and the Barrier Reef Coast into bustling holiday resorts.

The proprietor of this transport and tourist empire is a craggy,

creased-faced entrepreneur, who built his $150 million business
from a starting capital of $1 in cash and a $200 second-hand
Studebaker. Leaving school at 14, Reg Ansett worked in his
father's country bicycle shop, put himself through night school to
qualify as a mechanic, and then set off to seek his fortune in the
Northern Territory growing peanuts. After spending 18 months
in the outback at a time when the entire Qantas air services
amounted to one flight a fortnight between Darwin and southern
Queensland, Ansett decided to give up his agricultural activities
('My only achievement was that I learnt how to use an axe') and
founded a transport business. Beginning with one second-hand
jalopy, he created a flourishing taxi and trucking concern in
Victoria. He used an inherited $100 life-insurance policy to pay
for his own flying lessons in a beat-up Tiger Moth, and in 1929
he obtained the 419th pilot's licence to be issued in Australia.
Soon afterwards he started an air service between Hamilton and
Melbourne, using a 9-seat Airspeed Envoy, which he says was
'extremely sophisticated for those days. It even had a toilet and
a good pedigree as I bought it from Lord Nuffield.' In 1936
Ansett won the Brisbane–Adelaide air race, and the $1,000
prize was invaluable to him in financing the growth of his business.

Today, the business has grown into world-class dimensions
with capital assets of some $150 million, 11,000 employees, profits
of over $6 million and the equity 96 per cent in Australian
hands (an unusually high figure for such a capital-intensive industry).

Much of this success is due to a deal between Ansett and the
post-war Menzies government, by which Ansett's airline was
promised virtual exclusivity as an independent carrier over
Australia's major trunk routes. This deal, which has resulted in
the continuation for the last 15 years of the 'Two-airline policy'
(Ansett and TAA), is a matter of considerable political controversy, for many influential voices argue that the agreement has
been responsible for exorbitant fares and inadequate schedules.
This last complaint is the more serious, for the two airlines insist
on maintaining a 'one-timetable policy' by which Ansett and TAA
flights always take off for the same destinations at the same time,
thereby deliberately thwarting the convenience of busy travellers.
Yet whenever the two-airline policy has been challenged by some
entrepreneur such as Sydney's Gordon Barton, who wishes to start
up a more practical passenger air service, the Federal Government

muscles in with embargos on the importation of new aircraft. The justification for this prohibition of free enterprise is that new airline operators might bring about a price-cutting war on fares, which in turn would lead to Australia's internal airlines being unable to afford the large and expensive jets which are necessary for the long distances. This is a contentious point of view, but top executives in TAA and Ansett naturally swear by it, and have so far convinced the politicians of the merits of their case.

Perhaps as a result of being sheltered from the struggles of hot competition, Reg Ansett is today a multi-millionaire, commuting into his Melbourne office by helicopter, owning a string of race-horses and a race-course, promoting world championship boxing tournaments with personally guaranteed purse money of $80,000, developing his farm and cattle station and controlling a TV station. With his life covered by a $2 million insurance policy, he is no longer allowed to fly himself, but gets round the continent at least once a year (followed by direct lines to his office wherever he goes), and is optimistic about the prospects for Australian tourism.

'The Jumbo jets will change the face of this country, because the number of overseas visitors is going to be quite enormous. Already we can, without really trying, get over two thousand Americans to Dubbo on our Jolly Swagman tour, which is just barbecuing, a bit of boomerang-throwing and seeing sheep properties around Dubbo. Already we can offer Melbourne shop girls package deals like two weeks in Surfers Paradise (a return air trip of 1,800 miles) for $120. Already we've opened up big hotels in places like Hayman Island because we think it's our job to go out and develop an area. When the big money and the big numbers start coming in, the sky's the limit.'

Sir Reginald Ansett seems to have stretched a good many limits in his lifetime already. Today, Australians are the most air-minded people in the world, for out of a $12\frac{1}{2}$ million population, 5 million passengers fly by scheduled airline each year. Another record is that the utilization of aircraft in Australia is the highest in the world, for Ansett reckons on getting an average of 3,500 hours flying time a year ($9\frac{1}{2}$ hours a day) out of each of his machines. Most important of all, Ansett has made it possible for anyone to travel or move freight around Australia at the world's cheapest rates (it costs as little as $10 to make the 600-mile Sydney–Melbourne trip by one of his buses).

Such achievements have made Reginald Myles Ansett a legend

in his own lifetime, but this reserved tycoon looks forward to even greater results in the years ahead. 'If we can open up our resources in the right way by free enterprise,' he says, shrugging his rounded axeman's shoulders, 'Australia should become the playground of the world.'

8

THE CULTURAL SCENE

'When the picture of Australia abroad is of a country so endowed with natural resources that it has only to tap its surface for liquid gold to gush, is it to be a picture also of a lot of clownish shepherds without the grace of life to spend its wealth decently?'

This *cri coeur* from the former art critic of *The Australian*, Laurie Thomas, sums up the feelings of many Australian intellectuals and artists about cultural life in their own country. Similar notes of gloom are sounded in dozens of pessimistic interviews and articles every year. Typical of these was the comment of Sir Robert Helpmann, the international ballet star and director of the Adelaide Festival, who remarked at a recent airport departure, 'I don't despair about the cultural scene in Australia because there isn't one to despair about.' Melbourne's leading architect, Sir Roy Grounds, said in a 1968 interview with me, 'I suppose a cultural boom does exist, but only because there was nothing but philistinism before.' The maverick literary critic from Adelaide, Max Harris, wrote in 1969, 'We still believe the way to a man's mind is through his pocket. And we'll have to remain the Great Yahoo Society until we've outgrown this crude belief.' And when Arthur Koestler in 1969 condemned Australia's 'stifling conformism', claiming that the people were 'not a weird mob, but a dreary bunch', a surprising number of sophisticated Australians voiced support for the opinions of their vitriolic visitor.

It may seem unwise of an outsider to rush in where so many angels have trodden so squashingly, but faced with this barrage of masochistic self-depreciation, there is perhaps a need for an external observer to halt some of Australia's cultural Cassandras in their tracks with the vernacular cry 'Fair go, mate!'

It's fair to begin with the reminder that Australia has a population of barely 13 million people, which gives it approximately half the human resources of Canada (a real cultural wasteland!), a quarter of Britain's, and one-seventeenth of America's. Yet despite its smallness and its isolation there is a thriving, lively and economically viable cultural community in the antipodean continent. Compared to Britain without London, or the United States without the Eastern States and California, Australian culture is, in general terms, positively and plentifully swinging, and in some specific cases touches the highest peaks of artistic excellence. As positive a statement as that needs detailed defending in the light of the pejorative comments quoted above, but before getting down to the minutiae, it may be useful to give a short summary of the country's cultural activities which achieve good international standards.

Painting is the outstanding feature, for several Australian artists have won world acclaim, among them Sidney Nolan, Russell Drysdale, Arthur Boyd, Albert Tucker and William Dobell. They are among the leaders of a large army of professional painters with distinctive Australian styles, whose works are exhibited in over a hundred commercial art galleries throughout the country. In literature, the country's international authors include Morris West, Hal Porter, Patrick White and Thomas Keneally; while critics give high praise to some of the domestic poets such as Kenneth Slessor, A. D. Hope, Douglas Stewart, Randolph Stow and Judith Wright, and to playwrights like Ray Lawler. In drama, at least one company, the Melbourne Theatre, is widely acknowledged to be as consistently good as anything to be found on Broadway or London's West End. In music, each of the five states boasts a top-class concert orchestra financed by the Australian Broadcasting Commission. There is a successful National Opera Company and a National Ballet Company, which last year played to packed houses and much critical praise in London. As for institutions, such innovations, now under construction, as the Melbourne Arts Centre, the Sydney Opera House and the Canberra National Gallery are all symbolic of Australia's expanding artistic activity. This is further reflected by the recent increases in Government and State subsidies to the Arts, by the founding in 1967 of an Australian Council for the Arts (now with a budget of $2·85 million), by the setting up in 1970 of an Aboriginal Theatre Foundation, and by the continuing success of the outstandingly good Perth and Adelaide festivals.

There is both more and less than meets the eye in some of the labels in this compressed summary, but at least it should compel those who assert 'Australia is a cultural desert' to acknowledge the existence of several formidable oases. This analogy can perhaps be taken further, for with cultural as with real deserts, the traveller is frequently much more conscious of the watering-places than the resident. For example, I recall during one spell of my Australian travels seeing four plays, going to two concerts, attending a poetry reading and visiting a dozen art exhibitions all within the space of eight days. Admittedly I was moving between three cities at the time, but this mobility provided a more accurate perspective than that of a Brisbane-based critic who grumbled about having only one good art gallery and one orchestra, yet had no idea what was going on in Sydney and Adelaide. This artistic myopia is a common fault. If the whole of Australia was squashed together into a unit like Greater London (whose population is also 12 million), the combined cultural resources would look rather good. Because they are scattered over a land mass as big as the continental United States, the cultural activities are no less laudable, but the people are much less aware of what is available to them. At least a part of the pundits' despair derives from their habit of wearing geographical blinkers.

Another cause of gloom for the cultural Cassandras is the large number of talented Australians who become expatriates and perform their creative work abroad, thus enriching societies other than their own. Yet there is nothing inherently deplorable in this practice, for Australia's isolation makes it inevitable that any self-respecting creative artist will want to spend some time overseas, matching his or her work alongside the best that Europe and America has to offer. Because of the high costs of international travel, even a temporary overseas visit is likely to take several months, especially if the impecunious artist has to save up for the $500 fare home, but however long the break, most Australians regard the return to their homeland as being as inevitable as the original escape.

One intriguing aspect of Australia's cultural expatriates, which applies even to those who live abroad permanently, is that they remain fiercely Australian in their identity and style. One observer has written illuminatingly of 'the extraordinary tenacity with which people whose career opportunities or exogenous circumstances have forced them to leave the country hold on so desperately to their Australianism. Their Australian origins, no matter what the length of time, never become irrelevant to their sense of personal identity. Even if they can't come back, their Australianism becomes a proud and permanent stigma.'

Sidney Nolan, who has spent more than a quarter of a century away from the country of his birth, still speaks with passion of the dominant Australian influences on him: 'All Australians are bewitched by the environment, by the continent. We all live a life which is very similar to the life here [Britain], but it's impossible not to look out and see a quite different kind of life exemplified in trees, and animals, and the light, particularly the light . . . Even now that I've fallen for this light here, I can still evoke in my studio on the Thames the river that I saw as a boy. A big long river, with the sun coming through the leaves, the vertical leaves of the gum trees. I've never seen it anywhere else. . . . Forty or more years later, sitting in the studio, looking at the Thames with its fleeting light, and the industrial chimneys, and the townscape at the end of it, I can still go back to this thing on the Murray River and get it so that when I took the painting back to Australia and showed it to the people there by the river, the old boys came in and recognized it.'

Another expatriate who has been out of Australia for seventeen years is novelist Jill Neville, author of *Fall Girl, The Girl Who Played Gooseberry* and *Lady Lazarus.* Living now in Paris, Jill Neville still feels completely Australian, intends to return one day, and has no guilt feelings about her long absence: 'I don't see it as a betrayal of Australia to live in Europe for so long and I'm sad that people there seem to think of it in that way. It is essential for all the brighter, more intelligent young people in Australia to come here. Europe is the university of life. I see Europe and Australia in purely physical terms, Australia is like having an affair with a strong young Italian fisherman. Very physical but a bit boring mentally. Europe is an intellectual lover—stimulating mentally but without the virility of Australia. Australia's tragedy is her distance from Europe. But we are the last of the suffering Australians. In 10 years fares will be cheaper, travel will be faster. There will be none of this the-great-moment-of-decision business —to leave or not to leave, to return or not to return. We will be able to be Australians and world travellers at the one time. We will be able to leave Australia without feeling as though we are cutting off an arm.'

The feeling of cutting off an arm on the part of those who leave is equalled by the feeling of being cut off on the part of those who stay. Aspiring young Australians who dream of being an antipodean Leonardo da Vinci or William Shakespeare find their own cultural scene claustrophobic because there are too few discriminating fellow spirits around in their own cities. Despairingly, they pack their bags and set off in search of more sympathetic environments, only to find when they arrive that their Australianism alienates them from their new surroundings. They can be educated, influenced and overwhelmed by another nation's culture, but they can never be part of it, for the Australian artistic temperament includes few qualities of the chameleon. Spending some evenings in conversation with the more sophisticated residents of 'Kangaroo Valley' (the district around London's Earls Court which houses approximately 25,000 young Australians) one comes away with the impression that the strongest common emotion among expatriate intellectuals is the desire to remain an Australian, preferably by returning to the homeland. This is now much easier, because the homeland's cultural life has begun to flourish.

THE ART WORLD

It is an understatement to say that the Australian art world is flourishing. In fact, it is exploding away in a superboom that is comparable to the mineral rush, and often as recklessly speculative. In Sydney alone there are some twelve good permanent galleries, and forty or fifty little galleries in converted shops or home units. The other four state capitals contain at least as many galleries again between them, and as their owners have to make a living, there is always a frenzied rush of new openings, exhibitions and champagne previews. The public loves all the activity, thinks it is chic to be arty, and frequently pay ludicrously high prices for trash.

Hard on the heels of the exhibition-goers comes a large army of enthusiastic amateur painters, whose weekend activity is staggering. Just about every well-educated Australian family seems to have one member who sits down regularly in front of an easel and 'gives it a go'. The results are often absurd, yet one cannot help but admire the creative spirit which produces so many attempts. Any of these amateurs with a trace of talent will very quickly get the chance of becoming a professional, for it is almost fatally easy for young artists just out of art school to exhibit their work. In a country full of affluent citizens hungry for 'an original' to hang on the lounge wall, artistic quality quickly becomes subordinate to quantity. Yet out of all the second-rate activity there have mushroomed up several Australian artists of acknowledged talent.

Sidney Nolan's lonely visions of the bleak interior; Russell Drys-

L.O.F.—7*

dale's harsh but colourful outback; Arthur Boyd's Brueghelian
evocations of inter-racial passion; William Dobell's rich Renaissance portraits; and the tragic grimness of Albert Tucker's symbolic death birds and Intruders are images that have made a major
favourable impact on the international art community. But there
are several less renowned Australian artists with considerable gifts
whose work has been highly praised by experts. These include
landscape painters such as Clifton Pugh, John Perceval and Fred
Williams; urban realists such as John Olsen and Robert Dickerson;
and abstract impressionists such as Stanislaus Rapotec, Ian Fair-
weather and John Passmore.

There are two minor mysteries about Australian art. The first
is its lack of recognition by the outside world. Once critics have
actually been to the far end of the Pacific they usually come away
singing the praises of several Australian painters, but until this
peregrination has been made, they are apt to keep silent on the
subject, mainly because of the difficulty of seeing Australian work
outside Australia. In 1960 there was an exhibition of Australian
painting at London's Whitechapel Gallery which marked a turning
point in world appreciation of antipodean art, but there have not
been many international exhibitions since, particularly of the work
by the less celebrated artists. James Fitzsimmons, the American
editor of the world's most prestigious art magazine, *Art International*, criticizes Australia's own isolationist thinking for the
apparent failure of the country's painting to win more widespread
world acclaim: 'Australian artists are very little known in the rest
of the world, and Australian art isn't yet recognized internationally.
People like Nolan and Drysdale are thought of as exceptions—
there's no awareness that you may have a thriving art centre here.
Much of the blame lies with you, for Australian galleries have not
been very energetic sending out releases. In the 15 years I've had
my magazine, I've received some 30,000 catalogues from all over
the world. But from Australia, I've got maybe 20 items. If they don't
send them to me I figure they don't send them to any magazines,
so how can the magazines pay any attention to Australian art if
they're never told anything about it?'

The other mystery about Australian painting is why it should
be so good at the professional top level, and so wildly popular at
the amateur level. Sidney Nolan believes that it is due to Australia's
compelling light: 'It's a light that's worthy of Dante. It has this
transcendental intensity and incandescence that Dante is describing at the end of his poem. And one is always conscious of this

intensity in the light, it's always beating on you, and the fact that you don't have any objects, as yet, underneath that light, or on which this light can shine, that are worthy of Dante is bad luck, but it doesn't matter. There's always the hope that there will be, that there will be the psalms written, and there will be the painting painted one day, that will stand up to this light.'

Certainly one gets this impression of a celestial light-quality influencing Australian paintings, which often seem to erupt out of the canvas in a riot of colour and gaiety. Even when portraying grimness and bleakness, there is little of the gloom and sepulchral use of chiaroscuro that is apt to characterize European images of tragedy. Walking round an Australian art gallery, there is an over-powering feeling that the paintings have been fun to do. No one is awed by the skills of Old Masters, because there aren't many of them hanging in Australia to do the aweing. Australian artists have had the chance to make a solid impact without being burdened by comparisons alongside Rubens and Renoir, and they have seized their chance with both hands. The absence of high critical standards has, in this instance, been a benefit to Australian culture, for the artists have painted from instinct, and in many cases their instincts have been very beautiful.

In the wake (and sometimes in the van) of the creative artists come a bustling group of gallery owners, dealers, patrons and critics. Some of them, as in all artistic communities, are what the Australians call 'hyping larrikins' (rascals who inflate prices falsely for their own profit) but most are men of real taste and dis-crimination who have worked long and with dedication to put Aus-tralian art on the map. One dealer who has been called the 'Lord Duveen of the Pacific', is a larger-than-life character named Kym Bonython. In addition to being a motor-racing champion, owner of a speedway circuit, compère of a jazz programme, air ace war hero, submarine diver, speedboat and hydroplane enthusiast and a gourmet with a passion for marshmallows shaped like Derringer pistols, the wealthy 50-year-old Bonython is above all a serious patron of the arts. He owns the Paddington Art Centre in Sydney, whose 11,000 square feet of space make it the largest commercial gallery in Australia, another smaller gallery in Adelaide, and is the author of a scholarly opus *Modern Australian Painting and Sculpture 1960*. Bonython is one of the few men in Australian art dealing who is tuned to the international as well as the national wavelength. He specializes in putting on expensive imported art exhibitions (his opening show at the Paddington Centre came from

London's Marlborough Galleries) because he strongly believes
that Australians need to see more than their own art. But Bonython
does not neglect the domestic painters, and is Australia's biggest
and most powerful dealer. Hard on his heels come gallery owners
like Rudy Komon of Sydney, who cornered the market in Fred
Williams' pictures some years ago; Brian Johnston, whose Cintra
Road gallery provides Brisbane with regular three-weekly exhibitions of the best art in the country; and Barry Stern, who has a
reputation for getting the highest prices of all for his stable of
artists. These prices can be astronomical. A Drysdale will usually
go for around $15,000, although they have fetched as much as
$45,000. Tucker sells for approximately $3,000 a picture, while
Fred Williams, whose work a year ago fetched $500, is now in the
$4,000 a canvas class, and on a different level, large quantities of
the most appalling junk get sold in the $50–$150 price range.
In Australia, the impoverished artist is as rare as the impoverished
dealer.

If Bonython can be labelled Australia's Duveen, Australia's
Bernard Berenson is probably Mervyn Horton, a goatee-bearded
connoisseur and critic of substantial independent means who is
the unpaid editor of the country's most exalted art magazine *Art
and Artists*. Horton lives in an elegant terraced house near Sydney's
Kings Cross. His drawing-room is full of the finest French
furniture, and on his wall hang two magnificent Olsens and a
Drysdale. *Art and Artists* now has a world-wide circulation of over
3,000, selling to fellow-connoisseurs as far away as Moscow and
Budapest. 'I think I've had an influence on taste in this country,'
says Horton. 'Although we are basically an uncultured society, we
are changing fast. Art is now a compulsory subject in our state
high schools, there is an identifiable artistic community, and
public interest is mounting all the time.' This opinion would
probably be shared by other critics who have influenced Australian
taste, men like Donald Brook, Ross Lancell and Laurie Thomas,
whose newspaper columns reach a consistently high standard of
criticism.

The Australian art boom is thus the creation of an amalgam of
forces, for critics, dealers, connoisseurs, patrons and gallery proprietors have done almost as much as the painters themselves to
create the interest, excitement and financial viability of an artistic
gold rush. But the boom should not be seen as a creative or
economic South Sea Bubble even though some aspects of it come
into that category, for at the heart of the boom lies real artistic

talent, and a distinctive style and tradition. Because the 'Manhattan regionalism' which Albert Tucker and other Australians sneer at is the prevailing fashion in international art at the present time, Australian painting still tends to be slightly discounted in world terms, but in the opinion of many respected international critics the hour of 'Australian regionalism' as a major artistic force may not be long delayed.

THEATRE

No one can accuse the Australian theatre of being dull, although much of its excitement stems from the farcical absurdity of the authorities' stage censorship activities. In the last two years police raids and prosecution have been carried out on plays like *The Boys in the Band, America Hurrah, Norm and Ahmed, The Beard, When did you last see my Mother?* and *Oh Calcutta!* Tension is increased by regular visits to theatres by police officers who makes reports on a show's contents, performance styles and audience reactions, all for the benefit of the States' chief secretaries. These are Ministerial figures with power to prohibit or regulate public entertainment when they believe (to quote the words of the New South Wales Act) 'that it is fitting for the preservation of good manners and decorum so to do.' Since their interpretation of this power has led various chief secretaries to prosecute plays solely on the grounds that the script contains one of the four- or six-letter words that can be heard every night with monotonous frequency in any Australian pub, it can be seen that stage censorship in Australia has brought itself into ludicrous disrepute. As John Tasker, one of the country's leading stage directors and a prominent anti-censorship campaigner, puts it: 'A decision to ban a play or modify a performance is usually founded on the advice of one or two men, constables who last visited the theatre fifteen years ago, or for whom *The Sound of Music* is the acme of theatrical experience. But perhaps one should feel pleased that the police are now staunch regular theatregoers.'

The enforcement of the censorship laws, which is sometimes carried out amidst rich comedy scenes of policemen chasing actresses *en déshabille* across the stage, distracts from the real achievements of Australian drama. These are considerable. Over a million Australians go to the theatre each year. More than 100,000 of them attend the Melbourne Theatre Company, which plays to regular 98 per cent capacity audiences in its Russell Street headquarters. This is the most highly subsidized theatre in Australia and the best, for its performances are acknowledged to be on a level of artistic achievement which is generally equal and occasionally superior to that of Broadway and the West End. Other good theatres are the Old Tote in Sydney, the Perth Playhouse and the South Australian Theatre Company in Adelaide. All are subsidized from government funds, a benefit which is not conferred on any of the numerous commercial managements who nevertheless have been moving steadily into productions of serious drama. For example, two internationally successful plays, *Fortune and Men's Eyes* and *The Boys in the Band* were, in 1968, produced in Australia several months before they appeared in London. This suggests that some elements in the Australian commercial theatre are by no means backward in their attempts to achieve quality, although it must be admitted that such attempts are still comparatively rare.

The trouble is that Australian audiences love corn. The J. C. Williamson theatre group, believed to own the world's largest circuit of theatres, gives the people just the sort of corn they like by specializing in old spectacular musicals and light comedies. These are usually identical in direction to the Broadway versions, and all the more popular because of it. One prominent Australian actor said to me about 'The Firm' (as J. C. Williamson's is universally known), 'They're great people to work for, they delight their audiences, and they give steady employment to a lot of actors, but the trouble is their productions are totally uninspired and unoriginal.'

The same could be said of most commercial managements, for rare indeed is the Australian play that is genuinely Australian or directed in a creative way. One can find exceptions to this rule, some of which are mentioned above. But there is a serious dearth of national playwrights, although tribute must be paid to Ray Lawler, author of *The Summer of the Seventeenth Doll* (the first ever all-Australian play to gain international fame), Alan Seymour, who wrote *The One Day in The Year*, and among younger writers for the theatre, Alex Buzo, Bill Reed and Tony Morphett. Some of Australia's novelists, notably Patrick White, Hal Porter, Morris West and Thomas Keneally have also written the occasional fine drama, but true playwrights remain depressingly thin on the ground.

Perhaps the most original and exotic theatrical talent to emerge from Australia in the last few years is Barry Humphries, the

36-year-old Melbourne-born satirist. His genius is unclassifiable, for it ranges over a whole field of inspired mimicry and creative characterization, from slapstick lunacy to tear-jerking pathos. Humphries has invented a whole range of Australian suburban figures, which were seen at their best in his last London one-man evening at the Fortune Theatre *Just a Show*. There was the pathetic bore Sandy Stone, croaking about the loneliness of serious illness from the depths of a wheel-chair; Rex Lear, the self-made drunk tycoon boasting of the cost of his ungrateful daughter's wedding reception; Debbie Thwaite, the expatriate sheila living in Kangaroo Valley, chanting a litany about comparative meat prices in Earls Court and Melbourne; a barrel-chested surfie swilling countless tubes of Fosters Lager and chundering them up again every few moments; and most hilarious of all, Humphries' finest creation, Edna Everage, who bitches about her son Brucie's mixed marriage (to an English girl), waves flags outside Buckingham Palace, and in a side-splitting finale hurls dozens of gladdies (gladioli) into the audience, who are then made to 'thrust swing and tremble' the blooms in the air as they join Edna in the Gladdie song. 'One of the strangest and funniest quarters of an hour you could spend inside a theatre,' said a glowing review by the BBC's Julian Jebb in *The Listener*. It was just about the only good notice *Just a Show* received, because most critics found Humphries totally incomprehensible. So he is to all but those whose ears are finely tuned to the Australian idiom, but this makes him achieve the rare distinction of being a prophet with honour in his own country. Masochistically, packed houses in Australia adore even the most savage shafts of his viciously unpatriotic satires, simply because their observation is so keen and precise. Sadistically, Humphries doesn't even pay Australia the compliment of living there, preferring to draw cartoons for *Private Eye* in London. Whatever one can say about Humphries, he is certainly not typical of the Australian theatre, though he has claims to being its finest son.

What the Australian theatre lacks most is numbers. Numbers of writers, numbers of eccentrics like Humphries, numbers of talented performers and producers, above all numbers of theatregoers. Because of small populations and big distances, there is virtually no out-of-town coach audience in Australia. If Britain suffered from a similar deprivation, half the West End theatres would close in a week, for only 20 per cent of the West End audiences are Londoners. This statistic is illustrative of the big disadvantages the Australian theatre faces, yet despite its difficulties the overall quality of productions seems to be rising slowly, rather like a reluctant but tasty soufflé. The drama content of the Perth and Adelaide festivals gets better year by year. Subsidies to the theatre from State and Commonwealth Government funds are increasing. The University of New South Wales now has two professorial chairs of drama. The Elizabethan Theatre Trust (founded in 1954 as a permanent memorial of the Queen's visit, with the object of promoting a living theatre in Australia) is working hard to encourage new writers, producers and actors by giving them opportunities at its own theatres. Because of the small scale which makes it difficult to determine what is a trend and what is an exception, it is too early yet to do much more than reserve judgment on the future of the Australian theatre, but the omens look distinctly promising.

FILMS

The Australian film industry is a weak and puny infant, but is now showing signs of gathering strength. Until 1969 it was possible to deride Australia as the only sizeable trading nation in the world without its own film production industry. Even a nation like South Korea made more feature films in one year than Australia had made in twenty. Although Australia was the nation which produced the world's first motion picture (a Salvation Army production, *Soldiers of the Cross*, in 1901) and despite the making of 198 feature films on Australian soil before 1914, this booming industry was killed off by competition from Hollywood between the wars and never managed to recover. Even a healthy rise in the total of film-goers produced no renaissance in film-making. In 1951 the box-office takings of all Australian cinemas amounted to $80 million. By 1966 these takings had advanced to $200 million. Yet in both years the Australian film-producing industry's share of the market was a mere $600,000.

These figures underline the stagnation and foreign domination that characterized Australian film-making. But by the end of the sixties, a number of younger film-makers decided to stop the rot, and several new production companies mushroomed into existence. One of these was Goldsworthy Productions, founded in Sydney in February 1968. Its executive producer, Warwick Freeman, told me: 'In the last two years the film industry has got extremely active. This year [1969] at least twelve feature films will be made in Australia. We ourselves are making two of them, both on budgets of around $400,000. The reason for this sudden boom is that overseas producers are intrigued by our locations here, and attracted by the low costs. The main cause of these low costs is that there are no restrictive unions in the industry here, in fact there are no effective unions at all. Even the very best cameramen in Australia are lucky if they earn $200 a week—the top cameramen in Hollywood get at least three times that. Now that there are several companies in Australia prepared to work with overseas companies, there isn't a great shortage of money here. But there is a great dearth of talent. It's difficult to get highly trained crews, there's a shortage of experienced film actors, and everyone's crying out for decent scripts. We're still a bit of a colony as regards film-making—there's never yet been an Australian director of a big Australian film.'

This 'import everything' policy of overseas producers is the Australian industry's biggest curse. In 1967, Mr Eddie Davis, a TV director from Hollywood visiting Sydney to make a pilot drama series, said he knew plenty of people in America who would put money into an Australian film. 'Of course,' he added, 'it would mean bringing out a name star and a couple of directors to do it.' As long as the man who pays the distributor calls the tune, the Eddie Davis rule will always deny Australian talent the top jobs. Even the 'at least twelve feature films' referred to above by Warwick Freeman in fact fall into the B-movie category, while the one major feature film recently shot in Australia (Tony Richardson's production of *Ned Kelly*, starring Mick Jagger) is only the third of its kind in ten years.

One additional cause of the talent shortage in films is the heavy toll in expatriates. They are possibly more numerous than in any other branch of Australia's cultural life because of the huge differentials between film-industry salaries in Australia and elsewhere. Nevertheless, the expatriates often make their mark for Australia at foreign festivals. At the 1969 British Film Institute's International Festival of Short Films, there were over 3,000 entries, only 120 of which were accorded the compliment of being shown. Of these 120, Australia scored a creditable 8. The films by Don Levy and Barry Humphries drew much favourable comment, while another Australian entry, *Darling Do You Love Me* by Martin Sharp and Bob Whittaker, was the runaway success of the festival. Unfortunately for Australian nationalism, seven out of eight Australian entries were made by expatriates resident in Britain.

As one Sydney newspaper put it, 'Now we know. Australia does have a film industry—in London.'

But even if nationalism takes a knock over film making, it gets a huge bonus in cinema-going habits. Australians will flock in hordes to see anything about their own country. The all-time box-office smash hit in Australia was the film of Nino Culotta's book *They're a Weird Mob*. It told the story of an Italian migrant's bewildering introduction to the Australian working man's world of mateship, gambling and boozing. When shown in London it was an all-time flop, but this did not matter too much since Australians were so busy splitting their sides at their third, fourth or fifth visits to the film, that *They're a Weird Mob* grossed $750,000 in five Australian cities alone, thereby breaking all records and comfortably recouping its production costs. Against this success was the failure of a much-fancied 1969 Australian feature film *2000 Weeks*, which was savaged by the local critics because of the advanced intellectual nature of its labyrinthine plot. Australians, it seems, prefer their films to be simple and basic. Fred Crouch, Sales Manager of Australia's biggest film distribution company, Greater Union Ltd, told me, 'After *Weird Mob*, our biggest grossers have been films like *The Sound of Music*, the Bond films, *My Fair Lady*, *Cat Ballou* and *Born Free*. You'd be surprised too how much we still take on some of the older-style British films like *The Battle of the River Plate*, *Reach for the Sky* and *Doctor in the House*. Some of the arty stuff doesn't do so well these days. Laurence Olivier's *Othello* was even a flop in Melbourne —it couldn't run for more than four weeks.'

There are exceptions to these manifestations of simple taste. For instance, the cerebral French feature *Un Homme et une Femme* ran for 80 weeks at one Sydney cinema. Yet on the whole, suburbia's mindlessness reigns triumphant in cinema-going habits.

Looking ahead to the future of Australia's film-making industry, there are several encouraging signs. The Commonwealth Government has now become aware of the export potential of film production and is financing a national film and TV school. The Government has also agreed to set up a film and television development corporation along the lines recommended by the Australian Council for the Arts, with $1 million initial capital to make loans and grants to film makers. The most encouraging portent of all is the expanding pool of film-making talent in Australia. These film-makers are very young and totally unknown, but having worked myself alongside several of them while making TV documentaries in Australia, I for one am certain that the talent is there and that it will soon push Australia's film industry into international recognition.

BOOKS

Australians are the world's biggest book buyers. This does not necessarily make them a literary people. Although the statistics prove that sales are booming astronomically in per capita terms, a tour of bookshops suggests that the staple reading diet of the Australian public is nostalgia, navel-contemplation and natural history. Almost any publication that spins yarns about the convicts' rugged beginnings, or contains statistics proving Australians to be the southern hemisphere's record-holders in toothbrush use, or prints glossy technicolor pictures of the Great Barrier Reef, is automatically guaranteed a handsome commercial success. But on entering the homes of the affluent citizens who pile their coffee tables with these expensive pictorial volumes, one sometimes discovers that the owner's bookshelves are woefully bereft of more highbrow reading material. I have even been into the houses of wealthy and prominent Australians and have discovered that they possess no books or bookshelves at all! Yet it would be unwise to draw an unduly harsh conclusion from such experiences, for the best aspect of the continent's book boom is that it definitely does include some literature. Today, the hardback edition of a reasonably good second novel is likely to sell 3,000 to 5,000 copies in Australia—which may well be more than it will sell in Britain. Home-grown writers such as Patrick White, Hal Porter, Cyril Pearl and Thomas Keneally are well supported (to the tune of around 15,000 copies) by the domestic public, while the dramatic growth of the bookselling industry in the last few years has enabled some publishers to give a break to aspiring first novelists.

Says Dennis Wren, the Managing Director of William Heinemann Australia Pty Ltd: 'In the 15 years up to 1965, this company published three titles a year. In 1969 we published 27 titles, and our costs have remained stable because for short and medium runs we, like most publishers, now use Hong Kong printing, which is usually 50 per cent cheaper than Australian printing. Most of our titles are non-fiction, or history, or about floura and fauna, but the expansion will make it easier for me to take a chance on some young creative writer with talent.'

The country's young writers, all of whom naturally think they have talent, are by and large pessimistic about the opportunity Australia now offers them. They argue that writing in Australia is first and foremost a matter of economics and that only the lucky few who have access to foreign markets can hope to survive. Supporting this argument is the Australian Society of Authors, which claims that 83 per cent of its members have earnings below the Commonwealth Government's poverty line, who would starve if they did not have alternative sources of income such as teaching and journalism.

Another cause of concern is the Australian authors' long-standing winge that in order to get recognized in their own country, the first essential is to go overseas and achieve success there. This is still true, but growing noticeably less so. One recent break-through was the imaginative decision of the international literary agency, Curtis Brown Ltd, to set up an office in Sydney. This addition to Australia's literary landscape has in two years raised the hopes and pushed up the rewards for all categories of writers.

One group of Australian literary figures who have definitely not had their hopes fully realized or their rewards pushed up are the continent's poets. International connoisseurs of poetry have consistently praised work from the pens of A. D. Hope, Kenneth Slessor, Douglas Stewart, Randolph Stow, Judith Wright and James McAuley, to mention but a few who keep Australia's muse alive, but they are still unfortunately poets without much financial honour in their own country. Although this group has been quietly acknowledged in the international academic community as one of the finest contemporary sources of modern poetry, most of its members could not exist at all without the generous subsidies paid to poetry from the Commonwealth Literary Fund—a Government body. This amazes some outsiders, such as a correspondent for the *New York Times Book Review*, Harry Roskolenko, who wrote recently, 'Even a poet as fine as James McAuley, who teaches at the University of Tasmania, thanked the Fund for assistance in completing his current book of poems. Can you imagine Robert Frost, of whom McAuley often reminds me, thanking the Library of Congress for the same service?'

Comparisons between Australian writers and the literary giants of the world are by no means fanciful, for the country can be justifiably proud of its leading authors' achievements. Morris West, who sprang to fame when *The Devil's Advocate* won the James

Tait Black Memorial Prize in 1957 is today one of the top best-selling authors in all countries, and is profitably mining the rich vein of film-making, following the box-office success of *The Shoes of the Fisherman*. The acknowledged leader of contemporary Australian literature is Patrick White, author of *Voss*, *The Aunt's Story*, *The Tree of Man*, *Riders in the Chariot*, *The Solid Mandala* and *The Vivisector*. Of his own motives in writing *Voss* in 1957 White illuminatingly said, 'I was determined to prove that the Australian novel is not necessarily the dreary dun-coloured off-spring of journalistic realism.' Certainly he has produced his proof, for White's style is a convoluted, symbolistic and quasi-poetic verbal mosaic. He is obsessed with spiritual states and spiritual journeys, and often the reader is baffled by the complexity of the mosaic. One who felt enraged by this feeling of bafflement was the poet, A. D. Hope, who slammed White for his 'pretentious and illiterate verbal sludge' in a notorious review of *The Tree of Man* in the Sydney *Morning Herald*. Said Hope: 'Mr White has three disastrous faults as a novelist: he knows too much, he tells too much and he talks too much . . . for the most part he tries to write a novel as though he were writing poetry . . . However delightful at first, it produces in time irritation, then torture and finally a numbness of the brain.'

In the years since Hope fired this broadside, White's writing has become less obscure, although no less concerned with dis-covering the inner meaning of his plots and his characters. His prose mosaic is often highlighted by the brilliance of his sharp social observation, but the writing is still tortuous and gargantuan in the scale of its imagination. Yet even to those who criticize him most vehemently, White's imagination marks him out as his country's most prominent literary influence.

All developments in modern Australian writing can be dated back to 1948 when Patrick White published *The Aunt's Story*. The concern with spiritual suffering and deep metaphysical mean-ing can be traced through the styles of Randolph Stow, Christopher Koch and Hal Porter, three novelists whose writing is usually grouped with 'The White movement' in Australian fiction during the fifties and sixties. But the White disciple who has come nearest to achieving global success with his writing is Thomas Keneally, author of *The Place at Whitton* (1964), *The Fear* (1965), *Bring Larks and Heroes* (1967), *Three Cheers for the Paraclete* (1969) and *The Survivor*. Keneally's writing has developed over the last few years from an Alfred de Vigny-like acceptance of suffering as the most beneficial essence of the human condition into a much more optimistic and less spiritually melancholic attitude. Dr Maitland, the central character in Keneally's best-seller *Three Cheers for the Paraclete*, is a cheerful activist who wants to cure suffering and believes it can be done. This characterization marks a major break with the White movement, of which Keneally was once so loyal a follower, and opens a new phase in the development of the Australian novel.

One of the disadvantages of being an up-and-coming Australian novelist is that it is still surprisingly difficult to get established in world markets. This is, to some extent, due to an anomaly in the Anglo-Australian publishing industry. For example, Keneally's *Three Cheers for the Paraclete* deserved to have been extensively reviewed and sold in Britain. True, it was available in the northern hemisphere, but only through the London office of the Sydney firm of Angus and Robertson, and this outlet managed to sell merely a few hundred copies. It would have been far more sensible for a fully-fledged British publisher to have the British rights, and an Australian publisher to have the Australian rights. The same would certainly be true of a book like my own, which likewise would be much more profitable for all concerned if there were separately printed and promoted Australian and British editions. Unfortunately, there is no hope of such a breakthrough because all British publishers maintain the fossilized fiction that Australia is still a colonial appendage to Britain where publishing is concerned. This anomaly dates back to the 1930s, when a London publisher sold the Australian part of 'The Empire Rights' of a novel *North by Northwest* off to a Sydney publisher. To everyone's great astonishment *North by Northwest* sold over 25,000 copies in Australia. Panicked by this success, the British publishers formed a gentlemen's agreement that henceforth no further dilutions of the Australia market would be permitted, and the main effect of this has been that no British house will accept a book that has been previously or simultaneously published in Australia, because 'Australia is part of the British market'.

This neo-colonial approach was causing considerable resentment in Australia by the mid-sixties, and to soothe the nationalistic mutterings, several British firms registered separate Australian companies such as Macmillans (Australia). These are given quite a degree of local autonomy where local books are concerned, and usually the Australian offshoot has complete power on whether or not to publish a manuscript like *Wildflowers of Tasmania*, which will not have a large sale outside the antipodes. But for more important titles, the imprint has to be made in London, and merely shipped to Australia for distribution, thereby obeying the rule 'Australia is part of the British market.' It is a most unsatisfactory situation in terms of national pride, for it has resulted in the near-total extinction of the Australian-owned publishing industry.

The individual who has done most to hasten this extinction is a 44-year-old Englishman, Paul Hamlyn. He arrived in Australia for the first time in 1967, saying, 'I want to be the biggest bookseller in Australia': two years and ten visits later, he was. Using the flair that built up his own £3 million publishing empire in London, Hamlyn reorganized the Australian industry's methods of promotion and distribution, purchased a controlling interest in the Cheshire–Lansdowne–Jacaranda publishing houses, and a substantial part of the equity in Sun Books. He also embarked on an energetic publishing programme of his own, and organized remainder marketing in Australia for the first time.

There are some who see nothing but good both in this particular British invasion of Australian publishing, and in the general British domination of the whole industry. Max Harris said in a recent column in *The Australian*: 'It's been my business to watch closely the movement of London imprints into Australian companies to see if there has been a deleterious effect on the Australian writer, from popular novelist to esoteric poet and erudite academic. And of course the truth is that Australian manuscripts have been received with acute, even hysterical, enthusiasm. Certainly the British presence has been a participatory and developmental one. One can consider them publisher by publisher, and almost all have made a worthwhile contribution to the Australian intellectual scene.'

Besides the authors and publishers, Australia's book world is inevitably shaped by certain important critical influences. Strangely enough, the Australian critics do not, on the whole, make much intellectual impact on Australian literature, the reason being that the critics themselves tend to be intellectually lightweight. There is nothing in Australia comparable to the quality of the reviewing in overseas journals such as the *New York Review of Books*, the *Times Literary Supplement*, the *New York Times Book Review*, the *New Statesman*, the *Economist* or the *Spectator*. Occasionally one sees a heavyweight review from an academic in the *Sydney Morning Herald*, the *Age*, or *The Australian*, but these tend to be rare exceptions, as do some contributions to Australia's leading literary magazines, *Meanjin* and *Overland*.

One man who is generally acknowledged to have had a significant influence on Australian literature is Geoffrey Dutton, a 46-year-old poet, critic, biographer, novelist and publisher. He comes from a wealthy family of graziers, and to this day lives in one of Australia's few stately homesteads, a 28-room U-shaped gothic mansion 'Anlaby', which stands 60 miles north of Adelaide and was built by the owner's great-great-grandfather in 1838. Dutton was educated at Geelong Grammar and at Oxford, where he read English under C. S. Lewis. Soon after coming down, he wrote his first novel *The Mortal and the Marble*, and followed this by three travel books and two biographies, one of them on Colonel William Light, the founder of Adelaide. Dutton then spent six years travelling in Europe, but returned to lecture at Adelaide University, and over the next fifteen years produced two more novels, three children's books, two critical studies (on Patrick White and Walt Whitman), and three volumes of poetry. He also found time to launch a poetry magazine, and more importantly a highly successful, all-Australian paperback company, Sun Books ('We started it because we were fed up with Penguins'), which has produced several exceptionally literate best-sellers, including Yevtushenko's poems (20,000 copies sold), Russell Drysdale's *Journey Among Men* (17,000 copies) and Geoffrey Blainey's *The Tyranny of Distance* (18,000 copies). Rising every day at 5 a.m., Dutton devotes the early matutinal hours to his writing, and thereafter concentrates on running his 8,000-acre family estate, his publishing interests, his criticism, and his political campaign for an Australian Republic.

To an outsider, the silver-haired patrician from Anlaby seems a positively Byronic figure. Like Byron, he puts his poetry before anything else, is a hopeless romantic, and although dedicated to the highest literary standards has a mild horror of 'authors who are all author'. Hence his agriculturalist's love of the land, his tycoon's enjoyment of the business side of publishing, his schoolboy enthusiasm for his mustard-coloured 1907 Talbot (which his father drove across Australia in 1908) and his political involvement in republicanism. Talking in his magnificent private library at Anlaby, I received from Dutton a fascinating perspective of the literary scene: 'There is a great spirit of national confidence—not to be confused with nationalism—in Australia today, and this has certainly touched all sections of the community, particularly perhaps in their attitudes to cultural subjects like novels and poetry. One of the reasons I like living on the land is that I am in contact with non-literary non-intellectual people who keep you close to the realities. One big reality is that the men on the land round here no longer have the old attitude that culture is something cissy. Just recently, Russell Drysdale came over, and when they heard he was coming the gardener and the pig-man cut the lawn specially in his honour. Also, when Sidney Nolan came to lunch, all the labourers' kids for miles around queued up for autographs. This same enthusiasm is reflected in the Adelaide Festival's poetry readings. We held these in places like the docks, the abattoir and the car factories and got big crowds—five or six hundred people a time. It was a terrific success with the working men. You might think poetry was a minority interest the way the books sell, but that's often the publisher's fault. I dream that we'll soon have in Australia the equivalent of Russia's National Poetry Day with readings in schools and factories. There would be a great response, you know. This country isn't indifferent to literature, it's totally innocent about it. The new national confidence will steadily bring poetry and good prose to the forefront of the life here, as has already happened with painting.'

ARCHITECTURE AND ENVIRONMENT

The quality of the environment has become a literary and intellectual topic of merit in Australia. Concern started to grow from 1960, when Melbourne architect Robin Boyd first published a crusading volume *The Australian Ugliness*, a devastating attack on the environmental horrors of the continent's major cities. On the first page Boyd quotes Anthony Trollope: 'It is taken for granted that Australia is ugly.'

This ugliness is visible in painful abundance. The suburbs of the eastern cities sprawl higgledy-piggledy in obscene rashes of jerry-built matchboxes. The beautiful coastline is being ravaged by unchecked open-cast beach-mining operations, by indiscriminately planned honky-tonk concrete slabs masquerading as bars and beach huts, and by ribbon industrial developments such as the massive Japanese chip-mill operations which raze the natural landscape for hundreds of miles down the New South Wales seaboard. Denis Winston, Professor of Town and Country Planning at Sydney University, warned recently: 'The whole of accessible Australia will soon be smeared with the bungaloid and substandard industrial and commercial growth familiar to all who travel the main highways for 30 miles or so outside Sydney and Melbourne today,' while Sydney architect Milo Dumphy proclaims: 'It took the United States fifty years to produce 2,000 miles of continuous suburban smear on its eastern seaboard. Australia will reproduce the same effect within twenty years. But our blight will be longer, cheaper and nastier.'

Yet despite such prophecies of doom, the encouraging fact remains that the conservationist banner has now been well and truly hoisted in Australia, and this has been done at a comparatively early stage in the nation's development. Compared to the industrially ravaged landscapes of Britain and America, Australia has a good chance of becoming the world's first technological power to preserve its countryside's ecological balance. The cynical maxim of the old Australian bushman—'If it moves shoot it, if it don't move, cut it down'—has now, thanks to intellectual agitation, been discredited and replaced by gentler sentiments. These are simultaneously being matched by several architectural projects, which in their way are doing as much as conservation projects to improve the quality of Australia's environment.

One man who combines both creation and preservation is Sir Roy Grounds, the true and onlie begetter of Melbourne Arts Centre and the individual who has done more than anyone else to introduce modern architecture to Australia. His houses and institutional buildings, such as the Academy of Science at Canberra, are revered collectors' pieces throughout the nation, while his commitment to the conservationist cause has gone beyond agitation to practical methods of enforcement. Recently, Grounds and his close friend, Ken Myer, a Melbournian supermarket and department-store tycoon, stepped in to purchase a 5-mile virgin strip of the northern New South Wales coastline which was on the point of being subdivided into a mass of quarter-acre building plots. 'We were motivated by a desire to treasure the natural beauty of this wonderful land,' says Grounds, 'so we are declaring the area a forestry, flora and fauna reserve and are giving it to the nation.' As the Australian public's concern over the environment grows, it is expected that both state governments and wealthy private individuals will follow the practical lead that Grounds and others have already given in conservation.

While environmental control has now become a *cause célèbre* in Australia, with even the Governor-General, Sir Paul Hasluck, throwing his not inconsiderable weight on the anti-pollution band-wagon, Australian architecture is also starting to move forward in several interesting directions. Sir Roy Grounds' former partner and fellow-propagandist for conversation, Robin Boyd, has a string of attractive houses and beautiful institutional edifices to his credit, among them Menzies College at La Trobe University, McCaughey Court at Ormond College, and the mysteriously darkened space-age tube at the Osaka Expo '70. Boyd comes from one of Australia's most celebrated, ancient and creative families, having five distinguished artists among his close relatives, and being the only man in Melbourne who proudly admits to having had an ancestor on the first convict fleet. He studied architecture at Melbourne University, and later became a visiting professor at the Massachusetts Institute of Technology. As a fellow of the Royal Australian Institute of Architects, a member of the Australian National Planning Committee, and an author of several successful books, notably *The Walls Around Us, New Directions in Japanese Architecture* and *The Australian Ugliness,* Boyd is one of the leading arbiters of architectural and developmental taste in his country. He says of the present trends: 'There are now a lot of very good buildings going up in Australia. A tremendous step forward has been made by the enlightened commissioning policies of the Commonwealth Government, and other public bodies like the Public Works Departments of Sydney and Perth. Some of the commercial firms are less enlightened—right now in Melbourne three ghastly skyscrapers are being built at one intersection and all of them are by American architects. How on earth are we ever going to develop our own talent if big Australian companies don't give Australian architects the big jobs? Still, let's be thankful that the aesthetic appeal of architecture is now becoming a national concern, because this means that in future we should see much less of the dreadful vulgarity and shoddy imitations of American bad taste that I call 'Austerica', which still characterize large parts of most of our cities.'

In addition to Grounds and Boyd, there are many other Australian architects now making enlightened changes in the sky-lines of the big conurbations. Among them are Harry Seidler, who made inspired designs for several Sydney office and apartment blocks, including Australia Square, a sort of unleaning Tower of Pisa on the scale of Montreal's famous Place Ville Marie; Graham Thorp, whose work in Sydney's eastern suburbs so impressed the visiting Duke of Westminster that Thorp was promptly invited to Britain to re-design 270 acres of the Grosvenor estate in London's Mayfair and Belgravia; and Paul Ritter, the brilliant but controversial former City Architect of Perth. But the pride of place in modern Australian architecture must go to Joern Utzon's Sydney Opera House, whose splendid madness has inspired a few touches of welcome eccentricity from more conservative members of the antipodean architectural profession. Compared to Utzon's extravaganza, even the Parthenon would look a cautious and sober creation, and as a result the importance of the still unfinished Opera House lies in its inspiration to others. As so often happens in Australia, it took a bloke from overseas to get things started, but now that architectural creativity is a thriving movement, and with conservation fast becoming a national political issue, the future of the Australian environment looks decidedly healthy.

OPERA, MUSIC AND BALLET

Until the end of the Second World War there was not a single permanent orchestra of professional players in Australia. Today, each of the six states has a symphony orchestra, generously financed by the Australian Broadcasting Commission. All of them reach a high standard of musical excellence, while those in Sydney and Victoria have been favourably compared by knowledgeable overseas critics to the London and New York Philharmonics. Even the relatively small (65-piece) Queensland Symphony Orchestra won an unsolicited tribute from visiting conductor Sir Malcolm Sargent, who said of it to English friends privately in London, 'In proportion to its size, it was as good as anything I've ever conducted in my life.'

Outside the field of state patronage, there are several professional musical groups in all the big cities, and plenty of amateur activity as well. All these combinations of serious musicians rely heavily on European migrants and overseas conductors. These include Dean Dixon, the American Negro conductor of the Sydney Symphony Orchestra; Richard Goldner from Vienna, who founded the Musica Viva Society; Rudolph Pekarek, the Czechoslovakian conductor of the Queensland Symphony; and Robert Pikler from Hungary, who leads Australia's most prominent chamber music society. In the last few years, Australia has seen the rise of several young composers specializing in highly esoteric experimental music, of whom the most respected are Richard Meale, Peter Sculthorpe, Nigel Butterley and George Dreyfus. Many of the experiments flourish in Adelaide, where audio-visual arts patron Derek Jolly (see p. 75) is a major artistic influence and catalyst. One of Jolly's recent projects has been the importing of the revolutionary electronic music synthesizer 'The Moog', a strange, five-octave, science-fiction-style organ invented by New Yorker Peter Moog. Derek Jolly, together with music lecturer Peter Tahourdin of Adelaide University, is reported to have pioneered several new breakthroughs in musical composition on this bizarre $50,000 machine. The mere fact that it exists at all in Australia is a tribute to the present vogue in cultural experimentation.

Returning to more conventional artistic achievements, the Elizabethan Theatre Trust deserves much credit for its encouragement and patronage of the National Ballet and Opera companies. The Trust has its own fully professional orchestra, and since 1964 has sponsored a ballet school in Melbourne, under the direction of Margaret Scott, a former principal dancer of the Ballet Rambert. This school demands a standard of dedication and talent over its two-year course that is said to equal that of London's Sadlers Wells Ballet school and other comparable international equivalents. Four or five of the school's twenty graduating students get into the Australian Ballet Company each year, and these graduates now comprise over 60 per cent of the corps de ballet. Having seen the company dance both in Melbourne and in London (where it received a rapturous reception from the critics), I am one of its many devoted fans, and see it as one of the finest examples of modern Australian culture.

The National Opera Company, good though its standards are, does not perhaps equal the world-class achievements of the Ballet, for although Australia has provided many celebrated opera stars from Dame Nellie Melba to Joan Sutherland, they seem to prefer working in the international opera community, making only the occasional return to their birthplace.

Perhaps the most interesting development in Australia's worlds of opera and ballet is the remarkable rise of public interest in these refined arts. This rise is largely due to Harry M. Miller, a New Zealand-born impresario (the occupation given on his passport), whose Sydney office is the maddest shrine to pandemonium even in that fever-paced city. Miller is a 36-year-old ex-research chemist from Auckland, who ran away to sea as a teenager and ended up in the PR world of New Zealand pop music. From there he graduated to promoting pop concerts in Australia, and brought to the continent stars like Sammy Davis Jnr, Louis Armstrong, Shelley Berman, Ella Fitzgerald, the Kingston Trio and the Rolling Stones. From his op-art office decor, collar-length hair style, sideburned visage, and maniacal exuberance for the joys of life, one might assume that Harry M. Miller was still immersed in the pop promotion world. But since January 1967, when the Chairman of the Elizabethan Theatre Trust, Dr H. C. Coombs, in an inspired gamble invited Miller to take on the post of promotion and commercial consultant to the Opera Company, Mozart, Puccini and Verdi have taken up more of Australia's leading impresario's waking hours than Jagger, Lennon and McCartney.

'The Trust said my responsibilities were to devise and direct the creation of an audience for opera in Australia. Well, I didn't know much about opera myself, so I got hold of all the records of the series and for the next three months not more than five minutes a day of my leisure time was spent away from the gramophone. It was marvellous! I liked it so much I decided to expose opera for what it is—the best of everything. I sold the stories of opera plots with subscription tickets, I offered cut prices to the youngies so that anyone under 26 could see four operas for $3 in their first subscription year, I dug old Joan Hammond out of retirement to make TV commercials, and I created a snobbery about opera— that it was chic and intelligent to go. The results were fantastic. Audiences trebled, and in the capital cities every opera was a complete sell-out. Everyone went mad—even my housepainter started singing *Don Giovanni*. Then the Trust asked me to do the same job for ballet, so of course I took it on and did the same. I offered mini-subs to balletomanes of 13 years old and under, and this brought in the sticky-finger brigade in hordes. Ballet audiences have now trebled too. It's been a real smash hit.'

Harry M. Miller's popularization of these arts has indeed been incredibly successful. Although he descended to such promotional excesses as saying, '*Tosca* and *Don Pasquale* are just the sort of stories that go on every day in your own street', and although he has kept an energetic finger in other promotional pies, such as producing the Australian version of *Hair* ('no more pornographic than *Snow White and the Seven Dwarfs*, I told the censors') and managing several show-business personalities, nevertheless Miller's dedication to promoting opera and ballet remains real and total. His efforts may result in the biggest cultural breakthrough yet seen in Australia. For now Miller has puppet shows with opera plots in Enid Blyton dialogue supplemented by records touring schools;

shortened and simplified performances for children being put on throughout Australia by two trust companies, *Opera in a Nutshell* and *Ballet in a Nutshell*; a whole new awareness of the performing arts is being created among the younger generation; it seems highly possible that tomorrow's adult Australians will be far more receptive to high culture than are their parents. As Miller himself says, 'Cultural curiosity has erupted among the young in the last three years. When these kids grow up they won't be queueing for the poker machines, they'll be queueing for the Opera House.' If that is true, Australia will certainly be a changed country.

9

POLITICS AND POLITICIANS

The first and most striking aspect of Australian politics is that there are a lot of them. To be precise, there are 719 salaried politicians in the country, 184 of them in the two houses of the Federal Parliament in Canberra, and the remainder in the six lower houses and five upper houses of the State legislatures. This makes Australia just about the most over-governed nation in the world, with one elected representative to every 10,633 voters.

However, over-government is by no means equated with good government, for the second most striking aspect of the Australian political scene is its low repute among ordinary people. The patriotism that leads to exaggerated pride in almost all other antipodean achievements is conspicuously absent when it comes to politics. Perhaps the national philosophy of 'We don't like tall poppies' explains this lack of esteem for politicians, or perhaps Australians sense that men of excellence are much rarer in their politics than in other walks of life. In a country exploding with new developments, new excitements and new riches, the individual who takes the uncomfortable, unexciting and underpaid road to politics must either be very dedicated or very second-rate. The cynics believe that too many politicians fall into the latter category, and after listening to the abysmally low standards of parliamentary debates in both Federal and State legislatures, one is inclined to agree.

A third notable feature of Australian politics is that they have a strong right-wing bias. One could almost go so far as to say that there is no such thing as a left-wing political party in Australia, at least by European or North American standards. Voice this opinion in Sydney's eastern suburbs or Melbourne's Toorak and one will probably get a glass of champagne thrown in one's face and be denounced as 'a bloody Com'. Nevertheless, the fact remains that even the Australian Communist Party is the most

right-wing of its kind in the world, having unhesitatingly condemned the invasion of Czechoslovakia and issued strong anti-
Soviet statements on many other policy matters. The next most
left-wing political group is the diminutive Australia Party which
was founded in 1966 following a response to a newspaper advertisement opposing Australia's involvement in the Vietnam War. The
Australia Party's founder and guiding light is Mr Gordon Barton,
a Sydney multi-millionaire with extensive interests in transport
industries, hotels, publishing and mineral finance. Although Barton
holds a few fairly radical views on foreign policy, he is a good safe
drawing-room liberal with opinions to the right of Harold Wilson
on economic issues. Thus, even in the highly improbable event
of the Australia Party being returned to power (like the Communist
Party it does not have a single seat at present) it seems unlikely
to pose even the slightest threat to the established capitalistic social
order. The same can certainly be said for the official opposition,
the Australian Labor Party, which stands on an approximate
political par with the US Democrats. The ALP leader, Mr Gough
Whitlam (see p. 234), is the mildest of social reformers, concentrating his fire on safe targets such as city sewerage, states rights,
environmental improvements and the pace of independence for
New Guinea. Moving over to the present Liberal-Country Party
coalition government, which has been in continuous power since
1949, one finds it is well to the right of the present Republican
and Conservative administrations in America and Britain. After
its narrow victory in the 1969 elections, the present Liberal
government is only in power today because of redistributed preference votes from the extreme right-wing Democratic Labor
Party. This is a ferociously anti-Communist and anti-Socialist
breakaway faction from the Australian Labor Party, and it owes
most of its limited but geographically concentrated popularity to
fervent Roman Catholic support in Victoria. The DLP manages
to elect an occasional senator, but has a considerable influence on
account of its preference votes, and also because its extremism
makes all other right-wing views look acceptable.

From this brief résumé of Australia's political parties it is clear
that there are no deep ideological differences between the major
groups. Of course, various spokesmen for the parties do their best
to tarnish one another with labels such as 'neo-Communists',
'fifth columnists', 'socialists', 'racialists' or 'fascists', but these
have little relevance to the actual policy positions. Despite all the
harsh words, even the fattest stockbrokers in the country sleep

easily in their beds on the night of an Australian General Election, secure in the knowledge that a change of government will not seriously damage their profits. This situation could only change if a radical new leader emerged, for Australian politics are highly pragmatic, and are based on personalities rather than principles. The relationships between these personalities can have traumatic effects on the government. Australia has now been led by five different Prime Ministers in the last five years, even though the Liberal party retained its parliamentary majority throughout that period. Some of these changes at the top were directly attributable to individual rather than to political pressures. Thus in order to understand the changes that are now evolving on the present political scene, it is worth taking a brief look at some of Australia's most prominent politicians—past and present.

SIR ROBERT MENZIES

Sir Robert Menzies is Australia's only internationally recognized political giant. He first became Prime Minister in 1939 at the comparatively tender age of 44, and steered his country through twenty-eight turbulent months of the Second World War. After a period as Leader of the Opposition, he regained the Premiership in 1949 and held it for seventeen unbroken years until his voluntary retirement in 1966 at the age of 71. Such prolonged tenure of a democratic country's highest office is unprecedented in modern times, and it is hardly surprising that the post-war decades in Australia have been dubbed 'The Age of Menzies'.

Now that this age is over, an inevitable degree of reaction has set in. The fashionable view of Menzies today is that he had an antediluvian style of leadership whose hallmark was excessive colonial deference and admiration towards all things British. Certainly Menzies had a near-idolatrous attitude to the Royal Family (he once ended a speech of welcome to the Queen with a quotation from a Herrick love poem 'I do but see her passing by, And yet I love her till I die') and when, towards the end of his career, he became a Scottish Knight of the Thistle and the Warden of Britain's Cinque Ports, many egalitarian Australians saw his acceptance of these feudal trappings on the other side of the world as a risible absurdity. The Age of Menzies, it was said, was also the Age of Kipling—only Kipling had been dead for nearly half a century.

Because of his Kiplingesque style, the placing of Menzies in historical perspective is still difficult. His domination of the Australian political scene sprang from his skill as a speaker, for he could charm a court-room (Menzies was, at 34, the youngest King's Counsel ever appointed), cajole Parliament, and cudgel hecklers on the hustings with a wit and eloquence that would be difficult to hear equalled anywhere in the English-speaking world. This oratorical superiority, together with a ruthless record of suppressing able rivals, was the secret of his long ascendancy. But having got to the top of the greasy pole and remained there for almost two decades, did Menzies achieve anything of lasting value? Perhaps the harshest condemnation of the Menzies era is that most Australians have to think long and hard before they are able to give any answer of substance to that question. Yet although the memorials to Menzies' statecraft are somewhat obscure, they are not so absent as to justify either Donald Horne's popular labelling of the ex-Prime Minister as 'The Great Survivor' or the *bon mot* of Menzies' former parliamentary colleague, W. C. Wentworth, who described his leader in a cruel phrase of legal Latin as 'Vox et praeterea nihil' (a voice and nothing else).

At home, Menzies is revered by the cognoscenti for his far-sighted investment in high-quality university education. At a moment when Britain's university building was totally stagnant, and even US expansion was going ahead comparatively slowly, Menzies in 1949 increased Australia's spending on universities from $16 million to $110 million annually. Although he was criticized for this apparent élitist extravagance at the time, his policy of making the highest standards of graduate education available to large numbers of school-leavers has done more than anything else to bring about the conversion of Australia from a nation of mediocrity to a nation of potential excellence. Certainly Menzies himself feels that his university expansion policy is his finest achievement, and his pride must seem justified to anyone visiting the splendid new academic citadels like Monash near Melbourne or the Australian National University in Canberra.

Apart from his success with universities, Menzies would like to be remembered for his careful free-enterprise husbandry of Australia's economy, and for his enthusiastic support for the transformation of Canberra from bush village to showpiece national capital. He would also like to be regarded by posterity as a successful world statesman, but this claim is far more hotly contested by his critics.

The basis of Menzies' foreign policy was that Australia's interests were entirely linked to those of 'our great and powerful friends'—i.e. Britain and the USA. In the 1940s and early 1950s there was some merit in this approach, but for the last ten years of the age of Menzies it became increasingly clear that the Prime Minister was completely out of touch and sympathy with the smaller 'third world' nations in Australia's immediate region. Although making regular annual pilgrimages to London and Washington, the Prime Minister took very little interest in Asia, visiting Malaysia only twice, and Thailand, the Philippines and Indonesia only once during his entire career—the last of these Asian sorties being in 1959. This lack of sympathy for Australia's near neighbours was considerably resented. Prime Minister Nehru of India launched a fierce attack on Menzies at the United Nations in 1960, declaring his ideas as 'negative, untenable and verging on absurdity'. Several experts have commented that Menzies' total neglect of President Sukarno (who came to power in Indonesia the same month as Menzies came to power in Australia) was an omission which led indirectly to the tragedy of the 'confrontation' war in the early sixties. Other incidents, such as Menzies' 1956 Suez fiasco when he led an abortive mission to persuade Colonel Nasser to give back the canal he had just nationalized, and his 1966 refusal to attend an emergency meeting of Commonwealth Prime Ministers in Lagos to discuss Rhodesia, confirmed the impression that Australia's leader was at odds with the prevailing international pressures of his time. Menzies' standards and sympathies were those of a preceding generation's, and as the years rolled on his Anglo-Saxon attitudes became more fossilized.

From a British point of view, this fossilization made Menzies a wonderful ally. However, even his Anglophilia ran to excess on occasion, such as the time when he tried to christen the Australian dollar 'The Royal', or when he hawked the Governor-Generalship round a number of junior ministers in the British Conservative Government before reluctantly (but far more suitably) offering it to his own ex-cabinet colleague, Lord Casey. Another small incident illustrating his pro-British enthusiasm occurred in the closing months of his premiership when the then British Minister of Aviation, Mr Roy Jenkins, flew to Australia in 1965 to try and boost the export sales of the BAC 1-11 aircraft. This seemed to be a hopeless mission, as Australia's two domestic jet airlines, Ansett and TAA, had already ordered the Douglas DC 9 aircraft, and had declared the BAC 1-11 unsuitable for antipodean conditions. However, Sir Robert Menzies' criteria for purchasing airliners were on quite a different plane. As Roy Jenkins, who had recently published a successful biography of Asquith, entered the Prime Minister's office, Menzies greeted him with the words: 'I'm a great fan of yours. I've just been reading your *Asquith*. What can I do to help you?'

As a result of this literary interview, the Royal Australian Air Force's VIP fleet was equipped with BAC 1-11s.

As a minor personal beneficiary of this Anglophilia, I met Sir Robert Menzies only a few days before his long reign came to an end on an evening which vouchsafed some interesting clues to the character of his leadership and style of government. The occasion was the Prime Minister's 71st birthday party, given on December 20th, 1965 in the US Embassy, Canberra by the then Ambassador 'Cowboy Ed' Clark. 'Cowboy Ed', who before becoming a diplomat had been one of L.B.J.'s big financial backers in Texas, was a host of immense boisterousness and bonhomie. He pinned yellow roses of Texas on the lapels or bosoms of each of his guests, made everyone admire his collection of Texan memorabilia, including an eight-foot-long wristwatch ('jest abaat fits the typical wrist of a maan-sized Texan') and poured out lavish libations of Texan champagne. After a Lucullian banquet of Texan Prime Rib of Beef, we were treated to some Texan Oratory, as Ambassador Clark proposed the toast of the guest of honour, presented a one-candle birthday cake, and led the assembled company in the singing of 'Happy Birthday Prime Minister'. Sir Robert replied to these tributes with gracious eloquence. He extolled the United States of America, and then turning towards the British High Commissioner he was no less fulsome in his compliments to the United Kingdom, combining all the felicitations by suggesting that if these two great powers really got together and co-operated with Australia, there was nothing that the triumvirate of English-speaking peoples could not achieve. The Prime Minister then directed his post-prandial oratory towards Mr Selwyn Lloyd, who was then on a VIP tour of Australia, and sang the former British Foreign Secretary's praises for the courageous and gallant way he had conducted the Suez policy. If the Suez invasion had succeeded, Sir Robert intimated, there would be a lot less international disorder in the world today. With a few side-swipes at the more termagant Black African nations, some reverential references to the Queen and the President of the United States, and a loving tribute to his wife, Dame Pattie, Sir Robert sat down to sustained applause. It had been a gem of a speech, relaxed, witty and at times moving, although no one could say that the Prime Minister was moving with the times.

A few weeks after this occasion, Sir Robert Menzies handed in his voluntary resignation. Perhaps because of his long-standing and ill-disguised contempt for the Australian press, the farewell eulogies to him were somewhat less fulsome than he deserved, but perhaps this balance will be redressed when he finishes the final volumes of his memoirs. Today, Menzies lives in peaceful retirement, dividing his time between his native Victoria and the ceremonial apartments of the Warden of the Cinque Ports in Dover Castle which he dutifully visits every summer. As the acknowledged father of his country he is enjoying the sunset of elder statesmanship, and although some critics wish he had shown a little more political virility towards Asia and certain domestic problems also, the man-in-the-street consensus is that 'Bob's one of the great 'uns.'

LORD CASEY

Another Australian statesman of the Menzies era who deserves classification as 'a great 'un' is Richard Gardiner, 1st Baron Casey. A summary of his career makes Casey sound a distinguished, heroic but conventional establishment figure. In the 1914–18 War, bravery at Gallipoli won him the DSO and MC. In the Second World War he represented Australia in Washington, was Governor of Bengal and sat as a member of Churchill's War Cabinet from 1942–43. During 30 years in Australian politics, Casey held virtually all the major ministerial portfolios, including a decade (1950–60) as Minister for External Affairs. He was elevated to the House of Lords in 1960, but at 75 came back to Canberra in 1965 for three and a half demanding years as the first native-born Governor-General since the reign of King George V.

Baldly stated, this record gives little clue to the originality of approach that Casey has always brought to his high offices. During his 10 years at External Affairs he revolutionized Australian foreign policy by insisting that Australia's destiny was linked more with Asia than with London. Casey made a dozen major tours of Asian countries, formed genuine friendships with Asian political leaders, and published a book on Australia's Asian involvement, *Friends and Neighbours* which caused a significant change in Canberra's official attitudes towards what Australians call 'The Near North'.

Casey's views on Asia were, at the time, regarded by many as slightly eccentric, and he received only lukewarm support for them from his Prime Minister, Sir Robert Menzies. But now the wheel has turned full circle. With White Australianism on the wane (a policy Casey has always opposed), and Australia's major diplomatic involvement now being concentrated on Asia, Casey has the distinction of being a prophet with honour in his own country. He now intends to spend some of his octogenarian years making regular visits to Asia. 'My wife and I know all the leading political figures in Asia pretty well, and we intend to keep this going. We're going next year on a trip through all the capital cities of South East Asia, and I shall also have a try to get into Communist China,' he said in an interview with me in the late summer of 1969.

It is clear from such plans that Casey has lost none of the legendary energy that characterized his 16-hour days as Governor-General. The job of representing the Queen even in such a go-ahead part of the Commonwealth as Australia can easily be a tedious task of empty ceremonial. Lord Casey brought a style and verve to the office which made him the most popular Governor-General of recent times. When the appointment was announced, the *Barrier Miner*, an influential local newspaper in the mining town of Broken Hill, published a letter saying that Casey would be 'a national calamity' as Governor-General because he was a clapped out 75-year-old ex-politician. 'What Australia needs is someone with a bit of go in him,' said the correspondent.

Casey must have taken the advice to heart. He exhausted many an ADC by spending only half of his term of office at his official residence in Canberra. The other half he spent travelling within Australia (he logged 115,000 air miles in 3 years), putting special emphasis on visits to remote parts of the outback, which had shot to prominence as development areas because of new mineral discoveries. On such visits he was often warmly praised for his thoughtful and meticulously researched speeches. 'Every speech I made, and there were at least two a week, took me between five and ten hours to prepare,' he says. 'I could never put over a speech written by someone else. It's like cleaning another person's teeth.'

Casey as Governor-General had a crusty side to him. He refused to have a well-known publisher of a Melbourne newspaper inside Government House on account of the near-pornographic material which kept appearing in the paper. He occasionally criticized his guests for 'mumbling and sloppy diction' (although the fault may

well have been Casey's own partial deafness). He upbraided
Australian editors for not keeping their own permanent correspondents in Asia. Always a relentless interrogator of experts, he
could get distinctly irritable when his questions were inadequately
answered. On one occasion, a government scientist who failed to
come up with the right information when Casey toured Australia's
prawn-fishing centres in the swelteringly hot Gulf of Carpentaria,
was landed with the task of preparing a report on the life-cycle of
the prawn for the Governor-General. Such episodes, and the
hectic pace of Casey's tours, soon dispelled any ideas that a
75-year-old ex-politician hadn't got enough go in him.

The crustiness was offset by welcome touches of informality.
While some Government Houses in the Australian State capitals
still maintain standards of protocol which make Buckingham
Palace look distinctly bourgeois, Casey made some minor relaxations at Canberra, such as ending the walking-out backwards
performance at dinner parties. Lady Casey was particularly skilful
at setting visitors at their ease, so much so that she ended Sir
Francis Chichester's official call at Government House by giving
him a personal haircut with her nail scissors. Above all, the Caseys
widened the scope of those invited to the nation's first official
residence, and enlarged the Governor-General's duties to their
proper constitutional formula 'to advise, to encourage, and to
warn' in all matters from politics to prawning.

Lord Casey's success as Governor-General has had one possible
ironic effect. Because it has now been shown that Australia is able
to produce its own admirable Queen's Man, some observers have
predicted that the day of an Australian Republic and of an
Australian President have moved nearer. Casey disputes this. 'The
idea of a republic is not at any important stage in Australia now,
nor will it be in any measurable period of time. Only a few
unbalanced people talk about it. The position of the monarchy in
Australia was very much strengthened by the visit of Prince
Charles. This was a most successful project. His six months in
Australia did him good and did us good.'

The success of the 1970 Royal Tour has confirmed this state
of affairs, and with the Gallup Poll now showing 68 per cent of
the Australian population in favour of a continued monarchy,
Casey's prediction of the demise of republicanism seems well
vindicated.

Casey today sees Australia as a land of 'almost limitless potential
in its future development and economic wealth.' He will be

spending his retirement (apart from his Asian sorties) amidst this potential on his sheep farm at Berwick, Victoria, only a few miles from the great new Bass Strait offshore oil fields. As a speed enthusiast, he looks forward to driving his Porsche, Mini Cooper S, 18-year-old Bentley and Cessna 180 aircraft, all of which he was prohibited from using while in the office of Governor-General. He plans to edit his diaries of the last 40 years, and to do a considerable amount of reading and writing. His 1969 appointment to Britain's highest honour, the Order of the Garter, came as the crowning accolade of a life already rich in achievement. It is fitting that Australia's first Knight Companion of this 623-year-old Order should so decisively explode the myth of Lord Melbourne's dictum on the Garter that 'There is no damned merit about it.'

HAROLD HOLT

After the retirement of Sir Robert Menzies in January 1966, the first official photographs flashed round the world of Australia's new Prime Minister portrayed a muscular spear-fisherman, clad in goggles, snorkel and a rubber wet-suit, and surrounded by three glamorous models in diminutive bikinis. This was the Rt Honourable Harold Edward Holt relaxing with his daughters-in-law near his summer house on Portsea Beach, Victoria. The most obvious conclusion to be drawn from this new approach to prime-ministerial pictorial presentation was that the Holt style of leadership would be very different from that of the Menzies era.

These differences did not take long to become apparent, particularly in foreign affairs. The first changes concerned Holt's diplomatic initiatives towards Asia (which are discussed at length in Chapter 5) but even in dealings with Australia's 'great and powerful friends' the new Prime Minister seemed at times to be rushing in where Menzies would certainly have hesitated to tread. For not only did Harold Holt become the most idolized disciple of President Johnson for declaring publicly in Washington that he was 'all the way with L.B.J.' on Vietnam, he even flew on to London to give the British Labour Government a fearsome public wigging for their refusal to send troops to Saigon. 'America's critics are being entirely unreasonable . . . You people are coasting on the issue of US action,' were two memorable sentences from Holt's press conference statement at Australia House in July 1966, and he expressed further irritation with the Wilson administration over their restrictions on British investment in Australia and their plans to make a military withdrawal from Singapore. It was the first time in history that such a chastening smack of firm Australian Government had been felt on British bottoms.

Holt's pro-US militancy may have brought him a chilly reception in Whitehall, but it also brought him electoral victory in his own country. Late in 1966 he fought a general election almost exclusively on foreign and defence policies. Military support for America in Vietnam, with a promise of more if necessary, some degree of conscription, and higher taxation to meet the mounting defence bill were the main planks of his campaign speeches. The result of so unflinching a prescription was the largest electoral victory in Australian national politics.

But after this triumph, Holt's star began to wane. In domestic affairs his administration was rocked by a minor scandal involving the use of the RAAF VIP aircraft fleet by ministers for allegedly personal purposes, and a serious backbench revolt forced the government to appoint a Royal Commission into the collision between the destroyer HMAS *Voyager* and the aircraft carrier HMAS *Melbourne*. Holt was thought to have mishandled both these political dramas by trying to be all things to all men. Later in the year the word got round in Canberra that the Prime Minister was neglecting his paperwork, slowing down on decision-making and spending an excessive amount of time with his café society friends. Such criticisms were reflected in the Gallup Polls and in the near-defeat suffered by the government in the 1967 Senate elections. The image of the Prime Minister by December 1967 was that of an amiable and civilized man who did not seem to be quite tough enough for the role of national leadership.

Yet all heads of government have their bad patches, and it can be convincingly argued that Harold Holt's personal diplomacy in Asia, coupled with his determination completely to destroy the White Australia policy (he was Prime Minister when the first substantial relaxations were announced in 1966) might well have paid powerful dividends in world politics. The tragedy is that we shall never know, for when Harold Holt went for his last disastrous swim on December 17th, 1967 and vanished into the high waves off Cheviot Beach many of his policy plans vanished with him. History's verdict on Australia's 18th Prime Minister must thus be an open one, but in personal terms few would disagree with the percipient comment in the London *Times* obituary 'the man's strength and weakness both stemmed from a nature which was unusually agreeable for a politician.'

JOHN McEWEN AND THE WAR OF THE GORTON SUCCESSION

Within a few hours of Harold Holt's disappearance into the sea, a crisis erupted over the succession. Once the evidence conclusively suggested that the Prime Minister must be presumed drowned, the Governor-General, Lord Casey, decided that a new Prime Minister—even if only a temporary one—must be sworn in without delay 'to enable the Government of the Commonwealth to continue without the uncertainties which would otherwise exist.' Lord Casey accordingly sent for Mr John McEwen, Deputy Prime Minister, Trade Minister and leader of the Country Party.

Although 'Black Jack' McEwen had long been acknowledged as the ablest political performer in Australia, many constitutional experts were critical of Lord Casey's choice. They argued that Mr McEwen was only Deputy Prime Minister by virtue of his position as leader of the rapidly deteriorating minority party in the Coalition Government. The obvious rightful heir to the Premiership was the Deputy Leader of the Liberal Party and Federal Treasurer, Mr William McMahon, and this was the man who should there and then have been sworn in as Australia's 18th Prime Minister.

The Governor-General's preference for Mr McEwen rather than Mr McMahon has never been satisfactorily explained. In an interview with me in London two years after the event, Lord Casey said, 'I did what I believed was right for Australia and that is all I am going to say about it.' Investigations by political reporters at the time, notably by Alan Reid (whose admirable book *The Power Struggle* is the definitive work on this tortuous saga), showed that Lord Casey had been deeply concerned for some time over the apparent rift between McMahon and McEwen. This had been going on for several months, originating in political differences over trade and economic policies, but embittered by personal feuding over alleged leaks from Mr McMahon to the Canberra journalist, Max Newton. Lord Casey apparently took McEwen's side in the quarrel, and this is thought to be the reason why McMahon was not sent for and sworn in as Prime Minister on December 19th, 1967. Instead, McEwen was sworn in on a temporary basis until the Liberals had decided who they wanted as leader.

Within a few hours of Mr McEwen assuming the acting Prime

Ministership, he let his attitude to McMahon be known on the political and journalistic grapevine. Two days later, Mr McEwen gave his first and only Press Conference as Prime Minister.

The first question was: 'Are you prepared to say publicly, as you have apparently said privately, that you will not accept Mr McMahon as a Prime Minister, as Leader of the Liberal Party?'

Then in one of the most dramatic statements ever uttered in Australian political history Mr McEwen replied: 'Yes, I say to you that I have told Mr McMahon that neither I nor my Country Party colleagues would be prepared to serve under him as Prime Minister. Mr McMahon knows the reason. My senior Liberal Party colleagues not only know the reason, but knew the reasons before Mr Holt's death.'

The Acting Prime Minister's unexpected announcement caused great fury and indignation in the McMahon camp. The McEwen veto, which appeared to be a personal vendetta, meant that under no circumstances could the Coalition Government continue if McMahon was elected leader of the Liberal Party. As an act of retaliation, McMahon's supporters squashed the suggestion that McEwen should continue in office permanently as joint leader of the Liberal and Country Parties. Thus with the two most experienced and able men in the government completely at loggerheads, a compromise candidate had to be found. John Gorton at the time was a little-known Senator, but he ran a brilliant lobbying campaign and on January 8th, 1968, was elected the new Leader of the Liberal Party and Prime Minister.

The preceding narrative is important because the stormy events around the New Year of 1968 left traces of bitterness and enmity which were not purged until March 1971. Neither Mr McMahon nor Mr McEwen settled happily under John Gorton's leadership. They continued to scrap against each other over trade policies until Mr McMahon went from the Treasury to the Department of External Affairs in 1969. Both men challenged the authority of Prime Minister Gorton on certain policy issues, and they both on occasion did considerable harm to their leader by mildly disloyal acts of indiscretion. Mr McMahon made a direct personal assault on the Prime Minister by unsuccessfully contesting the leadership of the Liberal Party immediately after the 1969 General Election. Mr McEwen, until his retirement with a knighthood in 1970, became more and more critical of John Gorton, both in public and in private. With these three prima donnas of the coalition noticeably out of harmony, the increasingly comic opera of the

Gorton government lurched uncertainly onwards until it was ended when the Prime Minister skidded on his own political banana skin in early 1971.

JOHN GORTON

John Grey Gorton's thirty-eight months as Prime Minister gave Australia an erratic, unconventional, and at times eccentric period of government. Now that he has been deposed it is fashionable to say that Gorton should never have been his country's leader at all, but this view underestimates the highly beneficial social and psychological effects of his innovations.

The most striking characteristic of John Gorton was his individualism. Never before had an Australian Prime Minister set such a personal stamp on the conduct of government and as a result never before did an Australian Prime Minister come in for so much personalized comment and criticism.

When discussing Gorton with his own political supporters, the word they most frequently used to describe their leader was 'arrogant'. This harsh epithet resulted from numerous instances, notably over defence policy, foreign take-overs and states right, when Ministers were left to discover startling new developments and reversal in government policy by reading in the newspapers what the Prime Minister had been saying. Frequently these headlined thoughts of Chairman John had little or no relevance to the actual outcome of what the government did, but to have the head of government indulging in the activities of a verbal grasshopper was unsettling to many established Liberal supporters. As *The Bulletin* commented in an editorial fifteen months after Harold Holt's death: 'The Gorton style is characterized by an unpredictable tendency to speak out first and do the thinking later . . . Mr Gorton is temperamentally inclined to give things a burl off the cuff. He lets fly with a pronouncement of his inclination. He comes out publicly or semi-publicly with whatever propositions come to his mind. Where most politicians would get someone else to fly their trial balloons, Mr Gorton flies them himself.'

To some observers, the most unacceptable aspect of this style of government was that John Gorton did not regard himself as a trial balloonist, nor indeed did he ever regard the job of Prime Minister in its traditional concept of a 'first among equals'. Gorton clearly believed that Australia needed a form of presidential government, and he went to considerable lengths to establish himself as the unquestioned and unquestionable arbiter of the nation's destinies. His attitude to Cabinet government, which many of his Ministers found overbearing, was summed up by his own revealing comment: 'The Prime Minister should put to the Cabinet what he believes should be done, and if he believes strongly enough that it ought to be done, then it must be done.'

Another important indication of Gorton's enthusiasm for presidential government was his reorganization of the Prime Minister's Office along personal choice lines. Refusing to accept most of this department's civil servants when he first took over from Holt, Gorton shifted them to other ministries and installed his own team of hand-picked advisers, headed by his close friend, Mr Len Hewitt. This team intervened in other departments on an unprecedented scale, very much as the White House intervenes in and dominates Washington's departments of state on behalf of the US President. Nevertheless, enormous resentment was felt by Australian Ministers and Ministries at this new kind of direct control from the Prime Minister's department.

The main result of this more presidential form of Australian Government was the increased public attention to the personality of the national leader. In particular, John Gorton's private life came in for some close and rather unfavourable scrutiny. This was perhaps inevitable with a Prime Minister who openly admitted to being 'a bit of a larrikin' (strine for 'rascal'), loved parties, adored his beer, and enjoyed chatting up a pretty girl, yet whatever the alleged incidents and irregularities may have been, they certainly did not justify the vicious personal attacks that were made on him from some quarters. At one time the Prime Minister was under such heavy fire from puritanical critics that his American-born wife, Bettina, made a direct retaliation on the principal anti-Gorton spokesman, Mr Edward St John, then a Liberal backbencher. Mrs Gorton publicly quoted some lines from a poem *The Serpent's Tongue* by Sir William Watson in answer to some published rumours about the Prime Minister and a girl journalist at a US embassy party:

> The haggard cheek, the hungering eye,
> The poisoned words that wildly fly,
> The famished face, the fevered hand
> Who slights the worthiest in the land,
> Sneers at the just, condemns the brave,
> And blackens goodness in its grave.

The main effect of this quotation was to excite world-wide interest in Canberra's alleged scandals which, even if they were all true, would hardly raise an eyebrow in other national capitals. Not for nothing is Australia the land of 'the wowsers' (see Chapter 10) and in such an environment the freewheeling John Gorton had an unusually rough personal ride.

Yet despite all the hullaballoo about the ex-Prime Minister's private and public style, he is most likely to be remembered for his policy innovations.

John Gorton was something of a social reformer. He held strong, compassionate views on the need to improve Australia's meagre social services. He favoured giving handsome government sub-sidies to the arts. He was reluctant to increase defence spending. He wanted to reform the inequitable tax system which penalized the middle-income earners. An ardent nationalist by conviction, Gorton liked to present himself as a fair dinkum cobber who was bloody proud of Australia and Australian values even to the point of restricting the inflow of foreign capital and replacing *God Save the Queen* with *Waltzing Matilda*.

Although these innovations (most of which were never im-plemented anyway) do not sound earthshaking to outsiders, they certainly shook the Liberal Party. But as the rumbles of his sup-porters' discontent became more and more audible, John Gorton remained very much the cat who walked by himself. He was paranoically sensitive to criticism (he once suggested the CIA were trying to smear him), yet spurned the counsel of his Cabinet colleagues, and made little effort either to placate enemies or to win new friends. This form of isolation has not abated the attacks from his own right wing (who suspect Gorton of being a creeping Socialist), from Liberal Party constitutionalists (who dislike the shift towards Presidential government), from anti-Vietnam crusaders, from wowsers, and from the Labor opposition. In short, John Gorton was the most criticized leader Australia has ever had.

At the last election, this criticism rebounded badly. Despite a booming economy and no serious clouds on Australia's inter-national horizons, the Liberal-Country Party Coalition Govern-ment saw its solid majority of 38 washed away to a hairline 7. Even this Pyrrhic victory would not have been achieved without the complex system of preferences which made second votes swing to the Liberals from the defeated extreme right-wing candidates of the Democratic Labor Party.

The blame for this Liberal collapse was well and truly nailed to John Gorton, and rightly so, for he had conducted a presidential campaign based mainly on television, highlighting his own personal qualities. When the end result was shown to be an 8 per cent swing away from the Liberals, the Prime Minister had to fight off an immediate leadership challenge from his arch rival and Deputy Leader, William McMahon.

Although this particular onslaught failed, it was the first of many Gorton-must-go moves. These grew more formidable after the Liberals had made another dismal showing at the polls in the 1970 Senate elections. With the discontent being fanned by an increasingly critical press it seemed only a matter of time before the leadership changed hands, though when the actual crunch came in March 1971, the episode had a touch of farce about it.

The dismissal saga began when the Prime Minister was interviewed by an eminent political journalist, Mr Alan Ramsey of the *Australian*. During this interview, Mr Ramsey asked whether there was any truth in a story he had unearthed to the effect that a senior army general had complained to the Prime Minister about the Defence Minister. Mr Gorton refused to confirm or deny this story, thereby tacitly acknowledging its accuracy. The *Australian* not unnaturally splashed the story the following day whereupon the Defence Minister, Mr Malcolm Fraser (who at 40 was the rising star of the administration), promptly resigned. He accused his chief of gross disloyalty and added, 'He is not fit to hold the great office of Prime Minister.'

Faced with a subsequent Parliamentary uproar, Mr Gorton gave his version of what he had said to the *Australian*. In the middle of this account, Mr Alan Ramsey yelled from the gallery, 'You lie!' before being ejected. The next day at a private party caucus meeting, Liberal members of the House of Representatives voted 33–33 on a motion of no confidence in the Prime Minister, whereupon John Gorton promptly gave his casting vote against himself and resigned.

Perhaps it was a little unfair that this last incident, or even the sum total of previous incidents, should have brought down a Prime Minister. The underlying reasons for political changes in Australia are much more to be found in the excessively long reign of the Liberal Party and in the national rise of critical self-awareness, rather than in any one individual's faults and failings. Yet John Gorton had wanted to run a one-man band, so perhaps he did not have too much to complain about when his political music proved unacceptable.

BILLY McMAHON

John Gorton's successor as Prime Minister of Australia, 63-year-old William McMahon, is undoubtedly the most professional politician yet to hold his country's highest office. Every job he has ever held in government has been performed with unusual skill and dedication. His only failure is that he has never been too popular with his colleagues.

A Sydney lawyer of renowned application and talent, Billy McMahon entered Parliament in 1949. Although actively disliked by Prime Minister Robert Menzies, McMahon's ability was too great for him to be excluded from the Ministry, and he held the successive portfolios of Navy, Primary Industry and Labour. When Harold Holt became the new leader, McMahon's star was very much in the ascendant.

As Treasurer (Minister of Finance), he guided the economy through years of both boom and recession with much-applauded skill. After the McEwen-Gorton imbroglio had denied him the leadership following Holt's drowning, McMahon continued with somewhat emasculated powers as Treasurer, then moved to the Department of External Affairs where he concentrated on internal executive reforms while foreign policy was changed weekly by the obiter dicta of John Gorton.

Billy McMahon made his ministerial reputation as an outstanding administrator in the McNamara mould. He works a regular 16-hour day, has a tendency to exhaust civil servants, and is a stickler for attending to detail. He used to be a rather lonely man, having been brought up as an only child by relatives after the death of both his parents in his infancy. But at 58 he shed some of this austere image when he married one of the most beautiful models in Sydney. Matrimony appears to have made him more amiable and more indiscreet. He has long been renowned for making highly diverting private comments about the failings of his fellow Ministers, a habit which endears him to his audiences if not to his colleagues.

It is too early, at the time of writing, to say what sort of Prime Minister Billy McMahon will turn out to be. All that is certain is that he will be totally different from John Gorton, probably more conservative, more clinical, and much more clever in his handling of men and events. McMahon is the nearest thing in Australian politics to an intellectual. He has profound views on the direction in which society ought to be going, and the world can look forward to some interesting surprises in Australia's foreign and economic policy if he gets firmly in control. But until the 1972 elections Billy McMahon will be concentrating more on politics than on statesmanship, and in this role one can expect him to put up a characteristically professional performance.

GOUGH WHITLAM

Billy McMahon's opponent in the Australian political power struggle will be Mr Gough Whitlam, leader of the Federal Opposition, the Australian Labor Party. His troops have been in the wilderness since 1949, but thanks to Whitlam's leadership in the last election and the disarray of the Liberals under Gorton, Australia's political soothsayers are now tentatively predicting a Labor victory at the 1972 polls. Since the ALP has in its 22 years of exile built up a legendary reputation for snatching defeat from the jaws of victory, its performance next time is very much in the hands of its newly arisen leader.

Son of a solicitor, himself a barrister, and married to the daughter of a judge, there is nothing in Gough Whitlam's sober legal background to suggest that he might turn out to be one of the most tempestuous figures in Federal politics. But beneath those elegant pin-stripe suits, immaculately polished shoes and pointed silk pocket handkerchiefs there beats a passionate heart with a fiery temper. In the days when Gough Whitlam was the up-and-coming Deputy Leader of the ALP he was notorious for handing out the rough stuff. During one Parliamentary debate in 1965 he threw a glass of water over the Minister of External Affairs. On another occasion he called the Chief Justice 'a bumptious bastard', and at various times he has not shrunk from publicly describing his ministerial opponents by such epithets as 'lackey', 'liar' and 'queen'. Evidently Gough Whitlam has no inhibitions about using unparliamentary language, for he is reputed to have used even rougher words about his former boss and ALP Opposition Leader, Mr Arthur Calwell, who was eventually overthrown in 1969.

But since he took command of his party Gough Whitlam has mellowed. After intensive tuition in all the arts of modern political leadership, such as TV image-presentation, he fought a superlative campaign in the General Election of 1969 achieving an 8 per cent pro-Labor swing which brought him within a whisker of deposing the Liberals. Much of the credit for this success went personally to Whitlam, who was universally acknowledged to have outpointed John Gorton in every facet of electioneering. Indeed, the somewhat irrational factor which was thought to have prevented Whitlam from becoming the new tenant of Canberra's Lodge was the deep inbred suspicion on the part of the older members of Australia's electorate that the Labor Party was full of Communists and fellow-travellers. A decade ago, the Parliamentarians in the ALP tended to be such obscure neanderthal figures that they could have been anything, but out of today's 59 Labor Members of the House of Representatives 28 are newcomers brought into politics by Whitlam since 1969, and this intake (which includes ex-army officers, ex-diplomats, farmers and university lecturers) has freed the ALP of its extreme left working-class image and provided a much-needed pool of talent for future ministerial appointments.

If the ALP does become the next government of Australia under Prime Minister Gough Whitlam, what sort of changes can be expected? Domestically, the answer is almost no changes worth talking about, for the ALP is not a fierce socialist carnivore sharpening its teeth and claws for an assault on the commanding heights of the liberal-run economy; it could more accurately be compared to a friendly sheep dog whose policy is to keep the *laissez-faire* capitalists in vague order with a few gentle nips and nudges. At a London Press Conference at Canberra House in July 1970, Whitlam reflected this soft approach when he was asked what were the major socialist reforms he would introduce as Prime Minister. His reply was a dreary recitation of the drainage statistics in Australia, which he said proved that Perth and Brisbane were the least sewered cities in the world. After more of this sanitary inspector's lament, the Leader of the Opposition declared: 'We are the only Party in Australia that will ever reform this situation. Sewers are usually socialist!'

Perhaps it is a little unfair to quote this one reply to a reporter's question, for Whitlam has demonstrated some real concern for social justice in his campaigns. In particular, he wishes to spend more money on state education and to reform the Health Services. 'Why should Australia be the only country in the world where the rich pay less for their health schemes than the poor, and where those who do not belong to any scheme get almost nothing?' he asks. A Whitlam government would probably bring in a capital gains tax (ironically, a popular move with stockbrokers, who are fed up with being taxed at the top income-tax rates of 66 per cent as traders), improve housing subsidies slightly and increase old-age pensions, but these are all minor adjustments rather than radical changes. The one political field where Whitlam's philosophy does reveal flashes of radicalism is in foreign policy—although there are great areas of unawareness in some of his attitudes to contemporary problems. At the above-mentioned July 1970 Press Conference in London, Whitlam staggered the assembled reporters by his refusal to make any comment on the ALP's attitude to the Common Market negotiations, to British arms sales to South Africa, or to the future of the five-power force in Malaysia–Singapore. As the correspondents summoned to this non-conference grew restless, Whitlam attributed his silence to the protocols of statesmanlike discretion, but a probing interrogation soon revealed that the Opposition Leader's reluctance to comment sprang from ignorance as much as from intransigence. For instance, he clearly had no idea that Britain had re-applied for admission to the Common Market in 1969, and kept replying to questions on Australia's attitudes with puzzled references to the 1962 negotiations. The same fog of oblivion shrouded his views on the defence of Malaysia–Singapore, for he appeared to have no comprehension of Britain's present and future contribution to the Australian-backed five-power force. As for arms sales to South Africa, Whitlam's stonewalling statesman posture eventually slipped a little when he was provoked into a violent attack on the 'disgraceful racialist policies' of Rhodesia and South Africa. With mounting moral indignation he denounced the Australian Government's support of the Smith régime, declared that a government under his leadership would revoke the passports of Australian citizens in Rhodesia, castigated apartheid and land apportionment, but ended by saying he would not like to commit himself on whether it was right or wrong to sell arms to the Vorster government. The only foreign policy subject of which he showed a complete grasp was Vietnam, where he cogently explained his Party's reasons for favouring total Australian troop withdrawals within a few months.

In many ways this press conference provided some highly revealing indications of Whitlam's style of leadership, for it was difficult to avoid the conclusion that this handsome ex-barrister is more concerned with form than with substance. On the surface Whitlam looks and sounds good, and he knows how to master the TV media, but after listening to him perform under pressure, one is forced to think of him as something of a political lightweight with a tendency to get easily rattled. This will not stop him from achieving power in Australia, for he has a certain charisma based on his ability to present himself in a down-to-earth matey manner which goes over well even when he is following his penchant for saying nothing. It may well be that when Whitlam reaches the Lodge and is flanked by able advisers (not least of whom will be his highly intelligent wife, Margaret) his present gloss of super-ficial shallowness may deepen into a more profound and sub-stantial Prime Ministerial performance. But on present evidence, Gough Whitlam appears to be the kind of politician who, in today's English-speaking world, could only be thought of as a national leader in Australia, and could only become leader there if John Gorton was his opponent.

STATES RIGHTS

One complex but emotive Australian political issue which Gough Whitlam has skilfully exploited is the growing controversy over states rights. Summarized briefly, it can be said that Australia's six federal states are now rather ineffectively struggling for economic power against the central government in Canberra, much in the same way that the American and Canadian states struggled against their respective central governments in Wash-ington and Ottawa during previous eras. Gough Whitlam sees the present Australian situation as 'our greatest controversy since the days of the depression' and promises that 'The Labor Party is prepared to use the machinery of other federal systems to give the states their rights.' John Gorton, for all his polite disclaimers, is an out-and-out centralist.

In reality, the row about states rights is something of a phantom controversy, for the real issue of who controls the cash flow was decided long ago in Canberra's favour. Under the constitution, the states have no adequate powers of direct taxation of their own, but are required to come cap in hand to the Federal Treasurer (Minister of Finance) for their most vital funds. Whether the states return from Canberra with their caps empty, half full, or overloaded, the cries of protest and disappointment are always more or less the same, for no local politician is ever going to miss the opportunity of blaming the big bureaucrats 'down south', 'back east' or 'up north' for withholding the funds for projects which their constituents want.

Yet although the power struggle between the states and Canberra is in fact more honoured in the breach than the observance, nevertheless it would be wrong to see the conflict entirely in terms of parish-pump cheer-leaders hopelessly outflanked by powerful federal statesmen. For one thing unpopularity in the states can mean defeat at the federal by-elections, or even general elections. But even more important than this ultimate electoral deterrent are the pressures put on the central government by individual ministers from the states. Sometimes these states politicians are far more effective than their federal counterparts and their achievements in getting their own way are correspondingly more successful.

CHARLES COURT

As far as the states are concerned, the most impressive political figure in Australia is 50-year-old Mr Charles Court, Western Australia's legendary Minister for Industrial Development. Since he came into office in 1959, Court has been personally responsible for every major mineral and industrial development in the West, which means that he has guided and often negotiated the contracts for more than $1,200 million worth of capital investment into what was once known as 'the Cinderella State'. At the beginning of his Ministerial career, Court found it difficult to persuade overseas tycoons that a trip to Perth would be worth their while. He likes to recall his early technique of giving handsome tips to the switchboard operators in Sydney's leading hotels so that whenever an important international company chairman flew in from Britain or America, within seconds of his arrival in his room there would be a telephone call from Perth with Court saying 'Welcome to Australia. This is the Minister for Industrial Development of Western Australia speaking. I'd like to invite you to come over and see the investment opportunities in our state.' This approach sometimes worked wonders, but it is no longer necessary, for the West's 1970s 'everything rush' has brought the top magnates of world industry beating a path to Court's door.

This new influx of powerful overseas giants willing to invest millions in return for a share of the continent's mineral wealth has placed Charles Court in one of the most sensitive political jobs in Australia. Faced on one side by idealistic nationalists who protest whenever a foreign company takes a spadeful of raw material away from Australia, and on the other by avaricious developers who want the fastest possible gain for their money whatever the terms of the deal, Court has evolved a far-sighted philosophy for the development of his state's natural resources: 'we're after industries, not mines. Our objective in this generation is to reach the stage where we export metal instead of untreated ore. Already we're achieving this. For instance, Western Australia exports no bauxite at all. We process it, and sell it off as alumina, and the gain to us is staggering. $5 million worth of raw bauxite when treated sells off for $60 million worth of alumina. We want to do this throughout all our minerals, particularly to export steel instead of iron ore. With this in mind, the investors we're after most are the big men who are prepared to include as part of their investment a highly sophisticated metallurgical and industrial programme. I have seen to it that every major iron producer has written into his contract the obligation to install processing facilities at his mine or port of shipment which in 20 years' time will give us a full-scale steel industry. Some people say this is a risky course and that we'll become someone else's economic colony, but I think this is rubbish. The choice is between going slow and being frightened of the big fellows, or going fast and putting the big fellows to work for us. It's like having a good horse—ride him hard and he'll take you a long way fast. In my view, if Australian development is allowed to advance without restrictions from pseudo-nationalists, then in a generation's time we will be so strong economically that overseas funds won't mean a thing.'

Court's cutting reference to 'pseudo-nationalists' is aimed at certain Federal politicians, particularly Prime Minister John Gorton, who have aired some rather vaguely expressed political doubts about the wisdom of allowing the continent's resources to be developed by outside interests at the present rate. Such doubts have, on occasion, led Canberra to intervene in deals between Japanese and Australian consortia, a degree of interference which Court has always vehemently opposed. For example, when Canberra abrogated an early Hamersley iron contract, Court issued a statement saying, 'They not only want to umpire the game—they want to take part and change the rules as they go along.'

Such comments have not improved the personal popularity of Western Australia's Minister for Industrial Development in central government circles, but Court is a tough in-fighter who reckons he knows what's best for his own state, and doesn't give

a damn about his critics. Son of a plumber who emigrated from
Britain, Charlie Court started out in life as a professional cornet
player, earning enough money from his wages in an orchestra to
put himself through night school on a course in chartered
accountancy. On qualifying, he set up his own business and made
himself a modest fortune before entering politics. He has held
only one job in government, having steadily refused all offers of
preferment within the State or in Federal politics, and also all
enticements towards personal wealth through proffered director-
ships. A dynamo of energy, Court rises each day at 5.30 a.m. and
is frequently to be found working in his office after midnight. He
makes harsh demands on his staff, suffers fools badly, and can be
so arrogant that one of his colleagues wryly used on him a phrase
originally applied to Churchill: 'On the crest of a wave, Charlie
Court has in him the stuff of which tyrants are made.'

The forcefulness of his character has certainly made Court the
dominant figure both in shaping Western Australia's destiny, and
in challenging the right of the central government to control states
expenditure. His domination is guided by a clear, and perhaps
even great vision, for Court has a passionate faith in the creed of
opening up Western Australia's wildernesses, despite the extra
cost. As he puts it: 'More and more we must put our money into
things that are permanent. All minerals are ultimately expendable.
Communities, industries, roads and farms are lasting. That's why,
in the long run, schemes like the Ord River irrigation project are
the most rewarding of all, even though they are the hardest and
the most expensive. By 1980 we will have twelve irrigation projects
across the Kimberleys, creating a large farming community up
there and bringing a dead land alive. It's to achieve results like
this that we're now spending 26 per cent of the state's budget on
an area where 2·7 per cent of the population lives. No centralized
government would do such a thing, but here we're still able to do
it, because we reckon our priorities are right for Australia and for
Western Australia.'

Although there are a few figures of Charles Court's stature in
state or federal politics, they are hard to find. Mr Don Dunstan,
the young Labour Premier of South Australia, stands out as one
exceptional state leader, while the prize for cunning longevity
must go to Sir Henry Bolte who has led Victoria for nearly 15
years without a break. Nevertheless, apart from these and a handful
of other exceptions, Australia's big men seem to be woefully absent
from Australia's politics.

10

OLD-FASHIONED AUSTRALIA

THE ADELAIDE CLUB

At 165 North Terrace, Adelaide, stands a grey stone building with green cedar shutters and a brass plaque by the door inscribed 'Non-members please ring bell.' This is the Adelaide Club, by no means the last, but certainly the most formidable bastion of Queen Victoria's Australia.

The non-member who rings the bell and satisfies the suspicious major-domo that he has bona fide reasons for admittance enters a world that makes him feel like a Rip Van Winkle in reverse. The décor of the club appears to date back to its foundation in 1863, for the imposingly pillared entrance hall is hung with stags' heads, crossed swords, suits of armour and the skin of a tiger shot in India by a club member called 'Tiger Smith'. Sombre oak panelling and faded leather armchairs set the tone of the atmos-phere, and the only concessions to modernity are a portrait of the Queen in her coronation robes and a signed photograph of Field-Marshal Lord Montgomery, who stayed in the club in 1952.

Groucho 'who wants to join a club that would let in someone like me?' Marx would approve of this august institution. Although the membership list runs to 500 names (and the Governor of South Australia always gets made an honorary member) the Adelaide Club is famous for the severity of its exclusions. Geoffrey Dutton, a wealthy South Australian landowner, publisher and author was asked for his resignation (he gave it) when it was discovered he had committed the heinous crime of editing a paperback book of essays suggesting that Australia should replace the Monarchy with a Republic. The State's long-serving Liberal Premier, Sir Thomas Playford, was regularly excluded, according to him because 'I was considered much too socialistic. There wouldn't have been enough blackballs in the Adelaide Club for me.' There are several other powerful men in South Australia who express strong resentment at being rejected by the club, and even at having their expected rewards in honours lists blocked by an imagined conspiracy of jealous club members for reasons which they believe to be based on political, social or religious discrimination.

When I visited the Adelaide Club there was nothing to suggest that the members were worried by this resentment of excluded outsiders. My hosts were a group of the most venerable pillars of the Adelaide establishment, so venerable, in fact, that at 25 I was 41 years younger than the junior member present at the table, and 69 years younger than the most senior. Not that their age was in any way wearying them, for during a gargantuan meal which they tackled with the gusto of ravenous schoolboys they enthusiastically eulogized all the club's customs and traditions. Club servants always wear their military decorations, and never ask members to sign for their drinks; members usually wear regimental or old school ties, are expected to drink the loyal toast with the club cocktail (a lethal mixture of gin and curaçao) and occasionally to take snuff after meals; although overseas and out-of-state visitors are acceptable as guests of members, it is greatly frowned upon if a non-member from South Australia is brought into the club; most bizarre of all, ginger biscuits are served to the particular group of members who were entertaining me at the end of their lunch each day in memory of a deceased member who ate at their table for 20 years and was noted chiefly for his consumption of ginger biscuits.

After observing a reverential silence during the ginger-biscuit-munching ceremony, I put a few reporter's questions to the assembled company.

What were the most important developments now happening in Adelaide and South Australia?

'The best thing about this part of the world is that there aren't any of these wildcat development schemes you hear about in the west and back east. We take immense pride in the fact that things are quiet and peaceful here.'

Hadn't Australia's big mineral boom affected South Australia at all?

'What mineral boom? There aren't any more mineral finds than there were 20 years ago. This boom nonsense is all got up by the Press.'

What did they feel about the power struggle in South Australian politics? (At the time, the State Liberal government had a majority of one and seemed likely to fall over the Chowilla dam project controversy.)

'The forces of commonsense will soon quieten things down. This boy Dunstan (the 46-year-old Labor Opposition Leader, now Premier) is a menace. But he'll get nowhere.'

After much more in this vein, I finally put a question designed to stimulate a less complacent type of response.

'Several people have said to me that the Adelaide establishment in general, and this club in particular, is ruled by extremely conservative old families with strong prejudices about politics, religion and class, who do their best to keep everyone else down. What is your reply to such criticisms?'

Sir Lloyd Dumas, the 80-year-old chairman of the *Adelaide Advertiser*, who had been presiding over our lunch-table, raised his glass of cognac to the sunlight. 'Jealousy, pure jealousy,' he murmured. 'This is the best club in the world, and Adelaide is the best place to live in the world.' And with those words of wisdom, my lunch at the Adelaide Club ended.

It would perhaps be unfair to write at such length about the Adelaide Club but for the fact that its style is characteristic of an influential section of the Australian establishment. As Donald Horne has written in *The Lucky Country* in his chapter on Australian Industry: 'Those at the top (some of them are very old) instinctively resist the creation of what might finally prove to be a victorious new social class.'

The cliché that Australia is a young man's country is so implanted into the national and international consciousness that it comes as quite a shock to find the old men of Australia so firmly installed in so many saddles. A recent survey among a cross-section of public companies quoted on the Melbourne stock exchange revealed that two-thirds of the directors of the companies concerned were over the age of 60. As a young reporter I was constantly amazed by the number of septuagenarians and even octogenarians holding demanding jobs in high places, and was correspondingly surprised by the apparent dearth of bright young whizz-kids holding positions of responsibility.

This situation is inevitably changing, but the pace of change is being forced by young Turk entrepreneurs who start up their own businesses, rather than by enlightened promotion systems inside the big companies. Perhaps the Australian philosophy of 'Fair Go Mate' demands that young men rise slowly by the rule of Buggins' Turn; perhaps the Japanese system of *'nenko'* (promotion exclusively according to seniority) has spread southwards across the Coral Sea; or perhaps the Australian young are so busy enjoying their salad days on the beaches that they are content to leave the top jobs to the older generation and wait their turn. The effect of the Australian climate on Australian ambition should never be underestimated.

Whatever the explanation, no one can doubt that Australian business and social life provides limitless opportunities—for the old and for the old-fashioned. Those who search for reasons why large parts of Australia's economic, industrial, social and political affairs are still lagging behind their equivalents in other countries will find some of the answers within the four walls of the Adelaide Club and its counterparts.

MATRONS, DÉBUTANTES AND THE SQUATOCRACY

Australian social life in its upper echelons can still be surprisingly old-fashioned. One evening I was bidden to the Royal Sydney Golf Club (waiting list 10 years long; establishment prestige 10 miles high) to attend 'The Matrons Ball'—a function which takes place every April 'to introduce the country girls to the Sydney boys', as my hostess explained.

I had visions of a swinging rave-up between jolly apple-cheeked farmers' daughters and urbane young Pitt Street stockbrokers, but the reality proved more strait-laced than London's Queen Charlotte's Ball in the days of good Queen Charlotte. All the country girls were attired in long white gloves and full-length white silk gowns, which somehow gave them the appearance of lambs dressed up as mutton. In this garb they were sartorially indistinguishable from the formidable herd of senior matrons, who stood in a long receiving line for the presentation of the guests, and thereafter stationed themselves like sentries at fixed points on the edge of the dance floor, keeping eagle-eyed vigil over the activities of their rural protégées. Not that there was anything much going on to be vigilant about, since every ball-goer had been issued with a printed programme which he or she was required to fill in with the name of a partner for each of the twelve dances. The word had come down from the Head Matron that it would be bad form for anyone to have more than two dances with the same partner, so this antediluvian programme system (last heard of in pre-war days in England, except at the occasional Hunt Ball in the more feudal shires) certainly had the effect of preventing any promising friendship from blossoming into romance. The music also contributed to the atmosphere of dowagerian starchiness, for although there was an encouragingly hirsute group of rock merchants called the Ricochets, every time they struck a note that might have raised an eyebrow of recognition from Elvis Presley's grandfather, an assistant matron rushed over to demand that the next tune should be something akin to Sir Roger de Coverly or the Blue Danube.

My own most vivid recollection of the evening was foxtrotting (or was it minuetting?) with a pastoralist's daughter from Queensland who described her previous season as a débutante in Brisbane's high society. She explained that the season had not been too much of a success because there had been a distinct shortage of both suitable débutantes and escorts in Brisbane that year, but anyway she herself had resigned from the scene in protest after an attempt had been made to remedy the shortage by putting the following advertisement in the Brisbane *Courier-Mail*: 'Any Débutantes wishing to be presented to the Minister of Tourism at the Débutantes' Ball please get in touch with the Ball secretary.' As my partner put it, 'What's the point of being a débutante if it's that easy? My mother said I should come to Sydney where they know about things like presentations.'

A few days later I met Lady Kitto, the wife of a senior New South Wales judge, who told me a story that might have shaken the retired Brisbane débutante's faith in Sydney's social omniscience. Lady Kitto had been rung up and asked if she would take the presentation of Sydney's débutantes at a ball. When she declined, the caller said hopefully, 'Do you by any chance know another titled lady who might deputize?'

But snobbery of this kind is not characteristic of Australian life. Such pockets of it as exist are to be found mainly among the class known as 'the squatocracy', a well-heeled amalgam of graziers, landowners and pastoralists. By virtue of the number of acres they hold, and the number of years their families have owned them, members of the squatocracy tend to consider themselves something of a race apart. They are apt to look down both on the brash vulgarity of the nouveau-riche city-dwellers, and also on the hayseed simplicity of their fellow country-dwellers, the farmers (the difference between a farmer and a pastoralist or grazier is about a thousand acres), whom they derisively refer to as 'cockies'.

Living in large rambling houses (there is a memorably unlovely type of architecture known as 'Graziers' Gothic'), surrounded by semi-feudal courts of station hands, workers, jackeroos (young apprentices who live with the family) and impoverished relations, some squatocratic families seem to be deliberately parodying the dynastic chronicles of celebrated fictional tribes such as the Forsytes or the Whiteoaks of Jalna. The self-ascribed social prestige of these 'kings in grass castles', as one Australian author has dubbed them, dates back to the days when Australia's wealth was exclusively based on agriculture, thereby giving special importance to those who held title to vast tracts of land. Unfortunately, as sometimes happens in other parts of the world, Australia's broad acres are often owned by narrow minds, and many of the older pastoralists and graziers have not yet woken up to the fact that far greater financial and social success is now being achieved by those who lead Australia's worlds of mining, industry and finance. Indeed, even the properties of many members of the old-time squatocracy look somewhat inefficient and ramshackle compared to those of the 'Pitt Street Farmers'—investors who use their stock-exchange profits to buy land and are quick to make their managers implement all the latest and most lucrative techniques to improve agricultural productivity.

In short, one way and another, the squatocracy is very much a vanishing class. Yet the breed is taking an unconscionable time a-dying, and it shores itself up by continuing to indulge in these antiquated charades of débutante presentations and Matrons' Balls in the cities, while maintaining its own brand of condescending paternalism on country properties.

Although such nineteenth-century snobberies seem ludicrous to the 85 per cent of Australia's population who live in cities, yet the suburban masses are inclined to preserve at least one tradition of old-fashioned Australia which would seem to have its historical roots in the puritanism of seventeenth-century England. This tradition is known as 'Wowserism', a strine word said to derive from a slogan of nineteenth-century Australian nonconformists 'We Only Want Social Evils Righted.'

THE WOWSERS

Perhaps the best definition of a wowser is contained in a verse first published in *The Bulletin* in 1912.

> A long thin beast in a long black skin
> Armed with a gimlet and wearing a grin
> He has a very flat hat and a very fat brolly
> Supposed to hate everything pretty or jolly.

The last line sums it all up. Even though the pilgrim-father apparel of flat hats and black clothes have vanished from the Australia of the 1970s, the puritan soul goes marching on, particularly in the towns and cities of the 'Deep South'.

The three main wowser causes have always been temperance, public decency and censorship. The battle for temperance, which was a major Australian political issue at the turn of the century, has now been all but completely lost, although there is still an iron ban on Sunday drinking in many parts of Australia. Yet until three years ago both Victoria and South Australia had highly illiberal licensing laws, whose most unpopular provision was the rule that all pubs and bars must close by 6 p.m. One result of this regulation was an amazing spectacle known as the six o'clock swill, which I first witnessed in Melbourne early in 1966. As the city's shops, offices and factories closed on the stroke of 5.30, hordes of maniacal males would charge like dervishes at Omdurman in the direction of the nearest hostelry. On the counters of the pubs for which they were heading (and woe betide any innocent bystander who got in the way of the charge) stood row upon row of glasses brimming with ice-cold beer. Like thirsty robots demonstrating a high-speed manual refuelling operation, the drinkers would each front up to an individual line of glasses and systematically pour the cooling liquid straight down their throats, tumbler after tumbler. Apart from the imbibers' onomatopoeia of grunts, gurgles, sips, swallows and belches the entire operation was conducted in silence. Ruthless concentration was applied to the task of getting down as many 'middies'[1] (10-ounce glasses) as possible before the hour of six, and any diversions such as pleasant conversation were rudely discouraged. Provided the barmen were efficient in keeping the lines of glasses filled up, determined drinkers could probably consume eight or ten pints of the heady ale before closing time. But with the moment of departure came the moment of truth. Stepping from the saloon bar into the evening air, many a six-o'clock swiller would temporarily stagger or lose his balance completely. The sight of these inebriated customers reeling like eightsomes along the pavements and then getting into their cars to weave off home, demonstrated the alarming amount of truth in the saying that Australian drivers divide pedestrians into two classes—the quick and the dead. Certainly the evening traffic accident rates were an important factor in encouraging the licensing law reforms which now

---

[1] The word in the State of Victoria is 'pot'.

make it possible to buy a drink up to 10 p.m. in all Australian states.

Yet although the six-o'clock swill is mercifully a thing of the past, there are still many traces of temperance wowserism. After one busy afternoon's appointments in Melbourne, I had a beer with my taxi-driver. As we emerged from the bar he grabbed my arm and steered me through a circuitous route of back streets and alleyways to his cab which had all the time been parked a mere twenty yards from the pub's front door. 'Beg pardon, mate,' he said, 'but this town's full of people who if they see a driver coming out of a pub and getting into a taxi, they ring up the police to report him.'

Public-spirited wowsers do not confine their activities as coppers' narks to taxi-drivers emerging from pubs. Police vice squads in Australia have no need of professional informants with so many dedicated amateurs watching out for signs of public decadence and indecency. A Brisbane bookshop was last year reported (and succcessfully prosecuted) for obscenity because it hung on its walls a sketch 'Lysistrata and the three ladies' by the nineteenth-century English artist, Aubrey Beardsley. 'The trouble is,' said the magistrate, 'this poster was clearly visible to members of the public walking past the bookshop.' The same crazy logic resulted in the arrest last November of a Sydney bookshop owner who exhibited a poster of Michelangelo's famous nude statue 'David'. The curator of the New South Wales Art Gallery, Mr David Thomas, commented: 'The statue of David has been standing in an art gallery in a Roman Catholic city [Florence] in full view of adults and children for over 500 years—and this is Sydney 1969.' In Melbourne, following complaints from the public, a Supreme Court typist was in 1968 instructed by the judges to lengthen her 9 inches above the knee mini-skirt or look for another job. Two years earlier when international model Jean Shrimpton turned up at the Melbourne Cup ('The Ascot of the Southern Hemisphere') with a mini-skirt and her current steady boyfriend Terence Stamp, the disapproving clucks of Victorian matrons made world headlines. In 1964 a 17-year-old-girl was charged with offensive behaviour for dancing the shimmy shimmy shake during Melbourne's Moomba festival. 'She was not dancing, but shaking and twisting her body,' said a policeman in evidence before the magistrate, who however dismissed the charge.

Wowserism is inevitably on the decline as a result of absurdities like the above, but with Australian parks and beaches still being regularly patrolled by vigilant prudes apt to report couples for embracing, it can be said that the spirit of England's seventeenth-century puritans ('they were against bear-baiting not because it gave pain to the bear but because it gave pleasure to the spectators,' wrote Lord Macaulay) is still very much alive in twentieth-century Australia.

The field in which the wowser spirit is most triumphant today is that of censorship. Australia has some of the strictest censors in the world, who operate mainly through the long arm of the Customs Department. Customs clerks examine all imports of books and have the right to impound anything which they consider 'blasphemous, indecent or obscene'. Their interpretation of these words has led them in the last few years to ban books such as Nabokov's *Lolita*, J. D. Salinger's *The Catcher in the Rye*, D. H. Lawrence's *Lady Chatterley's Lover*, Ian Fleming's *The Spy who Loved Me*, John O'Hara's *Butterfield 8* and *Appointment in Samara*, and *The Kama Sutra*. After a series of challenges and controversies all these books have eventually been released from the ban, but the Australian Customs still maintains a proscribed list of about 200 titles which at the time of writing includes J. P. Donleavy's *The Ginger Man*, Philip Roth's *Portnoy's Complaint*, most of the works by Henry Miller and William Burroughs and most issues of *Playboy* magazine.

The long arm of the customs authorities extends to films also. During the last 12 months, for example, total bans have been clamped on the prize-winning Swedish film *I love, you love* (which was sent by a Swedish Government Agency as Sweden's official entry for the Sydney Film Festival), Otto Preminger's *Skiddoo* (starring Jackie Gleason, Groucho Marx and Burgess Meredith), *100 Rifles* (apparently prohibited because its theme was a white-coloured romance between Jim Brown and Raquel Welch), *The Bofors Gun*, Marianne Faithfull's *Girl on a Motor Cycle* and *Pretty Poison*, a much-praised thriller starring Tuesday Weld and Anthony Perkins. Apart from total bans, approximately one in three of the US and British feature films imported into Australia are severely cut. Recent victims of the censor's scissors include movies such as *Rosemary's Baby*, *The Boston Strangler*, *Blow-Up* and *If*, all of which received major excisions before they were deemed pure enough to show to Australian audiences.

Yet whatever the shortcomings of the Customs Department (who at their own discretion refer to an Advisory Board in cases where they think a book's literary merit may be relevant) they are far more lenient wielders of the blue pencil than the censors in individual states. In 1964, Victoria's vice squad seized copies of Mary Macarthy's *The Group*, even though it had been passed by the Customs. *America Hurrah* was banned in New South Wales during 1968, and in the same state parts of TV recordings in David Frost's *The Frost Report* had to be bleeped out because the humour was judged to be too risqué. Queensland, a banner's paradise if ever there was one, confined itself in 1969 to suppressing Aubrey Beardsley's posters and the record of *Hair*, a rather mild performance really from censors who are on record as saying their duties include defending 'the civilization of the West', and protecting youth against 'the fiery darts of the wicked'.

One surprising aspect of all this censorship is its popularity with the mass of the Australian people. Intellectuals and liberals may fulminate against the restrictions, but Gallup Polls indicate that approximately 60 per cent of all Australians favour the line being drawn just about where and how it is. The permissive society is still a very long way from getting a firm foothold in Australia.

BROKEN HILL

The capital city of Old-Fashioned Australia is Broken Hill, a mining town of legendary wealth standing 700 miles west of Sydney and 300 miles north of Adelaide in the heart of the New South Wales desert country.

The Hill has both the best and the worst reputation of any population centre in the antipodes. High wages (average worker's pay is $5,000 per annum compared to Australia's national average of $3,000), low crime rates, fiercely cherished community traditions, excellent working conditions and an unequalled contribution to the nation's mineral productivity are its good points. But to anyone who values basic freedoms such as the right to work, the right to trade and the right to free speech, the antiquated despotism of Broken Hill's neanderthal union bosses comes as a salutary shock.

This despotism comes from the town's ruling group of union leaders, collectively known as the Barrier Industrial Council. This unorthodox body, which holds far more sway over Broken Hill's 35,000 inhabitants than the State or Federal Governments, operates from a dilapidated office building locally known as The Kremlin.

There is an uncomfortable note of truth in this jesting sobriquet, for the Barrier Industrial Council, although militantly anti-Communist in its political outlook, at times enforces its own high doctrines of unadulterated unionism with all the dirigiste severity of an Iron Curtain régime. Some of the Council's most controversial edicts, which are rigorously enforced by trade boycotts and 'blacking' of individuals or firms, are as follows:

No outsider can work in Broken Hill's mines unless he was born in the town or has lived there continuously for 8 years. Even newcomers who marry local girls do not qualify.

Married women are not allowed to work in Broken Hill in case they take away jobs from union members. The only exceptions are teachers, nurses and widows. Single girls in Broken Hill are compelled to give up their jobs when they marry—the biggest inducement to living in sin in Australia.

Door-to-door salesmen and commercial travellers are banned from Broken Hill. Any firm wishing to do business in the town must open a shop, employ local labour and abide by the Barrier Industrial Council's rules. One of these rules requires companies to advertise in the union's own daily newspaper, *The Barrier Daily Truth*. Some years ago, Woolworths decided to defy this regulation and switched all their advertising to the free enterprise evening paper, the *Barrier Miner*. Immediately, the Barrier Industrial Council ordered all union members to boycott the store, with such effective results that Woolworths capitulated after ten days and has been advertising in *The Barrier Daily Truth* ever since.

The shaky position of press freedom in Broken Hill has been percipiently summed up by a celebrated young journalist, Bob Bottom, who wrote in his revealing book *Behind the Barrier*: 'At every step in Broken Hill a journalist is conscious of an extra commandment: Thou shalt not criticize the unions—right or wrong. If you do dare to criticize you do so at your own peril. Few people do, and so virtually anything done under the union aegis is condoned.'

Bob Bottom should know what he is talking about, for he was the journalist involved in a famous *cause célèbre* in which press freedom clashed with the Barrier Industrial Council's notorious autocracy. Bottom, in 1967, wrote an accurate news story about an industrial dispute in Broken Hill which was broadcast on a regional news bulletin by the Australian Broadcasting Commission. The Barrier Industrial Council, for some unexplained reason, took exception to the story, and peremptorily summoned Bottom to appear before it. Bottom very properly refused, whereupon he was 'fined' $10 in his absence and banned from the Council's premises. To make matters worse, all other press and radio representatives

were thenceforth banned as a reprisal from Barrier Industrial
Council negotiation meetings they had covered for 50 years, a
move which provoked the normally sedate editorial columns of
the *Sydney Morning Herald* into slamming the Council for exer-
cising 'its local prerogative of being prosecutor, judge and
executioner'. After a lot of tough talking, in which Bob Bottom
was threatened with being declared 'black' by the unions, the
dispute was swept under the carpet and ostensibly forgotten.
Bottom left the town to join a Sydney newspaper a year later, but
remains understandably bitter about the suppression of free
speech in Broken Hill. 'The price you pay to live in this workers'
Utopia,' he says, 'is that you lose that much-cherished sense of
liberty and personal freedom. The solidarity and loyalty demanded
by the Broken Hill trade union system has served to deaden that
indefinable will and conscience of the human mind.'

During my own visit to Broken Hill I found much evidence to
corroborate Bottom's thesis. The family with whom I stayed
received each morning through the letter box three copies of the
union newspaper, the *Barrier Daily Truth*. When asked why they
found it necessary to buy three copies of the same paper for one
breakfast table, they replied that union regulations compelled each
member to subscribe to the paper irrespective of his wishes or
convenience. I heard savage resentment being expressed over the
works ban on married women, and much criticism of other union
rules such as the monthly badge show—a compulsory display of
union badges which is so harshly enforced that one man who had
lost his badge through having his home burnt down the day before
was nevertheless turned away and docked a day's pay. Yet when
one asks why unionists do not protest against the obvious in-
humanities of these malpractices, the reply is, 'The Barrier
Industrial Council might declare us black.'

Declaring someone black is the union's most formidable weapon,
and they have not hesitated to use it and their powers of boycott
to bring peccant individuals into line. If a boycott is enforced, the
victim will be 'sent to Coventry' by Broken Hill's 9,000 unionists
and their families; he will not be served by any shopkeepers or
tradesmen; and his essential services, such as electricity, will soon
be cut off from him. Few people are heroic enough to withstand
such draconian pressures, and so the iron hand of the Council
remains unchecked.

In fairness to the union bosses of Broken Hill, it should be
stressed that their ruling methods are, on the whole, popular. For

the boycott has usually been enforced in 'good causes', such as the blacking of a pubkeeper who put up the price of beer, and dissenters from the system are comparatively rare. The general view is that the Hill is the best town to live in on the continent. Said one miner to me in the pub: 'It's true we don't like outsiders, particularly the Balts and the Grills. [Migrants from the Baltic and the Mediterranean.] It's true we don't stick to the usual State laws on gambling and drinking. (Broken Hill has a notoriously illegal two-up school and its pubs are open 24 hours a day.) And it's true the boys from the Kremlin can get a bit high-handed at times. But these are things that only worry outsiders. The wages and the conditions are the best in Australia, the air is so good it can cure chronic asthma in a few weeks, the town's full of fascinating characters like old Pro Harte, the famous artist, and there's a real sense of family and community tradition. We may be a bit behind the times, but we like it this way.'

THE ABORIGINES

Australia's oldest inhabitants are also her unluckiest, for the continent's 140,000 Aborigines (only 45,000 of whom are full bloods) are still, to a disturbing extent, the victims of serious discrimination, segregation and exploitation. Although there has been a recent awakening of concern among middle-class whites for the plight of the original Australians, nevertheless old-fashioned attitudes prevail to such an extent that major reforms are needed before the nation can rid itself of the taint of condoning second-class citizenship for those with dark skins.

An Aboriginal's luck starts to run out the day he is born. Although Aborigines account for only 2 per cent of the birth rate, they comprise 10 per cent of all infant deaths, 28 per cent of all deaths in the 1- to 2-year-old age group and 9 per cent of all deaths in the 2- to 4-year group. Survivors who reach childhood have often experienced malnutrition and endemic diseases which are likely to prove a lifelong handicap. As for education, Aborigines enter school at a later age than white children; they rarely get either the pre-schooling or the special coaching necessary for them to make progress at the same rate as their contemporaries, and as a result less than 20 per cent of all Aboriginal schoolchildren get any form of secondary education at all. Only 12 Aborigines in Australian history have had a university education.

The results of these early deprivations are tragic. Surveys show that even among young men in the 20–25 age group, one-fifth are illiterate and one-third are more or less permanently out of a job. Maladjustment, unemployment, alcoholism, prostitution, lethargy, irresponsibility, poverty and disease are rife throughout the entire Aboriginal community, and in certain States there is an alarming tendency on the part of the authorities to treat these social problems as crimes.

In Queensland, for example, the State Director of Native Affairs has the absolute power to confine any Aboriginal to a native reserve. The reserve manager can impose sentences of solitary confinement for four offences: indiscipline, escaping or attempting to escape, committing 'any immoral act or misconduct', and being 'idle, careless or negligent at work without just cause'. The reserve manager acts as prosecuting counsel, judge and jury in such cases and does not even have to report the solitary confinement for six months. After six months he has to get the State Director's permission to continue the imprisonment. An Aboriginal has no right of appeal, and it appears that a solitary confinement sentence can thus be continued indefinitely.

Queensland's discriminatory treatment of Aboriginals appears to be open to severe criticism, for in addition to the above regulations there are some startling examples of harsh administration. A 1970 Australian Broadcasting Commission television programme revealed that the authorities forcibly remove any baby born to an Aboriginal woman where the father is known to be a white man. The child is given to one of the religious welfare organizations to bring up. Queensland's welfare officers are also empowered to 'take possession of, retain, sell or otherwise dispose of' the property of 'assisted' Aborigines, and there is a regulation to the effect that no legal document executed by Aborigines can be held legally valid 'unless approved and witnessed by an official'.

But if Queensland is the worst State for black Australians, there is plenty of anti-Aboriginal discrimination elsewhere. The Native Welfare Board of Western Australia can and does revoke the citizenship of Aboriginals who are 'not adopting the manner and habits of civilized life'. Another cause for citizenship revocation is if an Aboriginal 'has contracted leprosy, syphilis, yaws or granulomas'. Also, the west is the only part of Australia where Aborigines are not legally entitled to buy alcoholic drinks.

Apart from archaic laws, the Aborigines frequently suffer a degree of humiliation and segregation which amounts to an antipodean form of apartheid. I myself have visited 'the Abo quarter' of many country towns and seen the sad little straggle of squalid tin shacks and broken down humpies, so reminiscent of the notorious shanty towns of Johannesburg in that they are quite separate geographically from the white residential areas, and quite distinct from the rest of the town in their atmosphere of misery and despair. Visit a local cinema in such towns and one finds the Aborigines herded off into a special section in the front rows. Visit a pub and the same often goes for the corner of the room in which the Aborigines do their drinking alone. Such delineations are neither automatic nor universal, but the fact remains that in a great many rural areas the White Australians do not disguise their contempt for 'the Boongs' and make no attempt to treat them as equal human beings.

A more contentious issue among the Aborigines themselves than either of the above examples of unjust legislation (which are often not enforced by wise and humane administrators) or the conditions amounting to apartheid (which do not exist everywhere) are the Aborigines' grievances about their right to own land. Throughout the continent there are numerous Aboriginal reserves which may vary in size from a few acres near a country town in the eastern states to several hundred square miles in the outback of the Northern Territory. The Aborigines want the ownership of these reserves to be vested in an Aboriginal trust. This form of ownership, which was long ago granted to North American Indians in the USA and Canada, is resolutely opposed by the present Federal Government of Australia. The justification for refusing to grant the Aborigines any title to land stems from a fear that the Federal Treasury may lose valuable mineral rights. At present, mining prospectors have free access to all native reserves (even when there is a moratorium on prospecting in all other areas—as happened in early 1970 in Western Australia) and in the event of a strike a mining company can get permission to move in and start full drilling and processing operations. If this means pushing the Aborigines off land where they have lived and hunted for centuries, parts of which may be sacred to them for religious reasons, the present Federal Government will nevertheless insist on mines taking precedence over people. Humanitarian voices all over Australia condemned an outrageous example of this practice when Prime Minister John Gorton's administration in 1969 refused to grant land rights to Aboriginals of the Gurindji tribe who were being turned off their reserve in the Northern Territory near Gove in order to make way for a bauxite mine.

But although the preceding account of Australia's treatment of her black minority makes depressing reading, there are certain glimmerings of hope for substantial social improvements in favour of the Aborigines soon being implemented. That such hopes exist at all is largely due to the present Minister in Charge of Aboriginal Affairs, Mr W. C. Wentworth IV.

Billy Wentworth is a political maverick who combines the foreign policy views of a John Birchite hawk with the domestic policy views of a compassionate Martin Luther King. The great-grandson of a celebrated Australian explorer, William Charles Wentworth, he inherited a fortune reported by one newspaper to be $21 million ('I hope I can persuade my bank manager that the rumour is true and can keep it from my wife'—was his comment) and won a First in Classics from Oxford. After a spell in the Army, during which he became a legend as a prankster after spoofing a serious wartime military exercise by leading his company to a spectacular capture of Sydney Barracks, he entered politics as a Federal Liberal member for a Sydney constituency. After getting elected, this gifted and articulate scholar spent 19 years languishing in the purdah of the back benches. Some thought his long exile was due to his obsession with Reds under the Australian bed, for Wentworth fiercely believes that 'the Com issue' is the greatest menace to his country's survival, reveres the late Senator Joe McCarthy, and when I interviewed him spent several minutes passionately advocating the immediate nuclear bombing of China. However, these views, which he holds as firmly as ever despite the ever-diminishing evidence of Communist influence on Australia, did not disqualify him from taking an eventual place in the government, and his long exclusion from high office is therefore almost certainly attributable to his personal feud with Sir Robert Menzies.

Despite the feud, Wentworth managed to get some useful legislation of his own on the Statute Book, and was directly responsible for the setting up of a referendum which, in May 1967, enabled the Federal Government to include Aborigines in the census and to over-ride the State Governments on some matters of Aboriginal welfare. In November 1967 fresh efforts by Wentworth (still a back-bencher) resulted in the founding of the Council for Aboriginal Affairs, a governmental advisory body, and in December 1968 with Wentworth's ministerial encouragement equal pay was granted to Aboriginal stockmen in the Northern Territory by the Arbitration Court. Other achievements of the Wentworth era are the beginning of a major drive to improve health, housing, education, and employment facilities for Aboriginals, a 50 per cent cut in Aboriginal infant mortality (although it is still three and a half times as high as among white Australians), the extension of the franchise to Aboriginals, and constitutional changes which should compel individual State governments to abolish all their discriminatory legislation by the end of 1972.

Yet despite these advances, Billy Wentworth has had a most frustrating time as Minister in Charge of Aboriginal Affairs. Ever since the post was created for him in January 1968 as a result of his own well-known passionate concern for improving Aboriginal welfare and preserving Aboriginal culture, he has run into complacency, lack of compassion and sometimes downright prejudice amidst the government of which he is a member.

Undoubtedly his unhappiest moment occurred over the previously mentioned expulsion of Gurindji tribesmen from their land by a bauxite mining company. At the time, Mr Alan Ramsey, the distinguished columnist of *The Australian*, commented: 'Cabinet to a man opposed Wentworth and although he virtually went down on his hands and knees to get Mr Gorton to over-ride the decision, he might as well have spared himself the effort and the anguish.

'The Gorton Government will not have a bar of the suggestion that Aboriginals have any claim to land rights as such and no minister upholds this contention more than does Mr Gorton.

'That, then, is Aboriginal welfare. It exists only as a catchphrase. It has no substance, no meaning. And Mr Wentworth hasn't been able to change a thing.'

These words are too harsh, seen in the perspective of time, for Billy Wentworth has, by virtue of his limited successes and also through his own mortifying defeats, completely changed the climate of Australian concern for Aborigines. Where there was once total disinterest there is now a thriving white middle-class protest movement, frequently raising its unexpected voice on the Aborigines' behalf. Newspapers and magazines are devoting a commendable amount of space to the issue of discrimination, and the Aborigines themselves have suddenly produced a tiny handful of sporting heroes (of whom Lionel Rose and Yvonne Goolagong are the most celebrated) and political leaders (such as Philip Roberts, Charles Perkins and Reg Saunders) whose efforts have helped to reduce the Aborigines' feeling of racial inferiority. Perhaps as a result of these pressures, and certainly as a result of Billy Wentworth's own tireless personal lobbying, Prime Minister Gorton did produce a supplement to his 1969 election policy speech in which he made several promises to the Aborigines including the abolition of all discriminatory legislation; equality of services in health and education; increased money for housing; and government spending on certain regional projects which will allow economic self-sufficiency for some Aboriginal communities. So far, none of these election promises have been honoured, and Billy Wentworth has been reported by *The Bulletin* as 'fuming over the delays in preparing legislation.' Some commentators are wondering whether the pledges will be honoured at all.

Recalling de Toqueville's dictum that the level of a nation's civilization should only be defined in terms of the provision that society makes for its most unfortunate members, it seems that until a major legislative assault is made to clean up the unfairness and inequalities which now exist against Aborigines, Australia will remain, despite the efforts of Mr W. C. Wentworth IV, a very uncivilized country.

MILITARY SENTIMENTALISM

Australia is a country where old soldiers show a marked reluctance to fade away. One reason for their durability is the Returned Servicemen's League, a formidable association of around a quarter of a million ex-military men with clubs throughout the country and immense influence as a pressure group. Emotionally, the RSL keeps military sentimentalism in the forefront of the Australian way of life. Politically, it keeps conservative defence and foreign policies in the forefront of Australia's government. The RSL maintains an impressively vast office and a large staff in Canberra specifically for political lobbying, and enjoys infinitely more power than international equivalents such as the British Legion or the US Veterans' Association.

In its time, the RSL has used its unique lobbying powers (unique because the RSL has the right of privileged direct access to Ministers) to oppose immigration from ex-enemy countries, Southern European countries and all non-white sources; it has requested the banning of literature published by communists, fascists, republicans and Jehovah's Witnesses; and it has demanded stiffer penalties for conscientious objectors. On the international scene, the League has recently deleted from its Oath of Allegiance all mention of the British Commonwealth of Nations because, in the words of the RSL's former New South Wales President, Sir William Yeo, in a speech to the National RSL Conference, Canberra, in 1968, 'some members of the Commonwealth are Wogs and Bogs'. The RSL's most successful lobbying activity has been its campaign for war service pensions and repatriation benefits. Under the present arrangements, any ex-serviceman (even from the 1914–18 War) who develops a chronic illness will receive a war disability pension unless the Government can prove that his condition was not due to war service. By putting the onus of proof on the Government, the RSL has, for example, regularly managed to obtain pensions for ex-servicemen with tuberculosis, even when the infection occurred twenty years after the war finished. Such preferential treatment is widely resented among civilians.

In Adelaide I was given lunch in a spacious, modern RSL club by Sir Arthur Lee, the League's National President. He told me, 'Until about 10 years ago the RSL was primarily a self-centred organization, but now it is much more outward-looking. We try to use our influence to make Australia a great nation. When some important issue arises we try to find out what our members think and then we pass on our view to the Government. The RSL has the right to convene a meeting of the ex-service members of the Cabinet who make up nine-tenths of it. Also, the RSL President has an automatic right of direct access to the Prime Minister. This is a considerable privilege, but we think we use it wisely.'

One of the less controversial activities of the RSL is its organization of Anzac Day parades. ('The Vietnam commitment has been very good for us,' said Sir Arthur. 'RSL membership is now rising again by 1 or $1\frac{1}{2}$ per cent a year, and at this year's (1968) Anzac Day parades 30,000 men marched in Sydney and 9,500 in Adelaide. Both were record totals.')

Anzac Day (April 25th) commemorates the appalling defeat (8,000 killed and 20,000 wounded) which was suffered by Australian and New Zealand troops at Gallipoli in 1915. It is Australia's most important National Day, and it is marked by a public holiday, religious services and military ceremonies in even the smallest country towns. In many homes the polarized attitudes to Anzac Day cause almost generational civil war, for the old tend to regard it as sacred, while the young tend to think it is a farce.

On the only Anzac Day I was in Australia I found myself in Darwin. The temperature by the city's war memorial was a sweltering 100° in the shade, but from the immensely formal clothes worn by the participants in the ceremony an observer might have thought we were in the chilliest months of the English winter. Veteran soldiers stood rigidly to attention in tweed suits,

bowler hats and medals. As the Union Jack and Australian flag
flew side by side, various similarly-attired dignitaries laid some
20 wreaths on the war memorial, while a contingent of kilted pipers
played Cameron's Lament, and an amateur brass band tootled its
uncertain way through a selection of unrecognizable funeral dirges.
The Administrator of the Northern Territory (in morning coat
and medals) presided over the ceremony, the high point of which
was an address by the RAAF Commander of the Darwin Air Force
base. It was one of the Commander's shorter speeches and the
rather elderly and perspiring audience of 1,000 (including about
100 presumably mystified Aboriginals) loved every hour of it, none
more so than the platoon of uniformed RAAF cadets. They were
stationed in the hottest part of the sunbaked square, and approximately a quarter of them had fainted before their Commander had
finished speaking. The ceremony ended with a bugler sounding
the Last Post and Reveille as the flags were lowered, followed by
the crowd singing 'O God our help in ages past.'

As the last note of this hymn died away, past and present members
of the Australian military moved off at a brisk trot in the direction
of the nearest pubs. I joined some of the veterans for a drink, lost
a dollar at Two-Up ('It's strictly speaking illegal, but we used to
play it in the war and so nobody objects on Anzac Day'), and
heard much excited betting on the ability of a noted local drinker
to consume 53 glasses of beer in the day—one for every year since
Gallipoli.

As I left the pub a 77-year-old ex-soldier raised his glass and
said with the utmost seriousness: 'Gentlemen, I give you a toast.
Long live the British Empire!' It seemed a fitting epitaph for
Old-Fashioned Australia.

11

THE AUSTRALIAN FAIRYTALE

Once upon a time there was a hot, parched island stuck in a southern corner of the world that no one wanted to visit or know about. The people who lived on this island were rather dull and parochial, and their manners were sometimes a little uncouth. They had lots of chips on their shoulders about being descended from convicts or colonial settlers and they used to get cross whenever an outsider said anything the least bit critical about their country. Because they minded criticism so much, the islanders tried hard to imitate the sophisticated people with skins as white as theirs who dwelt in the rich countries of the northern part of the world. This imitation often made the islanders look ridiculous, and in some ways it prevented them from having a real identity of their own. Indeed their inferiority complex about the old white countries was so bad that the islanders actually imported many of their most important governors, judges, chief priests, scribes and merchants, bringing most of them from the Northern Kingdom whose navy had first discovered and settled the island in 1770.

Although it was very costly, and perhaps a little demeaning, to have most of the island's rulers, customs, and manufactured goods being shipped across the oceans from several thousand miles away, nevertheless the islanders seemed determined not to have any contact with their true neighbours. The reason was that the next-door nations were populated by huge numbers of men with yellow and brown skins who the islanders feared greatly, dreaming that one day hordes of yellow and brown warriors might come across the sea to seize their country. This would be a simple task, for the island was large and empty, and could not possibly be defended by its small number of inhabitants living chiefly in the cities of the plain around the faraway corner of the south-east.

And so about 180 years after the island had first been discovered

by the gallant naval captain named James Cook (a famous navigator
from the Northern Kingdom which many islanders still called
'home' or 'the mother country' and whose monarch still reigned
over the island in absence), there was some despondency about
the future of the island among certain wise men and soothsayers.

These Cassandras proclaimed that the island (which James Cook
had christened Terra Australis and is now commonly known as
Australia) could never become a truly strong and independent
nation because of its political and economic difficulties. Its
prosperity, declared the prophets, was wholly dependent on the
island's 140 million sheep, a situation which was about to cause a
great poverty and depression as wool prices were on the point of
suffering a permanent slump thanks to a new scientific discovery
called 'man-made fibres' on the other side of the world. When this
wool substitute brought about the collapse of the island's economy,
all its standards of living would decline, all its developments would
perish and all its hopes of an independent national culture would
be dashed. Instead Australia would become a boring bucolic backwater for poor whites and philistines, ripe for invasion by the
yellow and brown warriors from the near north. If this invasion
occurred, said the clever soothsayers, the islanders would have
only themselves to blame, for their hostility to their neighbours
was such that they hardly ever allowed a man with a yellow or
brown skin to live among them or even to trade with them. However, the old chief minister of the island did not concern himself
with these gloomy predictions, preferring to make speeches about
his bootstraps which he was proud to have made by the cobblers
of the Northern Kingdom. He argued that a nation which bought
even its chief minister's bootstraps from the motherland would
always be defended by the motherland in time of trouble, and
there was therefore nothing to worry about. But others argued
that the motherland could not be counted on to cross the globe
in order to shed the blood of her young men in defence of the
island. The reasons for this were twofold. First the Northern
Kingdom was now old and ailing and becoming impoverished.
Secondly, many people in the Northern Kingdom despised the
island of Australia on account of its poor sense of nationhood, and
its poor cultural and economic prospects.

Such at least were the opinions of some of the more pessimistic
islanders, although they did not often voice their prophecies in
their own land, knowing perhaps that their angry compatriots
might throw them to the wild dingos for such sedition. Instead

they preferred to travel to the Northern Kingdom to take up residence in the capital city of London round a district hitherto known as Earls Court. This district was shortly renamed 'Kangaroo Valley' by humorous natives of the capital on account of all the moans and groans that went up there from the displaced islanders who loved to complain in the public prints and to all and sundry that their former home was a melancholic and uncivilized spot, lacking everything they called culture, a category covering all things from grand opera to naughty picture books.

But while the moaners and groaners were foretelling a bleak future for their homeland, mysterious changes were happening on the island itself. For as the island drew near to the 200th anniversary of its discovery, the earth revealed great riches, the revelations beginning by a most strange accident. For it happened that a mighty wool baron named Hancock lost his way in his flying machine when travelling through mountains in the north-west and after being forced to land for several hours in bad weather on an unknown plateau, he returned with lumps of red stone in his 'kerchief declaring that he had discovered a mountain of iron. At first no one believed him but Baron Hancock had the visage of an ogre and the roar of a lion and when he confronted the great merchants of far-away lands they came in haste. When they saw what Hancock had found they agreed that these iron mountains of the north-west were the richest of all the world. Then a demon politician named Court arose in the West, and he harangued more merchant princes from all corners of the earth until they built great railway lines, ports, townships, roads and factories around the bleak iron mountains where no islanders had ever dwelt before. Yet this did not satisfy the demon Court, for he built costly dams for farmers, and more towns and ports and roads and demanded from the merchants bigger factories called processing plants for the precious metals. All this excitement in the West caused more men to search for mountains like Hancock's, and soon many findings were made throughout the island of nickel and bauxite and uranium and many other precious stones. One clever searcher came across the ocean from the great northern republic of America saying that there were vast lagoons of oil under the sea in the little waters between the island of Australia and the island of Tasmania and to everyone's surprise it was true. For after the American searcher had sunk but one small hole in the waters the oil gushed forth in such a flood that the islanders no longer had to buy petrol for their cars and homes from far away lands, and this was a great saving in money for them all.

Now at about this time, the wise men and elders of the island began to scratch their heads to decide what should be done with these new riches. Hitherto the islanders had sold all their goods (these being largely meat and wool) to the white nations of the north, but now there came to the island little yellow men from the Emperor of Nippon offering piles of gold and silver for the metals from the province of the ogre Hancock and the demon Court. After long deliberations (for these yellow men had been great enemies of the island in times past), the elders of the island's Capital decided to accept the gold from the Nipponese Emperor's coffers, a move which opened the floodgates to much trade between the island and all her neighbours populated by men with yellow and brown skins. As this trade grew, the island's elders decided to allow men of yellow and brown skins to come and study in Australia's seats of learning and even to reside on the island in small numbers. This would have caused great gnashing of teeth in past days, particularly among the retired island warriors who had in olden days gone out to battle against the soldiers of the Emperor of Nippon, yet because the island's new and younger chief Minister now declared 'Australia is part of Asia,' all was peaceful, and the yellow and brown men were welcomed.

But it was not just the people of neighbouring countries who wished to come and live on the island (which by now was getting so proud of its riches that the islanders liked to speak of their home as 'The Continent'). When the news of the precious stones and the hot sun and the empty spaces became known in the cold and crowded northern part of the planet a big movement of peoples went southwards in search of the better and richer life that Australia was said to offer. Among them were many doctors of physick, clerks of the accounts ledgers, broking merchants for stocks and shares, breeders of cattle, and diggers for precious stones, all of whom found it easy to make great fortunes in the rich continent. Even the princeling son of the mighty Queen from the Northern Kingdom came to gain his education in Australia, a subtle and skilful decision on the part of the royal courtiers for the prince voiced so many flattering words about the continent's people that he hushed all rumbles of discontent which were then being noised abroad about his mother The Queen by those who wished to replace her by a President and Republic like that in America.

With so many people and benefits suddenly accruing to the

nation, several scribes in Australia wrote books and produced special journals in praise of their country. At the same time there was a great surge of painting and sculpture by artists endeavouring to reflect the glory of the changing scene. Palaces of drama and music were built (the Opera House of Sydney being one of the wonders of the world on account of its extravagance) and the elders decided to give part of the public taxes to painters, writers, musicians and makers of films. Although some embittered residents of the aforementioned Kangaroo Valley liked to sneer at these manifestations of cultural achievement, it was widely believed that these improvements were helping to present Australia with a new sense of national pride and an end to all former feelings of inferiority.

Thus it came to pass that when Australia celebrated the 200th year of her discovery by James Cook there was feasting and rejoicing throughout the land as never before. The Queen of the Northern Kingdom made a long visit saying many pretty words in speeches, although her majestic presence did not conceal from the prescient scribes and scribblers that the motherland whence she came had become a pauper in comparison to the rich continent. The President of the great Republic of America (whose predecessor had shown much partiality for Australia, making two special visits there) sent warm words of goodwill and despatched his hot-tongued Vice-President to make salutations. Leaders of nearby nations of Asia came in profusion to pay homage to their wealthy white neighbour, who was now their friend, and even God's Vicar in Rome flew across the world from the throne of St Peter to bless his Australian brethren. Meanwhile the crust of the continent revealed more precious stones, the cities put up more fine buildings, the soil gave forth more crops and more cattle and all the people of the land became more rich.

Now all these things seemed so strange to those older islanders who recalled the days when Australia was but a poor and humble farm that they had to pinch themselves to make sure it was not a dream about to end. Yet there were voices raised saying 'the dream has not yet begun'. So faced with this confusion when the author of this book made visits to the continent, he consulted the oracles and soothsayers to find out whither Australia would go during the future decade. And after much examination of the entrails, gazing into crystal, and reading of the signs and portents, the foretellers of Australia's future spoke thus: 'What you have written in your book is poor stuff, for when it is studied a few

years from now a wise reader will echo the saying of the Queen
of Sheba at the court of King Solomon and exclaim, "But the half
was not told me." Know now that our population grows four times
as fast as that of the Northern Kingdom and twice as fast as that
of the American Republic, meaning that in ten years' time we shall
have upwards of sixteen million. Perchance we may have many
more spread out across our land if the peoples from foreign climes
flock to our shores in even greater numbers than heretofore. Know
too that our economy now grows eight times faster than that of the
Northern Kingdom, and three and one half times faster than that
of the American Republic, meaning that our wages and standards
of life will in ten years' time be superior even to that of California.
As for our rocks and precious stones, be sure that they will increase
in value and that our discoveries will continue apace, making us
the wonder and envy of the world. As a consequence we shall
never have fears about that topic which agitates all northern
professors of economy so much—the balance of payments. Concerning the topic which most agitates our neighbours—that of
famine—our land will be able to provide one half of the peoples of
Asia with nourishing viands when all the pasture territory has
been sown and watered according to vision of our greatest breeders
of cattle and growers of corn. These foodstuffs, together with the
sale of our precious metals to the foundries and factories of the
Nipponese Emperor, will cause us to be much respected within
our region of the planet, for great trade, backed up by symbols of
friendship such as exchange of students, and the acceptance of a
small number of Asian people dwelling in our midst, will ensure
that we can live in peace and concord with our neighbours. Our
only fear will be that we may seem to be too rich and powerful,
for our country has since the beginning of time been as large as
the American Republic in size, and now within ten years we will
be the wealthiest nation in that vast quarter of the globe which lies
west of America, south of China, east of Africa, and north of
Antarctica. This sudden realization that we stand on the brink of
becoming a world power will effect many changes throughout our
continent. The uncouth customs which flourished in the days
when we were a small inward-looking island will wither away.
Our politics will, for the first time in our history, be reaching
outwards pulling our ancient but now dissipated Western friends
towards a greater understanding of the revolutionary Eastern
forces which theaten to sweep our region of the world. It may
be that Australia's role will be a mediating one between these

mighty juggernauts, or it may be that we shall have to stand up as a firm ally in the vortex of the whirlwind which ever threatens to move southwards from Moscow and Peking. In reluctant preparation for such possibilities, our military ranks will swell with numbers, vast monies will be spent on costly armaments, and it is most likely that we will begin to build our own nuclear weapons. But while such homage is paid to the gods of war, be sure that we will attend with no less devotion to our muse. Writers, painters, musicians, and all manner of men devoted to the arts will be raised up and glorified within our country, for already we have the wealth and the desire and soon we shall have the talent to develop a culture of an excellence to match our economic riches. For the hour will soon come when Australia is thrust to the forefront of the world stage. Whether our role will be to play the part of rich benefactor, courageous warrior, clear-headed mediator, cultural instigator or merely to be for several nations a sane, stable and loyal friend we know not. All that we have faith in is that Australia has some great work to do for mankind in the coming years. As one of our prophetic scribes, Robert Heanley, has written:

> Not only for the riches from her soil,
> Or wealth discovered in the deep-dug earth,
> Nor yet for all the wonders she has wrought
> Shall coming generations praise her worth.
> For they shall know a nation in its hour,
> A catalyst, a force made manifest.
> They shall behold a people proved, a power,
> A living bridge between the east and west.'

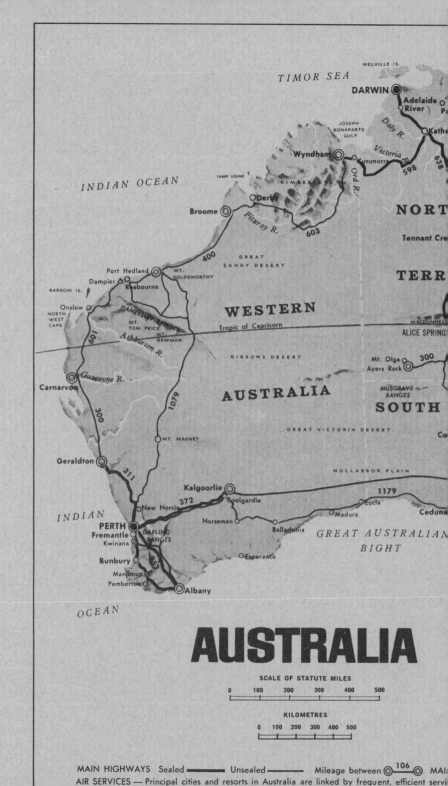

AUSTRALIA

SCALE OF STATUTE MILES

0   100   200   300   400   500

KILOMETRES

0   100   200   300   400   500

MAIN HIGHWAYS   Sealed ━━━━   Unsealed ━━━━   Mileage between ⊙¹⁰⁶⊙   MAI

AIR SERVICES — Principal cities and resorts in Australia are linked by frequent, efficient servi